Lecture Notes in Computer Science   11267

Commenced Publication in 1973
Founding and Former Series Editors:
Gerhard Goos, Juris Hartmanis, and Jan van Leeuwen

More information about this series at http://www.springer.com/series/7409

Roger Chamberlain · Walid Taha ·
Martin Törngren (Eds.)

Cyber Physical Systems

Design, Modeling, and Evaluation

7th International Workshop, CyPhy 2017
Seoul, South Korea, October 15–20, 2017
Revised Selected Papers

Springer

Editors
Roger Chamberlain
Washington University
St. Louis, MO, USA

Walid Taha ⓘ
Halmstad University
Halmstad, Sweden

Martin Törngren
KTH Royal Institute of Technology
Stockholm, Sweden

ISSN 0302-9743   ISSN 1611-3349   (electronic)
Lecture Notes in Computer Science
ISBN 978-3-030-17909-0   ISBN 978-3-030-17910-6   (eBook)
https://doi.org/10.1007/978-3-030-17910-6

LNCS Sublibrary: SL3 – Information Systems and Applications, incl. Internet/Web, and HCI

This Springer imprint is published by the registered company Springer Nature Switzerland AG
The registered company address is: Gewerbestrasse 11, 6330 Cham, Switzerland

Preface

This volume contains the joint proceedings of the Workshop on Design, Modeling and Evaluation of Cyber Physical Systems (CyPhy 2017) and the Workshop on Embedded and Cyber-Physical Systems Education (WESE 2017). The two events were co-located and coordinated with the goal of exploring opportunities for closer collaboration.

After the event, there was an open call for papers on the theme of the CyPhy workshop. Participants of the workshop were encouraged to submit, and in total there were 16 submissions. Of these, the Program Committee decided to accept ten. Each paper received at least two reviews, and most received three or more. The Program Committee was sizable and diverse, consisting of 30 members representing 11 different countries.

The WESE workshop had a vibrant program, and after the event selected one paper for publication.

The joint workshop featured a keynote address by Ichiro Hasuo entitled "Nonstandard Static Analysis: Literal Transfer of Deductive Verification Frameworks from Discrete to Hybrid."

We would like to acknowledge several efforts that were key to the success of the event, including the program co-chairs: William L. Harrison, Pavithra Prabhakar, Martin Edin Grimheden, and Falk Salewski, the Technical Program Committees, the external reviewers, the publicity chair, Abdelhamid Taha, and the organizers of ESWEEK 2017.

March 2019

Roger Chamberlain
Walid Taha
Martin Törngren

Organization

General Chair (CyPhy)

Walid Taha   Halmstad University, Sweden,
                               and University of Houston, USA

Program Committee Chairs (CyPhy)

William L. Harrison   University of Missouri, USA
Pavithra Prabhakar   Kansas State University, USA

Program Committee Chairs (WESE)

Martin Törngren   KTH Royal Institute of Technology, Sweden
Martin Edin Grimheden   KTH Royal Institute of Technology, Sweden
Falk Salewski   Münster University of Applied Sciences, Germany

Program Committee (CyPhy + WESE)

Julien Alexandre dit   ENSTA ParisTech, France
  Sandretto
Jakob Axelsson   Mälardalen University, Sweden
Christian Berger   Chalmers and University of Gothenburg, Sweden
Manuela Bujorianu   Leicester University, UK
Thao Dang   Verimag, France
Georgios Fainekos   Arizona State University, USA
Martin Fränzle   University of Oldenburg, Germany
Laurent Fribourg   CNRS, France
Antoine Girard   CNRS, France
Scott Hissam   Carnegie Mellon University, USA
Daisuke Ishii   Tokyo Institute of Technology, Japan
Mehdi Kargahi   University of Tehran, Iran
Zhiyun Lin   Zhejiang University, China
Nacim Meslem   Grenoble INP, France
Wojciech Mostowski   Halmstad University, Sweden
Mohammad Reza Mousavi   Halmstad University, Sweden
Tarek Raïssi   CNAM, France
Nacim Ramdani   University of Orleans, USA
Andreas Rauh   University of Rostock, Germany
Michel Reniers   Eindhoven University of Technology, The Netherlands
Bernhard Rumpe   RWTH University Aachen, Germany
Christoph Seidl   TU Braunschweig, Germany

Christoffer Sloth	Aalborg University, Denmark
Jack Stankovic	University of Virginia, USA
Martin Steffen	Oslo University, Norway
Rafael Wisniewski	Aalborg University, Denmark
Hugo Andrade	National Instruments, USA
Lucia Lo Bello	University of Catania, Italy
Saddek Bensalem	University of Grenoble, France
David Broman	UC Berkeley, USA, and KTH Royal Institute of Technology, Sweden
Daniela Cancila	Commissariat à l'Énergie Atomique (CEA), France
Janette Cardoso	Institut Supérieur de l'Aéronautique et de l'Espace (ISAE), France
Alex Dean	North Carolina State University, USA
Tei-Wei Kuo	National Taiwan University, Taiwan
Peter Marwedel	TU Dortmund, Germany
Jogesh Muppala	Hong Kong University of Science and Technology, Hong Kong
Bernhard Schätz	TU Munich and Fortiss, Germany
Erwin Schoitsch	Austrian Institute of Technology, Austria
Walid Taha	Halmstad University, Sweden, and University of Houston, USA
Shiao-Li Tsao	National Chiao Tung University, Taiwan
Jon Wade	Stevens Institute of Technology, USA

Additional Reviewers

Igor Shumeiko
Julia Kersten
Yue Kang

Advisory Committee (CyPhy)

Manfred Broy	Technische Universität München, Germany
Karl Henrik Johansson	KTH Royal Institute of Technology, Sweden
Karl Iagnemma	MIT, USA
Insup Lee	University of Pennsylvania, USA
Pieter Mosterman	McGill University, Canada
Janos Sztipanovits	Vanderbilt University, USA

Contents

Keynote

Nonstandard Static Analysis: Literal Transfer of Deductive Verification
Frameworks from Discrete to Hybrid. 3
  Ichiro Hasuo

Design

Local Descent for Temporal Logic Falsification
of Cyber-Physical Systems. 11
  Shakiba Yaghoubi and Georgios Fainekos

Memory Access Pattern-Aware DRAM Controller Design
for Mixed-Criticality Systems. 27
  Jeongyoon Eo, Kang-Wook Kim, and Chang-Gun Lee

Increasing Safety by Combining Multiple Declarative Rules in Robotic
Perception Systems. 43
  Johann Thor Mogensen Ingibergsson, Dirk Kraft,
  and Ulrik Pagh Schultz

Simulation

Template-Based Monte-Carlo Test Generation for Simulink Models 63
  Takashi Tomita, Daisuke Ishii, Toru Murakami, Shigeki Takeuchi,
  and Toshiaki Aoki

Reliable Simulation and Monitoring of Hybrid Systems Based on Interval
Analysis (Extended Abstract) 79
  Daisuke Ishii, Alexandre Goldsztejn, and Naoki Yonezaki

An Integrated Simulation Tool for Computer Architecture
and Cyber-Physical Systems. 83
  Hokeun Kim, Armin Wasicek, and Edward A. Lee

Safe At Any Speed: A Simulation-Based Test Harness
for Autonomous Vehicles. 94
  Houssam Abbas, Matthew O'Kelly, Alena Rodionova,
  and Rahul Mangharam

Formal Methods

Switching Delays and the Skorokhod Distance in Incrementally Stable
Switched Systems   109
  Kengo Kido, Sean Sedwards, and Ichiro Hasuo

Formal Analysis of Robotic Cell Injection Systems
Using Theorem Proving   127
  Adnan Rashid and Osman Hasan

Workshop on Embedded and Cyber-Physical Systems Education

FPGA Based Big Data Accelerator Design in Teaching Computer
Architecture and Organization.   145
  Chao Wang, Yuming Cheng, Lei Gong, Bo Wan, Aili Wang, Xi Li,
  and Xuehai Zhou

Author Index   159

Keynote

Nonstandard Static Analysis: Literal Transfer of Deductive Verification Frameworks from Discrete to Hybrid

Ichiro Hasuo[1,2]([✉])

[1] National Institute of Informatics, Tokyo, Japan
i.hasuo@acm.org
[2] The Graduate University for Advanced Studies (SOKENDAI), Tokyo, Japan

The talk summarizes our series of work [4,7,10,11]. Special thanks are due to my collaborators: Kohei Suenaga (Kyoto University), Swarat Chaudhuri (Rice University), and my (former) students Kengo Kido and Hiroyoshi Sekine (The University of Tokyo).

Towards the analysis, verification and control of hybrid systems, there are naturally two approaches: the *control theory* one that originates in the continuous world; and the *formal verification* one from the discrete world. For the formal verification approach, obvious challenges are: (1) to accommodate continuous *flow* dynamics in an existing verification framework that is originally developed for discrete *jump* dynamics; and (2) to do so at the lowest possible (theoretical) cost, so that the existing theory smoothly and correctly transfers to hybrid situations. A large body of existing work includes explicit differential equations for this purpose—as in *hybrid automata* [1,5] and in *differential dynamic logic* [8].

In our series of work [4,7,10,11] we adopt a different approach. Instead of explicitly using differential equations, we express continuous flow dynamics as infinitely many iterations of jump dynamics—each of which is infinitely small—by means of a `while` loop, a programming language construct that is well understood for us computer scientists. The idea is as simple as in the following example.

Let `elapse` be the program in Fig. 1. Here `dt` is a constant that stands for an *infinitesimal*—i.e. infinitely small—positive value. Our intention is that the program models continuous and smooth increase of the value of the variable t from 0 to 1: although a `while` loop carries a distinctively discrete flavor, each iteration changes the value of t only infinitesimally, and it is not impossible that the program models continuous dynamics.

This example, however, should raise a lot of questions to be answered. For one, the `while` loop in Fig. 1 does not terminate within finitely many iterations: for it to terminate within $n \in \mathbb{N}$ steps we need to have $\mathtt{dt} \geq 1/n$; however the constant `dt`, being "infinitely small," must be such that $\mathtt{dt} < \varepsilon$ for any positive real number ε. Therefore it would also make sense to regard the program `elapse`

The work summarized here is supported by JSPS Grants-in-Aid No. 24680001, 24800035, 25730040 & 15KT0012; Aihara Innovative Mathematical Modelling Project, FIRST Program, JSPS/CSTP; and JST ERATO HASUO Metamathematics for Systems Design Project (No. JPMJER1603).

R. Chamberlain et al. (Eds.): CyPhy 2017, LNCS 11267, pp. 3–7, 2019.
https://doi.org/10.1007/978-3-030-17910-6_1

$$t := 0 \, ;$$
$$\textbf{while } t \leq 1 \textbf{ do}$$
$$t := t + \mathtt{dt}$$

Fig. 1. A $\textsc{While}^{\mathtt{dt}}$ program `elapse`

$$t := 0 \, ;$$
$$\textbf{while } t \leq 1 \textbf{ do}$$
$$t := t + \tfrac{1}{i+1}$$

Fig. 2. The i-th section of `elapse`

in Fig. 1 *nonterminating*—in which case the value of t would be undefined, rather than 1 (that is our intention).

Another fundamental question is whether it is legitimate to use a constant `dt` that stands for an *infinitesimal* positive real. Existence of such a number immediately leads to contradiction in the theory of reals: for `dt` to be smaller than any positive real, we must also have $\mathtt{dt} < \mathtt{dt}$. In fact, when we take a mathematical view on the program `elapse` in Fig. 1, it looks like a naive definition of Riemann integrals, in the early age of calculus, before integrals (and derivatives, limits, etc.) were given rigorous (ε, δ)-style definitions by Bolzano and Weierstrass. It is therefore far from straightforward whether we can argue rigorously about such programs with an infinitesimal constant.

It is at this point that we appeal to *nonstandard analysis (NSA)*, a theory introduced by Robinson [9] in 1960s as a rigorous reincarnation of Leibniz's calculus that is described (naively) in terms of infinitesimals. There we work in the set $^*\mathbb{R}$ of *hyperreals*; the set $^*\mathbb{R}$ extends the set $\mathbb{R}$ of *standard* real numbers with infinitesimals, infinites (such as $1/\mathtt{dt}$), and others. We can then define: a positive hyperreal r is *infinitesimal* if it is smaller than any *standard* real number.

NSA is a fruit of model theory in modern mathematical logic—the construction of the set $^*\mathbb{R}$ relies on an *ultrafilter*, a highly nonconstructive mathematical entity whose existence is guaranteed by the axiom of choice. NSA comes with the powerful *transfer principle*: a logical formula is valid in $\mathbb{R}$ if and only if it is valid in $^*\mathbb{R}$. One contribution of our series of work [4,7,10,11] is NSA-based denotational semantics of programs like `elapse` in Fig. 1. That is: we introduce a language $\textsc{While}^{\mathtt{dt}}$ that extends a usual imperative language with a constant `dt`; and we define its semantics as transformations of memory states that store hyperreals. The semantics uses the idea of *sectionwise execution*, which we shall describe now.

For the program `elapse` in Fig. 1, we define its *i-th section*—denoted by `elapse`$|_i$—as the one obtained by replacing `dt` with the constant $\frac{1}{i+1}$. See Fig. 2. Informally `elapse`$|_i$ is the "i-th approximation" of the original `elapse`.

Note that the section `elapse`$|_i$ is a usual `while` program without peculiarities like an infinitesimal constant. Therefore its semantics is defined as usual; in the current specific case the section `elapse`$|_i$ terminates after $i + 2$ iterations and it yields $1 + \frac{1}{i+1}$ as the value of the variable t.

What we do now is to collect the outcomes of such sectionwise executions, for each $i \in \mathbb{N}$, and organize them in a sequence

$$\left(1 + 1, \; 1 + \tfrac{1}{2}, \; 1 + \tfrac{1}{3}, \; \ldots, \; 1 + \tfrac{1}{i+1}, \; \ldots \right) . \tag{1}$$

Intuitively we can think of the sequence as a progressive approximation of the actual outcome of the original program elapse in Fig. 1. In fact this intuition is almost precise: in NSA a hyperreal is defined as (a suitable equivalence class of) an infinite sequence of reals (like (1)); and the sequence (1), in NSA, represents a hyperreal that is infinitely close to 1. This is what is stored in the post memory state of the program elapse, for the variable t.

Let us now go back to the first "termination" question. Following the idea of sectionwise execution, we can argue as follows: each section elapse$|_i$ terminates after $i + 2$ iterations; and collecting these numbers, we can say that the original program terminates after

$$(0 + 2,\ 1 + 2,\ 2 + 2,\ \ldots,\ i + 2,\ \ldots) \tag{2}$$

iterations. In NSA the sequence (2), much like (1), stands for a *hypernatural number* that is greater than any *standard* natural number. Summarizing, we regard elapse to be terminating, but after an *infinite hypernatural number* of iterations.

This "sectionwise" semantics of WHILE^{dt}—an imperative language with while loops and an infinitesimal constant dt—might look useless: most "programs" in WHILE^{dt} are not executable on any physical device (their loops iterate infinitely many times). Our view on WHILE^{dt} is rather that it is a *modeling* language on which we can run deductive verification. Specifically we introduce a Floyd-Hoare style program logic HOARE^{dt} for inferring about WHILE^{dt} programs. This verification framework, being a *static* (as opposed to dynamic) one, does not require programs to be executable.

Floyd-Hoare style program logics—derivation systems for *Hoare triples* $\{A\}c\{B\}$ of a precondition A, a program c and a postcondition B—are commonly used for reasoning about imperative programs [3,6]; see also [12]. They feature compositional reasoning that is inductive on program constructs; in particular the rules for while loops rely on *invariants*.

In [10] we introduce a program logic HOARE^{dt} for the programming language WHILE^{dt}, and prove that it is sound and (relatively) complete. A remarkable fact is that the derivation rules of HOARE^{dt} are *literally the same* as those of a standard Floyd-Hoare style logic. One way to look at this fact is: our results extend the transfer principle of NSA with dynamics specified as programs.

With the language WHILE^{dt} and the logic HOARE^{dt}, our workflow is as follows.

- We first model the hybrid dynamics in question as a WHILE^{dt} program c. One example of such programs is elapse in Fig. 1. With the language WHILE^{dt}— although it is a simple extension of usual imperative languages merely with a new constant dt—we can express continuous as well as discrete dynamics.
- Our goal is to establish a certain property (a *specification*) of the hybrid dynamics; a specification is expressed in the form of a precondition A and a postcondition B, both given in a usual first-order language (we will introduce one that is called ASSN^{dt}). That is, we aim to establish validity of the Hoare triple $\{A\}c\{B\}$, where c is the WHILE^{dt} modeling of the hybrid dynamics.

– Towards our aim we try to derive $\{A\}c\{B\}$ in the Floyd-Hoare type logic HOARE^{dt}. This process of proof search is almost the same as with the usual combination of an imperative programming language and a Floyd-Hoare logic: recall that the derivation rules of HOARE^{dt} are precisely the same as the usual ones; and the only difference here is presence of the constant dt.

The above workflow of "hybrid system verification" is justified by the soundness theorem for HOARE^{dt}, and the underlying (sectionwise) semantics of WHILE^{dt} programs as models of hybrid systems.

   This has been the summary of the papers [4,10]. The idea of *nonstandard static analysis*—i.e. combining deductive verification (static analysis) and nonstandard analysis—has been pushed further to verification frameworks other than Floyd-Hoare logics. Specifically, in [11] we extend a stream-processing language into one that processes continuous-time signals; for verification a refinement type system is introduced. In [7] we extend *abstract interpretation* [2] with infinitesimals, towards automatic reachability analysis of hybrid dynamics.

References

1. Alur, R., et al.: The algorithmic analysis of hybrid systems. Theor. Comp. Sci. **138**(1), 3–34 (1995)
2. Cousot, P., Cousot, R.: Abstract interpretation: a unified lattice model for static analysis of programs by construction or approximation of fixpoints. In: Graham, R.M., Harrison, M.A., Sethi, R. (eds.) Conference Record of the Fourth ACM Symposium on Principles of Programming Languages, Los Angeles, California, USA, January 1977, pp. 238–252. ACM (1977). http://doi.acm.org/10.1145/512950.512973
3. Floyd, R.W.: Assigning meanings to programs. In: Colburn, T.R., Fetzer, J.H., Rankin, T.L. (eds.) Program Verification: Fundamental Issues in Computer Science. Studies in Cognitive Systems, vol. 14, pp. 65–81. Springer, Dordrecht (1993). https://doi.org/10.1007/978-94-011-1793-7_4
4. Hasuo, I., Suenaga, K.: Exercises in *Nonstandard Static Analysis* of hybrid systems. In: Madhusudan, P., Seshia, S.A. (eds.) CAV 2012. LNCS, vol. 7358, pp. 462–478. Springer, Heidelberg (2012). https://doi.org/10.1007/978-3-642-31424-7_34
5. Henzinger, T.A.: The theory of hybrid automata. In: LICS, pp. 278–292. IEEE Computer Society (1996)
6. Hoare, C.A.R.: An axiomatic basis for computer programming. Commun. ACM **12**, 576–580, 583 (1969)
7. Kido, K., Chaudhuri, S., Hasuo, I.: Abstract interpretation with infinitesimals. In: Jobstmann, B., Leino, K.R.M. (eds.) VMCAI 2016. LNCS, vol. 9583, pp. 229–249. Springer, Heidelberg (2016). https://doi.org/10.1007/978-3-662-49122-5_11
8. Platzer, A.: Logical Analysis of Hybrid Systems-Proving Theorems for Complex Dynamics. Springer, Heidelberg (2010). https://doi.org/10.1007/978-3-642-14509-4
9. Robinson, A.: Non-standard Analysis. Princeton University Press, Princeton (1996)

10. Suenaga, K., Hasuo, I.: Programming with infinitesimals: a WHILE-language for hybrid system modeling. In: Aceto, L., Henzinger, M., Sgall, J. (eds.) ICALP 2011. LNCS, vol. 6756, pp. 392–403. Springer, Heidelberg (2011). https://doi.org/10.1007/978-3-642-22012-8_31
11. Suenaga, K., Sekine, H., Hasuo, I.: Hyperstream processing systems: nonstandard modeling of continuous-time signals. In: Giacobazzi, R., Cousot, R. (eds.) POPL, pp. 417–430. ACM (2013)
12. Winskel, G.: The Formal Semantics of Programming Languages. MIT Press, Cambridge (1993)

Design

Local Descent for Temporal Logic Falsification of Cyber-Physical Systems

Shakiba Yaghoubi[✉] and Georgios Fainekos

School of Computing, Informatics, and Decision Systems Engineering,
Arizona State University, Tempe, AZ, USA
{syaghoub,fainekos}@asu.edu

Abstract. One way to analyze Cyber-Physical Systems is by modeling them as hybrid automata. Since reachability analysis for hybrid nonlinear automata is a very challenging and computationally expensive problem, in practice, engineers try to solve the requirements falsification problem. In one method, the falsification problem is solved by minimizing a robustness metric induced by the requirements. This optimization problem is usually a non-convex non-smooth problem that requires heuristic and analytical guidance to be solved. In this paper, functional gradient descent for hybrid systems is utilized for locally decreasing the robustness metric. The local descent method is combined with Simulated Annealing as a global optimization method to search for unsafe behaviors.

Keywords: Falsification · Hybrid systems · Optimization

1 Introduction

In order to address the need for providing safety and real-time analysis for Cyber-Physical Systems (CPS), a variety of search-based falsification methods has been developed (for a survey see [1]). In search based falsification methods, the working assumption is that there is a design error in the system, and the goal of the falsifier is to search and detect system behaviors that invalidate (falsify) the system requirements. Typically, such requirements are formally expressed in Metric (MTL) [2] or Signal (STL) [3] Temporal Logic (TL).

In this paper, we continue the progress on improving single shooting falsification methods for TL specifications [4]. This class of methods is guided by evaluating how robustly a system trajectory satisfies a TL specification [5]. Positive values mean that the system trajectory satisfies the specification, while non positive values mean that the specification has been falsified by the system trajectory. Single shooting falsification methods sample one or multiple system trajectories for the whole duration of the test time, they evaluate the TL robustness of each trajectory, and, then, they decide where to sample next in the search space. Ideally, at each iteration, the proposed new samples will produce trajectories with TL robustness less than the previously sampled trajectories. However, in general, this cannot be guaranteed unless some information is available about

© Springer Nature Switzerland AG 2019
R. Chamberlain et al. (Eds.): CyPhy 2017, LNCS 11267, pp. 11–26, 2019.
https://doi.org/10.1007/978-3-030-17910-6_2

the structure of the system. In [6], it was shown that given a trajectory of a non-autonomous smooth non-linear dynamical system and a TL specification, it is possible to compute a direction in the search space along which the system will produce trajectories with reduced TL robustness. This direction is referred to as *descent direction* for TL robustness.

Our main contribution in this paper is that we extend the results of [6] to computing local descent directions for falsification of TL specifications for hybrid systems. The extension is nontrivial since as discussed later in the paper, the sensitivity analysis is challenging in the case of hybrid systems. In particular, we focus on hybrid automata [7] with non-linear dynamics in each mode and external inputs (non-autonomous systems). Hybrid automata is a mathematical model which can capture a wide range of CPS. We remark that the descent directions computed can only point toward local reduction of TL robustness. Hence, we propose combining descent direction computations with a stochastic optimization engine in order to improve the overall system falsification rate.

We highlight that the contributions of this paper have some important implications. First and foremost, it should be possible to derive results for approximating the descent direction for hybrid systems without requiring explicit knowledge of the system dynamics. For example, in [8], we showed that this is possible for smooth non-linear dynamical systems by using a number of successive linearizations along the system trajectory. The method was applied directly to Simulink models. Second, the local descent computation method could be further improved by utilizing recent results on a smooth approximation of TL robustness [9]. Therefore, the results in this paper could eventually lead to testing methods which do not require explicit knowledge of the system dynamics, and could be applied directly to a very large class of models, e.g., Simulink models, without the need for model translations or symbolic model extraction.

2 Problem Statement

In order to formalize the problem that we deal with in this paper, we will describe the system under test and also the system requirements in this section.

2.1 System Description

Hybrid automaton (HA) is a model that facilitates specification and verification of hybrid systems [7]. A hybrid automaton is specified using a tuple $\mathcal{H} = (H, H_0, U, Inv, \mathcal{E}, \Sigma)$, where $H = L \times X$ denotes the 'hybrid' discrete and continuous state spaces of $\mathcal{H}$: $L \subset \mathbb{N}$ is the set of discrete states or locations that the system switches through (each location attributes different continuous dynamics to the system), and $X \subseteq \mathbb{R}^n$ is the continuous state space of the system, $H_0 = L_0 \times X_0 \subseteq H$ is the set of *initial conditions*, U is a bounded subset of $\mathbb{R}^m$ that indicates the input signals ranges, $Inv : L \to 2^{X \times \mathbb{R}^+}$ assigns an invariant set -a subset of continuous state and time space- to each location, $\mathcal{E}$ is a set of tuples (E, Gu, Re) that determine transitions between locations. Here,

$E \subseteq L \times L$ is the set of control switches, $Gu : E \to 2^{X \times \mathbb{R}^+}$ is the guard condition that enables a control switch (i.e., the system switches from l_i to l_j when $(x(t), t) \in X \times \mathbb{R}^+$ satisfies $Gu((l_i, l_j))$) and, $Re : E \times X \to X$ is a reset map that given a transition $e \in E$ and a point x for which $Gu(e)$ is satisfied, maps x to a point in the state space X. Finally, Σ defines the continuous dynamics in each location $l \in L$:

$$\Sigma(l) : \quad \dot{x} = F_l(x, u(t), t), \tag{1}$$

where $\dot{x} = \frac{dx}{dt}$, $x \in X$ is the system continuous state, and $u : [0, T] \to U$ is the input signal map which is chosen from the set of all possible input signals $U^{[0,T]}$ whose value at time t is denoted as $u(t)$. Also, $\forall l \in L$, $F_l : X \times U \times \mathbb{R}_+ \to \mathbb{R}$ is a C^1 flow that represents the system dynamics at location l.

A *hybrid trajectory* $\eta(h_0, u(t), t)$ starting from a point $h_0 = (l_0, x_0) \in H_0$ and under the input $u \in U^{[0,T]}$ is a function $\eta : H_0 \times U \times \mathbb{R}_+ \to H$ which points to a pair (control location, state vector) for each point in time: $\eta(h_0, u(t), t) = (l(h_0, u(t), t), s(h_0, u(t), t))$, where $l(h_0, u(t), t)$ is the location at time t, and $s(h_0, u(t), t)$ is the continuous state at time t.

We write the dynamical equations for the continuous system trajectory as:

$$s(x_0, u(0), 0) = x_0$$

$$\frac{ds(x_0, u(t), t)}{dt} = F_l(s(x_0, u(t), t), u(t), t) \quad \text{while } (s(x_0, u(t), t), t) \in Inv(l) \tag{2}$$

$$s(x_0, u(t), t^+) = Re((l_i, l_j), s(x, u(t), t^-)) \text{ if } \left\{ \begin{matrix} (s(x_0, u(t), t^-), t) \in Gu((l_i, l_j)) \\ (s(x_0, u(t), t^+), t) \in Inv(l_j) \end{matrix} \right. \tag{3}$$

If the point $(s(x_0, u(t), t^+), t)$ lies outside $Inv(l_j)$, there is an error in the design. We assume that such errors do not exist in the system. The times in which the location l and consequently the right-hand side of the Eq. (2) changes, are called *transition times*. In order to avoid unnecessary technicalities, in the above equations we use the notation of [10] and denote transition times as t^- and t^+, where t^- is the time right before the transition and t^+ is the time right after that. However in more technical analysis of hybrid systems, one needs to consider the notion of hybrid time explained in [11] where a hybrid trajectory is parametrized not only by the physical time but also by the number of discrete jumps. When we consider the trajectory in a compact time interval $[0, T]$ and η is not Zeno[1], the sequence of transition times is finite.

Assumption 1. *We assume our system is deterministic, it does not exhibit Zeno behaviors and given (h_0, u) there is a unique solution $\eta(h_0, u(t), t)$ to the system.*

Remark 1. The input signal map u, should be represented using a combination of finitely many basis functions. In this paper we use piecewise constant signals.

---

[1] η is *Zeno* if it does an infinite number of jumps in a finite amount of time. A hybrid system is Zeno if at least one of its trajectories is Zeno.

2.2 System Requirements

Temporal logic formulas formally capture requirements concerning the system behavior. Requirements can be expressed by Boolean abstractions of the behavior using atomic propositions as in MTL [2], or directly through predicate expressions over the signals as in STL [3]. Since the differences are only syntactic in nature (see [12]), in the following, we will just be using the term Temporal Logics (TL) to refer to either logic.

TL formulas are formal logical statements that indicate how a system should behave and are built by combining *atomic propositions* (AP) or predicates using logical and temporal operators. The logical operators typically consist of *conjunction* ($\wedge$), *disjunction* ($\vee$), *negation* ($\neg$), and *implication* ($\rightarrow$), while temporal operators include *eventually* ($\Diamond_\mathcal{I}$), *always* ($\Box_\mathcal{I}$) and *until* ($\mathcal{U}_\mathcal{I}$) where the index $\mathcal{I}$ indicates a time interval. For example, the specification "The value of the trajectory s should reach the bound ($s_{ref} \pm 5\%$) within δ seconds and stay there afterwards" can be formulated as $\Diamond_{[0,\delta]}(\Box(|(s - s_{ref})/s_{ref}| < 5\%))$.

The robustness of a trajectory $\eta(x_0, u, t)$ with respect to a TL formula is a function of that trajectory which shows how well it satisfies the specification (see [5] for details on how the robustness is defined and calculated). The function creates a positive value when the requirement is satisfied and a negative value otherwise. Its magnitude quantifies how far the specification is from being satisfied for non-positive values, or falsified for non-negative values. Software tools such as S-TaLiRo [13] compute the robustness value of a TL formula given a trajectory $\eta(x_0, u, t)$. In order to detect unsafe system behaviors, we should falsify the specification, which means we need to find trajectories with non-positive robustness values. As a result, in a search based falsification, the effort is put on reducing the robustness value by searching in the parameter space.

It can be easily shown that given a TL formula ϕ and a trajectory $\eta(h_0, u, t)$ of a hybrid automaton $\mathcal{H}$ that satisfies the specification, if Assumption 1 holds, then there exists a *critical time* $t^* \in [0, T]$ and a *critical atomic proposition* (or *critical predicate*) p^* with respect to which the robustness is evaluated [14]. For example, in practice, the tool S-TaLiRo [13] computes the critical time t^* and atomic proposition p^* along with the robustness value of the specification. Reducing the distance of the trajectory $\eta(h_0, u, t)$ from the set defined by p^* at the critical time instance t^* will not increase the robustness value; and in most practical cases it will actually decrease it. As a consequence, the TL falsification problem can be locally converted into a safety problem, i.e., always avoid the unsafe set $\mathcal{U}$ defined by p^*. Hence, we need to compute a descent vector (h_0', u') that will decrease the distance between $\eta(h_0', u', t^*)$ and the unsafe set $\mathcal{U}$.

2.3 Problem Formulation

Let $H_\mathcal{U} \subseteq H$ denote the system unsafe set, if $\eta(h_0, u(t), t)$ enters $H_\mathcal{U}$ then system specification is falsified. To avoid a digression into unnecessary technicalities, we will assume that, both the set of initial conditions and the unsafe set are each included in a single control location, i.e., $H_0 = \{l_0\} \times X_0$, and $H_\mathcal{U} = \{l_\mathcal{U}\} \times \mathcal{U}$, where $l_0, l_\mathcal{U} \in L$, and $X_0, \mathcal{U} \subseteq X$.

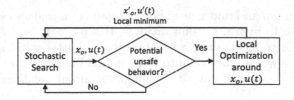

Fig. 1. 2-stage falsification: The stochastic search will search for the global optimizer while the local search improve the search speed.

Definition 1. *Let $D_{H_\mathcal{U}} : H \mapsto \mathbb{R}_+$ be the distance function to $H_\mathcal{U}$, defined by*

$$D_{H_\mathcal{U}}((l, x)) = \begin{cases} d_\mathcal{U}(x) & \text{if } l = l_\mathcal{U} \\ +\infty & \text{otherwise} \end{cases} \tag{4}$$

where $d_\mathcal{U}(x) = \inf_{u \in \mathcal{U}} ||x - u||$.

Given a compact time interval $[0, T]$, $h_0 \in H_0$, and the system input $u \in U^{[0,T]}$, we define the robustness of the system trajectory $\eta(h_0, u(t), t)$ as

$$f(h_0, u) \triangleq \min_{0 \leq t \leq T} D_{H_\mathcal{U}}(\eta(h_0, u(t), t)) \tag{5}$$

and the respective critical time as $t^* = \mathrm{argmin}_{t \in [0,T]} D_{H_\mathcal{U}}(\eta(h_0, u(t), t))$. Since all trajectories start at $l = l_0$, we will write $f(h_0, u)$ as $f(w)$ where $w = (x_0, u)$. Trajectories of minimal robustness indicate potentially unsafe behaviors, and if we can reduce the robustness value to zero, we have a falsifying trajectory. As a result robustness value should be minimized with respect to w. Our problem can be formulated generally as follows:

$$\text{minimize } f(w) \text{ such that } w \in X_0 \times U^{[0,T]} \tag{6}$$

Finding falsifying trajectories can be done in 2 stages. In the first stage, a higher level stochastic sampler determines a hybrid trajectory -a sequence of locations and state vectors- that exhibits system's potential bad behavior, and in the second stage, out of all the neighboring trajectories that follow the same sequence of locations, we find the trajectory of minimal robustness (see Fig. 1). This can be done using local minimization. In this paper, we focus on solving the problem in this stage: we will find the trajectory of minimum robustness in the neighboring of a previously created trajectory in the first stage.

Before we address our special problem of interest we should impose further assumptions on our system stated below:

1. The system is observable, i.e. we have access to all the system states, or we have a state estimator which is able to estimate them.
2. In the local search stage, we are always able to find a neighboring tube around each trajectory such that none of the trajectories inside that tube hit the guard tangentially. This ensures that trajectories of the system $\mathcal{H}$ starting

close enough to x_0 and under neighboring inputs of u undergo similar transitions/switches. In hybrid systems analysis, this property is called trajectory robustness (not to be confused with trajectory robustness in this paper) and is guaranteed if we can find an auto-bisimulation function of a trajectory and the trajectories starting from its neighboring initial conditions and under neighboring inputs [15].

3. The system is deterministic and the transitions are taken as soon as possible. In order to have a deterministic system, if two transitions happen from the same location, their *Guards* should be mutually exclusive.

4. *Guards* are of the form $g(x,t) = 0$ and *Reset* maps are functions of the form $x' = h(x)$, where g and h are C^1 functions. For all the states that satisfy a *Guard* condition the corresponding *Reset* map should satisfy $\frac{\partial h}{\partial x}\big|_x \neq 0$.

5. The trajectory $\eta(h_0, u(t), t)$ returned by the first stage, from which we descend, enters the location of the unsafe set.

The last assumption is made so that our problem be well-defined (note that the objective function (5) will have finite value only if trajectory enters unsafe location). The task of finding such an initial condition h_0 is delegated to the higher-level stochastic search algorithm within which our method is integrated (Fig. 1). If finding such a trajectory for the higher-level stochastic algorithm is hard, we can still improve our trajectories locally by descending toward the guards. This will be discussed more in the next section.

The problem is addressed in the following:

Problem 1. Given a hybrid automaton $\mathcal{H}$, a compact time interval $[0,T]$, a set of initial conditions $H_0 \subseteq H$, a set of inputs $U^{[0,T]}$, a point $h_0 = (l_0, x_0) \in H_0$ and an input $u \in U^{[0,T]}$ such that the system trajectory satisfies $0 < f(w) < +\infty$, find a vector $dw = (dx_0, du) \in X \times U^{[0,T]}$ that satisfies the following property:

$\exists \Delta_1, \Delta_2 \in \mathbb{R}^+$ such that $\forall \delta_1 \in (0, \Delta_1), \delta_2 \in (0, \Delta_2)$, $h_0' = (l_0, x_0 + \delta_1 dx_0) \in H_0$ and $u' = u + \delta_2 du \in U^{[0,T]}$, $\eta(h_0', u'(t), t)$ undergoes the same transitions as $\eta(h_0, u(t), t)$, and also $f(w + \delta dw) \leq f(w)$ where $\delta = min\{\delta_1, \delta_2\}$.

Finding such a descent direction can help improve the performance of stochastic algorithms [4] that intend to solve the general problem in Eq. (6).

Note that for the piecewise constant inputs u that we are working with in this paper, du is also a piecewise constant signal whose variables should be computed. Variables of du show the desired changes in that of the input signal u.

3   Finding a Descent Direction for the Robustness

In this section, given a trajectory $\eta(h_0, u(t), t)$, we find dx_0 and du such that the trajectory $\eta(h_0', u'(t), t)$, where $h_0' = (l_0, x_0 + \delta dx_0)$, $u'(t) = u(t) + \delta du(t)$, attains a smaller robustness value; i.e. $f(w') = f(x_0', u') < f(x_0, u) = f(w)$. The robustness function in Eq. (5) is hard to deal with as it is non differentiable and non convex [14]. To solve this issue we calculate the descent direction with respect to a convex, almost everywhere differentiable function, and show that decreasing the value of this function yields a decrease in the robustness function:

Theorem 1. *Let $x_0, x_0' \in X_0$, $u, u' \in U^{[0,T]}$, and assume that the critical time for the continuous part of the hybrid trajectory $s \triangleq s(x_0, u(t), t)$, is t^*. Define*

$$J(x_0', u') = \begin{cases} \|s(x_0', u'(t^*), t^*) - z(x_0, u(t^*), t^*)\| & \text{if } l = l_{\mathcal{U}} \\ +\infty & \text{otherwise} \end{cases} \quad (7)$$

where l is the first argument of $\eta(h_0', u'(t^*), t^*)$, and

$$z(x_0, u(t), t) = argmin_{z \in \mathcal{U}} \|z - s(x_0, u(t), t)\|. \quad (8)$$

If we find a trajectory $s' \triangleq s(x_0', u'(t), t)$ such that $J(x_0', u') < J(x_0, u)$, then the robustness of the trajectory s' is smaller than that of s, i.e.: $f(x_0', u') < f(x_0, u)$.

Proof. By Eq. (5) we have $f(x_0', u') = \min_{0 \leq t \leq T} D_{H_{\mathcal{U}}}(\eta(h_0', u'(t), t)) \leq J(x_0', u') < J(x_0, u) = f(x_0, u)$. $\qquad \square$

Let $x_0' = x_0 + dx$ and $u' = u + du$. Consider J at the unsafe location and define:

$$J(x_0', u') = G(s(x_0', u'(t^*), t^*)), \quad (9)$$

where $G(x) = \|x - z(x_0, u(t^*), t^*)\|$. Notice that the definition of G is based on a primary trajectory from which we want to descend. The total difference of a multi variable function shows the change in its value with respect to the changes in its independent variables while its partial differential is its derivative with respect to one variable, while others are kept constant. In the following, dx and du are calculated using the chain rule, such that $J(x_0', u') - J(x_0, u) = J(x_0 + dx, u + du) - J(x_0, u) = dJ(x_0, u) < 0$:

$$dJ(x_0, u; dx, du) = \frac{\partial G^T}{\partial x} ds(x_0, u, t^*) \quad (10)$$

where $\frac{\partial G}{\partial x} \triangleq \frac{\partial G}{\partial x}\big|_{s(x_0, u(t^*), t^*)} \in \mathbb{R}^{n \times 1}$ is the steepest direction that increases distance from the unsafe set, i.e., $-\frac{\partial G}{\partial x}$ is along the approach vector mentioned in [14] that shows the direction of the shortest distance between $s(x_0, u(t^*), t^*)$ and the unsafe set. Now observe that:

$$ds(x_0, u, t^*) = D_1 s(x_0, u, t^*) dx_0 + D_2 s(x_0, u, t^*) du \quad (11)$$

where D_i denotes the partial differentiation with respect to the ith argument (for instance $D_1 s = \frac{\partial s}{\partial x_0}$). Here, $D_1 s(x_0, u, t^*)$ and $D_2 s(x_0, u, t^*)$ are the sensitivity of the trajectory to the initial condition and input at time t^*, respectively. In the next section we show how to calculate sensitivity for a hybrid trajectory. Using Eqs. (10) and (11), we choose:

$$dx_0 = -c_1 \left(\frac{\partial G^T}{\partial x} D_1 s(x_0, u, t^*) \right)^T, \quad du = -c_2 \left(\frac{\partial G^T}{\partial x} D_2 s(x_0, u, t^*) \right)^T \quad (12)$$

for some $c_1, c_2 > 0$. As a result, we have $dJ(x_0, u) = -c_1 \| \frac{\partial s}{\partial x_0}^T \frac{\partial G}{\partial x} \|^2 -$ $c_2 \| \frac{\partial s}{\partial u}^T \frac{\partial G}{\partial x} \|^2 \leq 0$ and the equality holds if and only if $\frac{\partial s}{\partial x_0} \big|_{(x_0, u, t^*)}^T \frac{\partial G}{\partial x} =$ $\frac{\partial s}{\partial u} \big|_{(x_0, u, t^*)}^T \frac{\partial G}{\partial x} = 0$.

All the above calculations are based on the assumption that the trajectory enters the unsafe location, but even if finding a trajectory that enters the unsafe location using stochastic higher level search is hard, we can still improve trajectories locally by descending toward the guard Gu^* that takes the trajectory to the location with the shortest possible path to the unsafe set. This is shown in Fig. 2. For instance if the guard Gu^* is activated when $g(x) = 0$, we can easily use zero finding methods to find a set $M = \{x \mid g(x) = 0\}$ and replace $\mathcal{U}$ in all the previous calculations with the set M.

4   Sensitivity Calculation for a Hybrid Trajectory

Extending sensitivity analysis to the hybrid case is not straightforward and even in the case that there is no reset in transitions and the state stays continuous, a discontinuity often appears in the sensitivity function that needs to be evaluated [10]. In order to make the results comprehensive, in this section we analyze the sensitivity for trajectories of a Hybrid automaton. Without loss of generality, in order to focus on the complexity that happens under transitions, we consider a hybrid automaton with only two discrete locations ($|L| = 2$) and one control switch, also we assume $l_0 \neq l_\mathcal{U}$. There are 2 scenarios:

1. $(s(x, u(t), t), t)$ is either inside $Inv(l_0)$ or $Inv(l_\mathcal{U})$
2. $(s(x, u(t), t), t) \in Gu((l_0, l_\mathcal{U}))$

Let us use p_{x_0} and p_u to denote the sensitivity of the trajectory to changes in x_0 and u respectively, i.e., $p_{x_0}(t, t_0) = D_1 s(x_0, u, t)$ and $p_u(t, t_0) = D_2 s(x_0, u, t)$. It can be shown easily that in the first scenario, while $(s(x_0, u, t), t) \in Inv(l_i)$ and $i \in \{0, \mathcal{U}\}$:

$$\dot{p}_{x_0}(t, t_0) = D_1 F_{l_i}(s(x_0, u, t), u(t), t).p_{x_0}(t, t_0), \tag{13a}$$
$$\dot{p}_u(t, t_0) = D_1 F_{l_i}(s(x_0, u(t), t), u(t), t).p_u(t, t_0) + D_2 F_{l_i}(s(x_0, u(t), t), u(t), t), \tag{13b}$$

with the following initial and boundary conditions:

$$p_{x_0}(t_0, t_0) = I_{n \times n}, \ p_u(t_0, t_0) = 0, \tag{14a}$$
$$p_{x_0}(\tau^+, t_0) = r_{x_0}, \ p_u(\tau^+, t_0) = r_u. \tag{14b}$$

where τ^+ is the right hand side limit of the transition time τ that satisfies $(s(x_0, u(\tau), \tau), \tau) \in Gu((l_0, l_\mathcal{U}))$. We will calculate r_{x_0} and r_u in the following subsection. Consider that even if there is no reset, this jump happens in the state triggered transitions since neighboring trajectories have different transition times and as a result they are under different dynamics during the time between their transition times (see Fig. 3).

4.1   Sensitivity Jump Calculation

Assume that if $g(s(x_0, u(t), t), t) = 0$ then $(s(x_0, u(t), t), t) \in Gu((l_0, l_U))$. Let us denote the transition time by $\tau(x_0, u)$, which reminds us that this transition time differs for different trajectories; if the dependence was clear from context, we will write down τ, for brevity. Assume that $Re(x, (l_1, l_2)) = h(x)$, we have:

$$s(x_0, u(\tau^+), \tau^+) = h(s(x_0, u(\tau^-), \tau^-)) \tag{15}$$

To calculate the value of p_{x_0} at τ^+ we take derivatives with respect to x_0 from the above equation. We have:

$$\frac{ds(x_0, u, \tau^+)}{dx_0} = \frac{\partial h}{\partial x} \frac{ds(x_0, u, \tau^-)}{dx_0} \Rightarrow$$

$$D_1 s(x_0, u, \tau^+) + D_3 s(x_0, u, \tau^+)\frac{\partial \tau}{\partial x_0} = \frac{\partial h}{\partial x}(D_1(s(x_0, u, \tau^-)) + D_3 s(x_0, u, \tau^-)\frac{\partial \tau}{\partial x_0})$$

$$\Rightarrow p_{x_0}(\tau^+, t_0) = D_1 s(x_0, u, \tau^+) = \frac{\partial h}{\partial x}p_{x_0}(\tau^-, t_0) + (\frac{\partial h}{\partial x}f^- - f^+)D_1\tau \tag{16}$$

where $\frac{\partial h}{\partial x} = \frac{\partial h}{\partial x}\big|_{s(x_0, u(\tau^-), \tau^-)}$, and f^- and f^+ are equal to $F_{l_0}(s(x_0, u(\tau^-), \tau^-), u(\tau^-), \tau^-)$ and $F_{l_U}(s(x_0, u(\tau^+), \tau^+), u(\tau^+)), \tau^+)$ respectively. To calculate $D_1\tau$, consider that τ satisfies $g(s(x_0, u, \tau), \tau(x_0, u)) = 0$, taking the derivatives with respect to x_0, we have:

$$D_1 g^T(D_1 s(x_0, u, \tau) + D_3 s(x_0, u, \tau).D_1\tau) + D_2 g.D_1\tau = 0$$

$$\Rightarrow D_1\tau = \frac{\partial \tau}{\partial x_0} = -\frac{D_1 g^T.p_{x_0}(\tau^-, t_0)}{D_1 g^T.f^- + D_2 g} \tag{17}$$

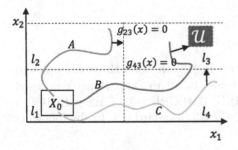

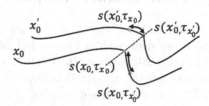

Fig. 2. Trajectories B, A and C improve locally by descending toward the unsafe set, guard g_{43} and guard g_{23} respectively.

Fig. 3. Assuming $\tau_{x_0} < \tau_{x_0'}$, trajectories are under different dynamics for all the times $t \in [\tau_{x_0}, \tau_{x_0'}]$, where τ_{x_0} and $\tau_{x_0'}$ are transition times for $s(x_0, .)$ and $s(x_0', .)$ respectively.

Using similar analysis we have:

$$p_u(\tau^+, t_0) = \frac{\partial h}{\partial x} p_u(\tau^-, t_0) + (\frac{\partial h}{\partial x} f^- - f^+) D_2 \tau^T \tag{18}$$

$$D_2\tau = -\frac{D_1 g^T . p_u(\tau^-, t_0)}{D_1 g^T . f^- + D_2 g} \tag{19}$$

Using a hybrid automaton, sensitivity and system states can be calculated simultaneously (see Fig. 4). This will easily let us calculate the sensitivities by reseting their values at transition times. Note that using Eqs. (16) to (19), for a system with time triggered transitions $(g(x,t) = g'(t))$ whose reset map is identity $(h(x) = x)$, there are no jumps in sensitivities, i.e., $p_{x_0}(\tau^+, t_0) = p_{x_0}(\tau^-, t_0)$ and $p_u(\tau^+, t_0) = p_u(\tau^-, t_0)$. These types of hybrid systems can be handled using our previous work in [8] where we showed how to use system linearized matrices to approximately calculate the decent direction. However to have these kinds of gray box analysis for hybrid systems with state dependent transitions, we also need to have some information about the guards or be able to approximate them in order to model the jumps in the sensitivity. In the future we will work on the descent calculation using gray box models of the general hybrid systems.

An algorithm to find the gradient descent (GD) directions for hybrid systems is mentioned in the technical version of the paper [16].

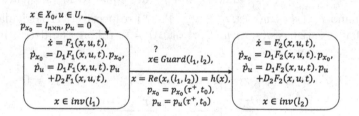

Fig. 4. HA of the system and trajectory sensitivity

5   Experimental Results

In order to show the utility of our method, in [16] we used three examples in which we deal with nonlinear hybrid systems. In all the experiments we used MATLAB 2015b on an Intel(R) Core(TM) i7-4790 CPU @3.6 GHZ with 16 GB memory processor with Windows Server 2012 R2 Standard OS. In the following we present one of the examples:

Example 1. Consider the motion of a rigid object on a plane that uses a pair of off-centered thrusters as the control input. Since these thrusters are not aligned with the center of the mass, they will create both translational and rotational motions on the vehicle [15]. The system is supposed to satisfy the requirement in Eq. (20) which implies that the vehicle should avoid the unsafe sets $\mathcal{U}_1$ and $\mathcal{U}_2$

(shown in Fig. 5 with red boxes) and reaches the goal set G (shown with a blue box) within the simulation time $T = 10$. Here (x_1, x_2) is the vehicle position.

$$\varphi_2 = \square_{[0,10]} \neg ((x_1, x_2) \in \mathcal{U}_1 \vee (x_1, x_2) \in \mathcal{U}_2) \wedge \Diamond_{[0,10]} (x_1, x_2) \in G \qquad (20)$$

The location-based dynamics of the vehicle are mentioned in Eq. (21), where $j \in \{1, 2, 3\}$, x_1, x_2 are the positions along the x and y axis, x_3 is the angle with the x-axis and x_4, x_5 and x_6 are their derivatives. The hybrid model consists of 3 locations, where $inv(l = 1) = \{x | x_1 < 4\}$, $inv(l = 2) = \{x | 4 \le x_1 \le 8\}$, and $inv(l = 3) = \{x | x_1 > 8\}$. The guards are shown using dashed lines in Fig. 5. The unsafe sets have attractive non-centered forces in their corresponding locations. In particular, $\mathcal{U}_1$ is located in location 2 and $\mathcal{U}_2$ is located in location 3. At location 1, $s_1(l = 1) = s_2(l = 1) = 0$, at location 2, $s_1(l = 2) = -1$ and $s_2(l = 2) = 0$, and at location 3, $s_1(l = 3) = 0$ and $s_2(l = 3) = -2$. (α_1, β_1) and (α_2, β_2) are the centers of $\mathcal{U}_1$ and $\mathcal{U}_2$, respectively.

$$\begin{bmatrix} \dot{x}_j \\ \dot{x}_4 \\ \dot{x}_5 \\ \dot{x}_6 \end{bmatrix} = \begin{bmatrix} x_{j+3} \\ 0.1x_4 + \Sigma_{i=1,2} s_i(l)(x_1 - \alpha_i) + F_1 \cos(x_5) - F_2 \sin(x_5) \\ 0.1x_5 + \Sigma_{i=1,2} s_i(l)(x_2 - \beta_i) + F_1 \sin(x_5) - F_2 \cos(x_5) \\ -\frac{b}{I} F_1 + \frac{a}{I} F_2 \end{bmatrix} \qquad (21)$$

Our search is over the initial values in $[0, 1] \times [0.5, 1]$, and the input signals $F_1(t), F_2(t) \in [-1, 1]$; other states are zero initially. Since the search over all the continuous input signals is a search in infinite dimension, here, we used piecewise constant inputs with 11 variables for each $F_1(t)$ and $F_2(t)$. So the overall search is over 24 dimensions. Starting from a trajectory that satisfies Eq. (20) with the robustness value equal to 0.2950, our method improves the robustness value to 0.8599 (Note that while in a falsification problem we try to decrease the robustness value, in a related problem called satisfaction problem increasing that value is desired). The projection of the trajectories into the $x_1 - x_2$ plane is shown in Fig. 5, where dark gray trajectories are refined to light gray ones.

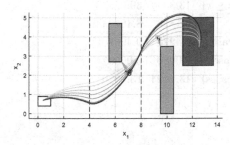 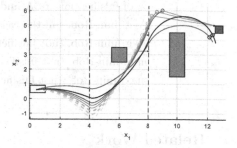

Fig. 5. Improving the robustness of the trajectories of the system of Eq. (21) with respect to the specification φ_2 from 0.2950 to 0.8599. Red arrows show the steepest ascent direction. (Color figure online)

Fig. 6. Trajectories that do not enter the goal set location (dashed trajectories here) can still improve by descending toward the guard set (dashed line at $x_1 = 8$).

In Fig. 6, one can see that even if the trajectory from which we want to descend does not enter the goal set location, we are still able to improve the trajectory by descending toward the adjacent guard with the least distance from that set.

In order to determine the effect of applying GD local search method to global search methods like Simulated Annealing (SA), we performed a statistical study in which we compare the combination of SA and GD (SA+GD) with SA only. To combine SA and GD, we apply GD algorithm whenever the samples taken by SA return a robustness value less than some threshold value r_T.

In our experiment we ran SA and SA+GD for 150 times with equal total number of samples $N = 100$ and $r_T = 2.5$ to automatically search for initial conditions and inputs that satisfy the specification φ_2 with $\mathcal{U}_1 = [5.5, 6.5] \times [2.5, 3.5]$, $\mathcal{U}_2 = [9.5, 10.5] \times [1.5, 4.5]$, $G = [12.5, 13] \times [4.5, 5]$ for the system in Example 1. In order to satisfy φ_2, we try to falsify its negation $\neg\varphi_2$. The results are shown in Table 1. The improvement in finding falsifying trajectories is clear from the total number of falsifications in the first row. Also, since GD gets a chance to improve the performance only if SA finds a robustness value less than r_T, we added the second row which shows in how many percents of the cases falsification is achieved if SA finds a robustness value less than r_T. While average of the best robustness value for all the tests is better for SA+GD algorithm, it is slightly better for SA if we only consider non-falsified cases. We can conclude that even if SA finds small robustness values, it is hardly able to further decrease it. As the constant budget in the comparison is "equal total number of simulations", we can claim that SA+GD can help improve the results if simulations/experiments are costly. Choosing different design parameters might lead to even better experimental results.

Table 1. Comparing SA and SA+GD results for the system of Example 1

Optim. method	SA	SA+GD
num. of total falsification	4/150	16/150
% of falsification if SA finds $r \leq r_T$	13.33%	39.02%
Avg. min-Rob. (all the cases)	9.1828	8.4818
Avg. min-Rob. (not falsified cases)	9.4278	9.4968
min. min-Rob. (not falsified cases)	0.0080	0.0059
max. min-Rob. (not falsified cases)	13.1424	13.0880

6   Related Work

One possible categorization for falsification approaches divides them into Single Shooting (SS) vs. Multiple Shooting (MS) methods. The technique of numerically solving boundary value problems is called shooting. SS approaches search over the space of system trajectories initiated from the set of initial conditions and under possible inputs. S-TaLiRo [13] and Breach [17] lie in this category. In contrast, MS approaches create approximate trajectories from trajectory segments starting from multiple initial conditions (not necessarily inside the initial set). Hence, the trajectories contain gaps between segments. The works [18,19] fall in this category. MS techniques cannot handle general TL requirements.

Motion planning approaches such as Rapidly-exploring Random Trees (RRT) lie in a category between SS and MS approaches. Starting from an initial condition, the tree grows toward the unsafe set (or vice versa) to find an unsafe behavior of a non-autonomous system [20,21]. The applicability of these methods, however, is limited since it depends on many factors such as the dimensionality of the system, the modeling language, and the local planner.

The performance of SS falsification methods can be improved using different complementary directions. One direction is to provide alternative TL robustness metrics [22]. Another direction is to compute guaranteed or approximate descent directions [8,14] in order to utilize descent optimization methods. Our method in this paper is a SS approach that uses optimization and robustness metric to solve the falsification problem. In [6,14] robustness-based falsification is guided using descent direction; however, that line of work is only applicable to purely continuous systems. In [23], descent direction is calculated in the case of linear hybrid systems using optimization methods.

In [19] authors use a MS approach to find falsifying trajectories of a hybrid system. Providing the gradient information to an NLP solver, they try to reduce the gaps between segments. Like our approach, they require knowledge of the system dynamics and solve a local search problem. Unlike our method, in their approach, falsifying trajectories are segmented trajectories which are not real system trajectories unless the gaps between segments become zero in the optimization procedure (for systems with identity reset maps), which may not be the case, in general. As a result, falsification cannot be concluded unless they can randomly find a neighboring real system trajectory that violates the specification. We think that our approach can help their method to effectively search over real trajectories neighboring the segmented trajectory. Furthermore, the specifications they have focused on in [19] are safety properties and because of the nature of the search, their method cannot easily be extended to search for system trajectories that falsify general MTL formulas.

The general idea of using sensitivity to explore the parameter space of a problem that deals with robustness of a TL formula was first introduced in [24]. To solve a verification problem, they propose using the sensitivity of a robustness function to a parameter assuming that the function is differentiable to that parameter. There are however multiple factors which result in non-differentiability of the robustness function with respect to a parameter: First of all, the predicates themselves might be non smooth and non-differentiable. Secondly, hybrid systems may have non smooth and non-differentiable trajectories. Finally, logical operators in the TL formula impose min and max operators to robustness function. The paper suggests using left and right hand derivatives for dealing with min and max operators, but it does not propose solutions for the first two cases. In our framework, by introducing Eq. (7), we solve the non differentiability issue in the first case and the analysis in Sect. 4 deals with this issue in the second case. Also, the problem we try to solve is a different problem (a falsification problem).

In [25], a smooth infinitely differentiable robustness function is introduced which solves – to some extent – the non-differentiability problem of the robustness function to parameters. In the case of hybrid systems however, we still deal with this problem as the non-differentiability is caused by the system model rather than the robustness function itself. In the future, we will investigate if the results in [25] could further improve the performance of gradient descent falsification methods as formulated in our work.

In [26], an algorithm to approximate reachable sets using sensitivity analysis is introduced. Sensitivity of hybrid systems without reset maps is used to verify safety properties. Like all approaches that try to solve a coverage problem, the method suffers from the state explosion issue which happens when one tries to cover the high dimensional spaces induced by the variables in the input signal parameterization. Our framework solves a different problem and it is applicable to hybrid systems with reset maps under general TL formulas. Furthermore, as we are not solving a coverage problem, we do not face the state explosion issue.

7   Conclusion

TL robustness guided falsification [4] has shown great potential in terms of black or gray box automatic test case generation for CPS [27–29]. In this paper, we presented a method that locally improves the search for falsifying behaviors by computing descent directions for the TL robustness in the search space of the falsification problem. Our proposed method computes such descent directions for non-linear hybrid systems with external inputs, which was not possible before in the literature. Using examples, we demonstrated that our framework locally decreases the TL robustness at each iteration. Furthermore, our preliminary statistical results indicate that it is possible to improve a global test-based falsification framework when the proposed local gradient descent method is utilized.

Currently, the proposed framework requires a symbolic representation of the non-linear dynamics and the switching conditions of the hybrid automaton in order to compute the descent direction. As future research, we expect that we can relax this requirement by numerically computing approximations to the descent directions similarly to our work for smooth non-linear dynamical systems [8]. This will enable the application of the local descent method to a wide range of Simulink models without explicit extraction of the system dynamics.

Acknowledgments. This work was partially supported by the NSF awards CNS-1319560, CNS 1350420, IIP-1361926, and the NSF I/UCRC Center for Embedded Systems.

References

1. Kapinski, J., Deshmukh, J.V., Jin, X., Ito, H., Butts, K.: Simulation-based approaches for verification of embedded control systems: an overview of traditional and advanced modeling, testing, and verification techniques. IEEE Control Syst. Mag. **36**(6), 45–64 (2016)
2. Koymans, R.: Specifying real-time properties with metric temporal logic. Real-Time Syst. **2**(4), 255–299 (1990)
3. Maler, O., Nickovic, D.: Monitoring temporal properties of continuous signals. In: Lakhnech, Y., Yovine, S. (eds.) FORMATS/FTRTFT - 2004. LNCS, vol. 3253, pp. 152–166. Springer, Heidelberg (2004). https://doi.org/10.1007/978-3-540-30206-3_12
4. Abbas, H., Fainekos, G.E., Sankaranarayanan, S., Ivancic, F., Gupta, A.: Probabilistic temporal logic falsification of cyber-physical systems. ACM Trans. Embed. Comput. Syst. **12**(s2), 95 (2013)
5. Fainekos, G., Pappas, G.: Robustness of temporal logic specifications for continuous-time signals. Theoret. Comput. Sci. **410**(42), 4262–4291 (2009)
6. Abbas, H., Winn, A., Fainekos, G., Julius, A.A.: Functional gradient descent method for metric temporal logic specifications. In: 2014 American Control Conference, pp. 2312–2317. IEEE (2014)
7. Alur, R.: Principles of Cyber-Physical Systems. MIT Press, Cambridge (2015)
8. Yaghoubi, S., Fainekos, G.: Hybrid approximate gradient and stochastic descent for falsification of nonlinear systems. In: American Control Conference (2017)
9. Pant, Y.V., Abbas, H., Mangharam, R.: Control using the smooth robustness of temporal logic. Technical report MLAB paper 98, University of Pennsylvania Scholarly Commons (2017)
10. Donzé, A., Maler, O.: Systematic simulation using sensitivity analysis. In: Bemporad, A., Bicchi, A., Buttazzo, G. (eds.) HSCC 2007. LNCS, vol. 4416, pp. 174–189. Springer, Heidelberg (2007). https://doi.org/10.1007/978-3-540-71493-4_16
11. Goebel, R., Teel, A.R.: Solutions to hybrid inclusions via set and graphical convergence with stability theory applications. Automatica **42**(4), 573–587 (2006)
12. Dokhanchi, A., Hoxha, B., Fainekos, G.: Metric interval temporal logic specification elicitation and debugging. In: 13th ACM-IEEE International Conference on Formal Methods and Models for System Design, September 2015
13. Annpureddy, Y., Liu, C., Fainekos, G., Sankaranarayanan, S.: S-TaLiRo: a tool for temporal logic falsification for hybrid systems. In: Abdulla, P.A., Leino, K.R.M. (eds.) TACAS 2011. LNCS, vol. 6605, pp. 254–257. Springer, Heidelberg (2011). https://doi.org/10.1007/978-3-642-19835-9_21
14. Abbas, H., Fainekos, G.: Computing descent direction of MTL robustness for nonlinear systems. In: 2013 American Control Conference, pp. 4405–4410. IEEE (2013)
15. Winn, A., Julius, A.A.: Safety controller synthesis using human generated trajectories. IEEE Trans. Autom. Control **60**(6), 1597–1610 (2015)
16. https://sites.google.com/a/asu.edu/s-taliro/local-descent-temporal.pdf
17. Donzé, A.: Breach, a toolbox for verification and parameter synthesis of hybrid systems. In: Touili, T., Cook, B., Jackson, P. (eds.) CAV 2010. LNCS, vol. 6174, pp. 167–170. Springer, Heidelberg (2010). https://doi.org/10.1007/978-3-642-14295-6_17
18. Zutshi, A., Deshmukh, J.V., Sankaranarayanan, S., Kapinski, J.: Multiple shooting, CEGAR-based falsification for hybrid systems. In: Proceedings of the 14th International Conference on Embedded Software, p. 5. ACM (2014)

19. Zutshi, A., Sankaranarayanan, S., Deshmukh, J.V., Kapinski, J.: A trajectory splicing approach to concretizing counterexamples for hybrid systems. In: 2013 IEEE 52nd Annual Conference on Decision and Control (CDC). IEEE (2013)

20. Dreossi, T., Dang, T., Donzé, A., Kapinski, J., Jin, X., Deshmukh, J.V.: Efficient guiding strategies for testing of temporal properties of hybrid systems. In: Havelund, K., Holzmann, G., Joshi, R. (eds.) NFM 2015. LNCS, vol. 9058, pp. 127–142. Springer, Cham (2015). https://doi.org/10.1007/978-3-319-17524-9_10

21. Plaku, E., Kavraki, L.E., Vardi, M.Y.: Falsification of LTL safety properties in hybrid systems. In: Kowalewski, S., Philippou, A. (eds.) TACAS 2009. LNCS, vol. 5505, pp. 368–382. Springer, Heidelberg (2009). https://doi.org/10.1007/978-3-642-00768-2_31

22. Akazaki, T., Hasuo, I.: Time robustness in MTL and expressivity in hybrid system falsification. In: Kroening, D., Păsăreanu, C.S. (eds.) CAV 2015. LNCS, vol. 9207, pp. 356–374. Springer, Cham (2015). https://doi.org/10.1007/978-3-319-21668-3_21

23. Abbas, H., Fainekos, G.: Linear hybrid system falsification with descent. arXiv preprint arXiv:1105.1733 (2011)

24. Donzé, A., Maler, O.: Robust satisfaction of temporal logic over real-valued signals. In: Chatterjee, K., Henzinger, T.A. (eds.) FORMATS 2010. LNCS, vol. 6246, pp. 92–106. Springer, Heidelberg (2010). https://doi.org/10.1007/978-3-642-15297-9_9

25. Pant, Y.V., Abbas, H., Mangharam, R.: Smooth operator: control using the smooth robustness of temporal logic (2017)

26. Donzé, A., Krogh, B., Rajhans, A.: Parameter synthesis for hybrid systems with an application to simulink models. In: Majumdar, R., Tabuada, P. (eds.) HSCC 2009. LNCS, vol. 5469, pp. 165–179. Springer, Heidelberg (2009). https://doi.org/10.1007/978-3-642-00602-9_12

27. Fainekos, G., Sankaranarayanan, S., Ueda, K., Yazarel, H.: Verification of automotive control applications using S-TaLiRo. In: Proceedings of the American Control Conference (2012)

28. Strathmann, T., Oehlerking, J.: Verifying properties of an electro-mechanical braking system. In: Frehse, G., Althoff, M. (eds.) ARCH14-15. 1st and 2nd International Workshop on Applied veRification for Continuous and Hybrid Systems. EPiC Series in Computing, vol. 34, pp. 49–56. EasyChair (2015)

29. Sankaranarayanan, S., Kumar, S.A., Cameron, F., Bequette, B.W., Fainekos, G., Maahs, D.: Model-based falsification of an artificial pancreas control system. In: Medical Cyber Physical Systems Workshop (2016)

Memory Access Pattern-Aware DRAM Controller Design for Mixed-Criticality Systems

Jeongyoon Eo, Kang-Wook Kim, and Chang-Gun Lee[✉]

Seoul National University, Gwanak-ro 1 Gwanak-gu, Seoul 151-744, Korea
{jyeo,kwkim}@rubis.snu.ac.kr, cglee@snu.ac.kr
https://rubis.snu.ac.kr/

Abstract. Mixed-criticality systems integrate tasks with various levels of criticality onto the same hardware platform. Critical tasks require tight bounding of worst case latency at any cost, yet for non-critical tasks it is important to provide high performance as much as possible. In this paper, we take workload-driven approach and propose a novel *workload-aware* DRAM controller design for mixed-criticality system that can successfully achieve both of the conflicting demands in the presence of memory-intensive workloads. By using bank partitioning and request batching with prioritization, we provide tighter worst case latency bound for critical tasks and high performance and fairness for non-critical tasks. Our evaluation shows that the design achieves maximum 18% of performance improvement.

Keywords: Memory access pattern · Mixed-criticality system · DRAM controller

1 Introduction

Mixed-criticality systems are real-time systems where tasks of different criticalities are integrated onto the same hardware platform [2]. The mixed-criticality systems should guarantee strict safety assurance to critical tasks while providing high performance to non-critical tasks at the same time. These conflicting demands impose a difficult challenge to mixed-criticality system design. For strict safety assurance, it should guarantee *performance isolation* of critical tasks from others. But for high performance, allowing *efficient sharing* of underlying hardware resources is necessary.

In this paper, we take a novel workload-driven approach in designing DRAM controller for mixed-criticality systems with two criticality modes, i.e., critical and non-critical. It guarantees deterministic memory access latency for the critical tasks (tasks in critical mode) and provides high performance for the non-critical tasks (tasks in non-critical mode) at the same time. In order to achieve this goal, the proposed DRAM controller adopts request batching [13]. On top

© Springer Nature Switzerland AG 2019
R. Chamberlain et al. (Eds.): CyPhy 2017, LNCS 11267, pp. 27–42, 2019.
https://doi.org/10.1007/978-3-030-17910-6_3

of this, we classify tasks into three classes according to tasks' criticality modes and their memory access patterns as follows:

– **Latency-sensitive tasks:** critical tasks whose memory access latency should be guaranteed. For latency-sensitive tasks, the proposed DRAM controller design guarantees their memory access latency by immediately preempting memory access requests of non-critical tasks and processing the requests of the critical tasks as in [7].
– **Locality-sensitive tasks:** non-critical tasks that exhibit high DRAM bank locality. In order to preserve DRAM bank locality of tasks, dedicated DRAM banks are allocated to each task in this class.
– **Capacity-sensitive tasks:** non-critical tasks whose performance is sensitive to the amount of DRAM banks they can access. For capacity-sensitive tasks, multiple shared DRAM banks are assigned to entire tasks in this class for them to enjoy large memory capacity. Since capacity-sensitive tasks have low locality, the gain from increased memory capacity outweighs the loss from memory conflict at the shared banks.

We present the worst case latency analysis of tasks in each class. Our simulation study shows that this design improves the performance of tasks by maximum 18%.

The rest of the paper is organized as follows: Sect. 2 presents brief background of DRAM memory. In Sect. 3, we introduce our observation according to the DRAM memory access pattern. Section 4 defines the system model and proposes our DRAM controller design. Section 5 reports the simulation study of the proposed design. Section 6 presents the related work. Finally, Sect. 7 concludes the paper and brings up future work.

2   Background

In this section, we provide basic background knowledge of modern DRAM architecture. For more details, we refer readers to [6,8].

2.1   DRAM Architecture and Characteristics

Modern DRAM consists of multiple units called *banks*. A DRAM bank is a two-dimensional array. Data are stored in its cells, the interconnection point of a row and a column of the array, as in Fig. 1 To read or write data, first the whole row that contains the desired cell should be loaded into a *row buffer* inside the bank. To access data located in another row, the row buffer should be emptied before that row is loaded, which takes additional time. Due to this fact, row buffer acts as an *internal cache of a DRAM bank*. A DRAM bank enjoys cache hit benefit when it is a *Row Hit* case and suffers from cache miss penalty when it is a

Row Miss or a Row Conflict case. In terms of latency, the benefit and penalty can be analyzed as follows (See Table 1 for the DRAM timing parameters):

- *Row Hit*: The request accesses data contained in the row buffer. In this case, only *RD/WR* command is needed to access the data. Thus, the bank access latency becomes t_{CL}.
- *Row Miss*: Either the row buffer is empty or contains another row. If it is empty, the desired row is first loaded with *ACT* command and accessed with *RD/WR* command. The resulting bank access latency is $t_{RCD} + t_{CL}$. If it contains another row, it is emptied, loaded, and accessed with *PRE*, *ACT*, *RD/WR* commands. The bank access latency becomes $t_{RP} + t_{RCD} + t_{CL}$.

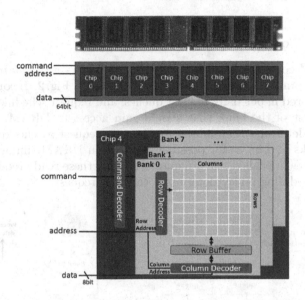

Fig. 1. DDR3-SDRAM organization

Banks operate independent of each other, thus access to different banks can be served in parallel. This allows a level of parallelism at the DRAM. *Bank-level parallelism* denotes for the average number of banks to which there are outstanding requests, when the thread has at least one outstanding request [9]. For memory-intensive workloads, exploiting bank-level parallelism to hide DRAM access latency is critical for high average performance. This becomes ever more important as the gap between CPU clocks and DRAM access latency keeps increasing.

Table 1. DRAM timing parameters

Parameters	Symbols	DDR3-1333
DRAM clock cycle time	t_{CK}	1.5 nsec
Precharge latency	t_{RP}	9 cycles
Activate latency	t_{RCD}	9 cycles
CAS read latency	t_{CL}	9 cycles
CAS write latency	t_{WL}	7 cycles
Burst length	t_{BL}	8 columns
Write to read delay	t_{WTR}	5 cycles
Write recovery time	t_{WR}	10 cycles

2.2   DRAM Controller

Modern DRAM controllers largely consist of two parts - *per-bank request queues and schedulers* and a *channel scheduler* as shown in Fig. 2. Incoming DRAM requests are stored in per-bank request queues, and request schedulers determine the next request of the bank that should gain access to DRAM. The channel scheduler first determines candidates for the next request by checking the status of DRAM banks and buses for possible violation in DRAM timing constraints. These candidates are called *ready* requests. Among these ready requests, DRAM controller's scheduling policy determines the next request.

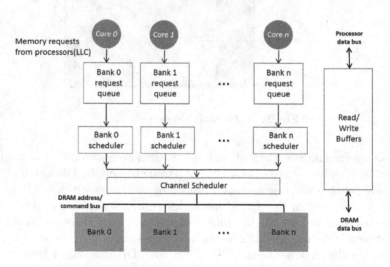

Fig. 2. DRAM controller architecture

Modern Commercial Off-The-Shelf (COTS) DRAM controllers adopt a request scheduling policy called First Ready-First Come First Served (FR-FCFS)[16]. Among the *ready* requests, they prioritize row-hit requests; if multiple such requests exist, then they apply FCFS policy among them. FR-FCFS scheduling policy well exploits row buffer locality, and proven to achieve highest average throughput in single-core systems [15,16]. However, in multi-core systems, multiple threads access the DRAM in parallel as a *shared resource*. In this environment, it is shown that FR-FCFS policy incurs unfairness problems between threads which harm overall performance as well.

3   Observation

In this section, we explain our observations that lead to key features of workload-aware DRAM controller design.

Observation 1. Request batching enables *both* preserving bank-level parallelism and tight bounding of worst case latency.

Parallelism-Aware Batch Scheduling (PAR-BS) [13] introduces buffers of requests called *batches* to exploit bank-level parallelism. By reordering requests inside a batch such that bank-level parallelism is maximized and preventing interference from requests in other batches, it maximizes bank-level parallelism of tasks and prevents unbounded interference from co-running tasks. In this paper we call this *request batching*.

In order to fully exploit bank-level parallelism, merely providing multiple banks is not enough. Even if there exist a stream of requests that can be processed by multiple banks in parallel, requests from tasks in other cores can arbitrarily interfere with them at the channel scheduler which destroys the potential parallelism.

By forming *a batch of memory requests*, we can construct a flexible granularity that allows us to preserve bank-level parallelism within it [13]. This batch of requests can be thought of as a 'pseudo request' due to its atomicity; requests inside a batch are treated as a single request, so that they're not preempted by requests outside the batch. By adopting batch granularity instead of plain single request granularity, we can preserve potential parallelism per this 'pseudo request' unit. Our DRAM controller attempts to maximize the parallelism inherent in the capacity-sensitive tasks by request batching, and maximize the locality inherent in the locality-sensitive tasks at the same time by isolating them from other tasks with bank partitioning.

In addition to preserving parallelism, request batching allows us to devise a scheduling policy with greatly reduced pessimism compared with FR-FCFS scheduling, widely adopted in most commodity DRAM controllers for performance. Under our DRAM controller design, worst case interference delay of tasks in locality-sensitive class is statically determined *regardless of memory intensity of the co-runner tasks in capacity-sensitive class*. However, FR-FCFS scheduling aggressively reorders requests such that row buffer hit requests are served earlier than any other requests [16]. Under FR-FCFS scheduling, bounding worst case interference delay is complicated and conservative because maximum possible requests that can be generated by any job of a task should be counted as a worst case interference. For example, as shown in Fig. 3(a), under FR-FCFS worst case interference that a single request suffers is the sum of maximum number of requests that can be generated by any job of each co-running task. In this case, each co-runner's interfering requests can be row hit and can be served earlier even if they arrived late. However, if we bound maximum number of requests that a co-running task can generate as a static batch size R as in Fig. 3(b), the worst case interference is statically bound, regardless of how memory intensive each co-running task is.

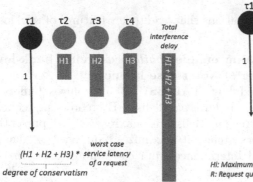

(a) Worst case interference delay under request granularity

(b) Worst case interference delay under batch granularity

Fig. 3. Request batching eliminates pessimism of request-based worst case interference analysis

Thus, by restricting the maximum number of possible interfering requests as a constant which is multiple of batch size, we can achieve much simpler and tighter worst case interference delay analysis for tasks in locality-sensitive class.

Observation 2. Memory access pattern-aware bank partitioning maximizes performance and fairness by providing the right amount of DRAM banks.

Bank partitioning is an OS-level mechanism that physically isolates a set of DRAM banks from the rest of the DRAM, thus eliminating interference between threads which access different dedicated parts of the DRAM. Modern OS uses virtual memory that maps thread's virtual address to physical address. Physical address contains *bank bits*, which designate the DRAM bank that the data with this address is stored. We can allocate pages that have specific bank bits to each thread by controlling the virtual-physical address mapping. This results in dedicated *bank partitions* for each thread. By wisely creating and allocating dedicated bank partitions of various size to threads in the workload, we can not only achieve performance isolation but also efficient utilization of DRAM bandwidth as a shared resource by providing the right amount of bank-level parallelism.

Recent works in real-time systems field that adopt bank partitioning as a way of performance isolation generally overlooked the fact that the number of allocated banks can significantly affect a task's performance. In these works, banks are equally allocated *regardless of tasks' memory access patterns*, focusing only on eliminating inter-core interference to achieve performance isolation [8,12,19,20]. However, we observed that the number of banks clearly affects tasks' performance depending on its memory access pattern as shown in Fig. 4. Especially for a capacity-sensitive application, where the number of banks that can serve requests in parallel is critical to its performance, performance dropped linearly as the number of banks decreased (Fig. 4(b)). For a locality-sensitive task, even though reducing the number of banks doesn't affect performance as much as capacity-sensitive one, a small number of private banks are definitely needed to maintain certain level of performance (Fig. 4(a)).

This preliminary result well supports the intuition that by allocating capacity (number of banks) and bandwidth (number of memory requests allowed per unit time) according to each task's memory access pattern, efficient resource usage would be possible, instead of blindly allocating equal amount of them. Also, some previous works [11,18] have demonstrated that 8 to 16 banks are enough for an arbitrary application to gain around 90% of its maximum performance.

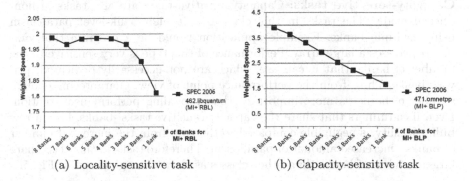

(a) Locality-sensitive task   (b) Capacity-sensitive task

Fig. 4. DRAM capacity affects performance of locality-sensitive and capacity-sensitive tasks

4   Memory Access Pattern-Aware DRAM Controller Design

4.1   DRAM Controller Architecture

In our proposed method, according to tasks' criticality modes and memory access patterns, tasks are classified into three classes, i.e., latency-sensitive class, locality-sensitive class, and capacity-sensitive class[1]. The tasks in each class have following properties:

- **Latency-sensitive tasks:** Latency-sensitive tasks are tasks in critical mode. The memory requests from these tasks should be processed without interference of non-critical tasks (tasks in other classes). Therefore, each task in this class has its own dedicated private bank as shown in left-most of Fig. 5. Also, when the memory requests from this class are issued, the proposed DRAM controller immediately evacuates backlogged requests of other banks to prevent interference from accessing channel scheduler which is shared by all bank schedulers (see Fig. 2) as in [7].
- **Locality-sensitive tasks:** Locality-sensitive tasks are tasks in non-critical mode, which enjoy high row buffer locality. An intuitive example application of this type is a program that *sequentially* accesses a large array. This type of tasks require relatively fewer banks compared to capacity-sensitive tasks, but guaranteeing performance isolation is much more critical than them. If co-runner tasks share and freely access locality-sensitive tasks' banks which will arbitrarily flush and reload the row buffer, high locality that ensures short access latency are destroyed. Thus, as shown in middle of Fig. 5, each task in this class access its own dedicated private bank.
- **Capacity-sensitive tasks:** Capacity-sensitive tasks are also tasks in non-critical mode. The tasks in this class exhibit high bank-level parallelism using multiple banks. Example application would be a program that *randomly* accesses a large array. Performance of this type is very sensitive to the number of banks that it can use, which are not necessarily dedicated, private banks. Thus, from the performance point of view, guaranteeing enough number of banks is more important than providing performance isolation. Even if co-runners that share the capacity-sensitive tasks' banks, loss in row buffer locality is negligible compared to the gain from the increased number of banks—increased amount of parallelism. Therefore tasks in this class share larger number of banks than other classes as shown in right-most of Fig. 5.

Memory Access Pattern-Aware Bank Partitioning. For capacity, latency-sensitive and locality-sensitive classes provide small number of private banks, as tasks of these memory access patterns don't need large amount of banks but require isolation from co-runner tasks on other cores. Capacity-sensitive class provides large number of shared banks because for tasks of this type number of banks that can serve requests in parallel is critical to performance. At the same time, due to low row buffer locality strict isolation is often not needed.

---

[1] There are various ways of categorizing memory access patterns [9, 21]. Among these, we follow the one introduced in [9], hence it is based on DRAM as a shared resource in multi-core machines and well captures memory behavior of memory-intensive workloads.

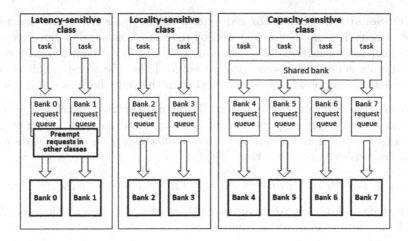

Fig. 5. Memory access pattern-aware DRAM controller design

Class-Based Prioritization and Request Batching. For bandwidth, providing right prioritization is important. Requests from latency-sensitive class gets the highest priority, since tasks of this type seldom generate memory requests but keeping their latency short is critical. Requests from capacity-sensitive class has the next highest priority, since prioritizing capacity-sensitive requests over locality-sensitive requests is proven to be more fair than vice versa [9]. Requests from locality-sensitive class has the lowest priority, since they suffer the least fairness degradation from inter-core interference.

For requests from capacity-sensitive class that use large number of shared banks, we use request batching. As in observation 1, it is important to *effectively guarantee* bank-level parallelism inherent in capacity-sensitive tasks, and merely providing sufficient number of banks is not enough. Request batching unit forms maximum $MarkingCap$ number of requests per each core, generating maximum $Number of cores in capacity-sensitive class * MarkingCap$ size batch each time. Next batch is formed only after current batch is completely served, as in [13].

4.2   Worst Case Interference Delay Analysis

We assume the following task model:

$$\tau_i = (C_i, T_i, D_i, H_i)$$

- C_i: WCET of any job of τ_i under single-core environment
- T_i: the minimum inter-arrival time of τ_i
- D_i: relative deadline of τ_i
- H_i: the maximum number of requests generated by any job of τ_i

Latency-Sensitive Class. For requests in latency-sensitive class, due to its highest priority it is neither preempted by requests from locality-sensitive class nor from capacity-sensitive class. The only potential delay comes from the previous requests sent to the same private bank. Thus, the worst possible delay occurs when the previous request serviced from the same bank is a row miss.

- **Worst case latency for row hit**: Read's data transfer takes $t_{CL} + t_{BL}/2$ and additional 2 cycles for data bus turn-around time and write's data transfer takes $t_{WL} + t_{BL}/2$ and additional possible $max(t_{WTR}, t_{WR})$ for the data bus turn-around/write recovery time [8].

$$L_{hit} = max\{t_{CL} + t_{BL}/2 + 2, t_{WL} + t_{BL}/2 + max(t_{WTR}, t_{WR})\} \cdot t_{CK}$$

- **Worst case latency for row miss**: Row miss requires all three of PRE, ACT and data read or write commands.

$$L_{miss} = (t_{RP} + t_{RCD}) \cdot t_{CK} + L_{hit}$$

Iterative response time test for the requests from latency-sensitive class can be rewritten as below, where $hp(\tau_i)$ denotes tasks of higher priorities than τ_i:

$$R_i^{k+1} = C_i + \sum_{\tau_j \in hp(\tau_i)} \left\lceil \frac{R_i^k}{T_j} \right\rceil \cdot C_j + H_i \cdot L_{miss} + \sum_{\tau_j \in hp(\tau_i)} \left\lceil \frac{R_i^k}{T_j} \right\rceil \cdot H_j \cdot L_{miss}$$

Capacity-Sensitive Class. For requests in capacity-sensitive class, it can be preempted by latency-sensitive class's requests. And in the worst case, a request can arrive right after the formation of a batch ended, thus scheduled to the next batch. Hence, the worst delay it can suffer occurs when it is preempted by the maximum possible number of memory requests that any job of latency-sensitive class's task can generate, and then their exist an already-formed batch from capacity-sensitive class. Since it's the worst case, we assume all of these requests are row miss.

$$R_i^{k+1} = C_i + \sum_{\tau_j \in hp(\tau_j)} \left\lceil \frac{R_i^k}{T_j} \right\rceil \cdot C_j$$

$$+ H_{latency-sensitive} \cdot L_{miss} + \sum_{\tau_j \in hp(\tau_i)} \left\lceil \frac{R_i^k}{T_j} \right\rceil \cdot H_j \cdot L_{miss}$$

Locality-Sensitive Class. For requests in locality-sensitive class, it can be preempted by requests from both latency-sensitive class and batches of requests from capacity-sensitive class. In the extreme scenario where capacity-sensitive class continuously generates requests, requests from locality-sensitive class suffer from starvation due to the continuous preemption by the batches. To prevent this, we put a limit on the maximum number of batches that can be consecutively served, which we call $MaxConsecutiveBatches$.

The worst delay locality-sensitive class can suffer occurs when it is preempted by the maximum possible number of memory requests that any job of latency-sensitive class's task can generate, and then there exist $MaxConsecutiveBatches$ number of already-formed batches from capacity-sensitive class. Here too, we assume all of these are row miss.

$$BatchSize = MarkingCap \cdot CapacitySensitiveClassCores$$

$$R_i^{k+1} = C_i + \sum_{\tau_j \in hp(\tau_j)} \left\lceil \frac{R_i^k}{T_j} \right\rceil \cdot C_j$$

$$+ (H_{latency-sensitive} + MaxConsecutiveBatches \cdot BatchSize) \cdot L_{miss}$$

$$+ \sum_{\tau_j \in hp(\tau_i)} \left\lceil \frac{R_i^k}{T_j} \right\rceil \cdot H_j \cdot L_{miss}$$

5 Evaluation

5.1 Experiment Setup

We used $Ramulator\#$, a cycle-accurate DRAM simulator with representative latency-sensitive (444.namd), locality-sensitive (462.libquantum), capacity-sensitive (471.omnetpp) workloads from SPEC 2006 [5]. Table 2 shows the characteristics of workloads. MPKI determines memory intensity, which denotes the number of DRAM requests per kilo instructions. RB Hit Rate denotes row buffer hit rate, which is the number of row buffer hit divided by total DRAM requests. BLP denotes bank-level parallelism and is the number of total banks that received at least one DRAM request when any one of the banks received memory requests.

Table 2. Characteristics of SPEC 2006 benchmarks used

Benchmark	MPKI	RB Hit Rate	BLP	Classification
444.namd	0.33	86.6%	1.27	latency-sensitive
462.libquantum	50.00	98.4%	1.10	locality-sensitive
471.omnetpp	22.15	26.7%	3.78	capacity-sensitive

For $Ramulator\#$ system setting, we used 3-core where each benchmark run and 4G DDR3-DRAM with one channel, one rank, 8 banks, and 1333 MHz memory clock. `MarkingCap` is set to 5, `MaxConsecutiveBatches` is set to 2.

5.2   Performance Result of Non-critical Tasks

We experimented FR-FCFS, FR-FCFS with bank partitioning, and our proposed solution. As the metric for system throughput we used *weighted speedup* [17] and for fairness we used *maximum slowdown* defined as follows:

$$WeightedSpeedup = \sum_i \frac{IPC_i^{shared}}{IPC_i^{alone}}$$

$$MaximumSlowdown = \max_i \frac{IPC_i^{alone}}{IPC_i^{shared}}$$

We compared different combination of bank allocation and tested the performance and fairness under the condition. For performance, we can see that even if banks are allocated against tasks' memory access patterns, our proposed method wins FR-FCFS and FR-FCFS with bank partitioning as shown in Fig. 6. The main gain came from the fact that the performance gain of tasks in locality-sensitive class outgrows the performance loss of tasks in capacity-sensitive class. This result shows the importance of performance isolation to locality-sensitive tasks—namely, guaranteeing enough number of private banks is very important for locality-sensitive tasks' performance.

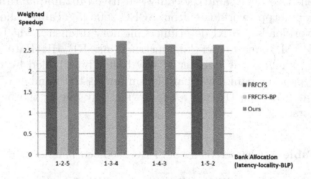

Fig. 6. Weighted speedup under various bank allocations

On the other hand, when we look at the maximum slowdown as in Fig. 7, we can see that fairness is paying the price. Even though the net performance gain increased due to locality-sensitive tasks, capacity-sensitive tasks suffer from severe slowdown as the number of allocated shared banks drops. This is due to the bank allocation ignorant of memory access pattern.

By testing various bank allocation and finding the best trade-off point between performance and fairness, our memory access pattern-aware DRAM controller can provide both performance isolation and efficient sharing to tasks with various memory access patterns' needs.

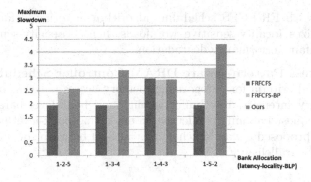

Fig. 7. Maximum slowdown under various bank allocations

6   Related Work

Bank Partitioning. Bank partitioning has been widely researched as a software-level solution for inter-core interference at main memory level. [10,11] proposed a way to profile bank address of commodity hardware, and implemented bank partitioning as a linux kernel page allocator. [12,19] adopted bank partitioning as a way of main performance isolation mechanism for real-time tasks running on COTS (commercial off-the-shelf) hardware.

Bounding Memory Interference Delays. Tightly bounding worst case interference delays at main memory have gained importance along with migration to multicore architecture. [8] developed worst case response time analysis that captures interference delay due to reordering effect of row buffer hit requests, which is adopted in most commodity DRAM controller hardware today [16]. [20] extended [8] and took various factors that define memory-level parallelism such as number of MSHRs into consideration.

DRAM Controller Design for Mixed-Criticality Systems. [14] first suggested bank privatization method, which achieves predictable bank access latency by scheduling accesses to each banks in a TDM way and generating DRAM commands in a predetermined way. [4] took a step forward and proposed a run-time reconfigurable DRAM controller that takes suitable trade-offs between bandwidth, response time and power. [1] provided a shared-resource abstraction for predictable and composable memory. [7] adopted bank privatization to have bounded worst case latency for critical tasks, and FR-FCFS aimed at maximized performance for low critical tasks. [3] viewed DRAM as a set of virtual devices and provided a partitioning mechanism to run mixed critical workloads to each virtual device.

While research on DRAM controllers for mixed-criticality system mainly focused on performance isolation for critical tasks [1,3,4,14], [7] first suggested a way of providing maximized performance to low critical tasks, but overlooked known issues with FR-FCFS scheduling algorithm in terms of fairness; i.e. it blindly prioritizes locality-sensitive workloads, hence capacity-sensitive workloads suffer unfair performance degradation.

Memory Access Pattern-Aware DRAM Controller Scheduling. [9] first proposed several criteria for categorizing memory access patterns of a program such as memory intensity, row buffer locality and bank-level parallelism. [13] showed that request batching is effective in exploiting bank-level parallelism of programs and proposed a way of achieving trade-off between row buffer locality and bank-level parallelism.

7 Conclusion

In this paper, we introduced a DRAM controller architecture that can achieve both performance isolation and efficient sharing of resources, which are two compelling goals of mixed-criticality systems. Our design guarantees strictly bounded worst case latency for critical tasks and maximizes performance by exploiting locality-sensitive and bandwidth-sensitivity for non-critical tasks. For future work, we're planning to develop a run-time program that analyzes each non-critical task and parses a task into locality-sensitive and capacity-sensitive *blocks*. Programs from real world workloads usually consist of locality-sensitive *parts* and capacity-sensitive *parts*, while program itself as a whole is often difficult to be clearly classified as locality-sensitive or capacity-sensitive. By parsing each programs into *blocks* that well fit the underlying partitions, much more efficient sharing of resources would be possible.

Acknowledgement. This research was partly supported by the MSIT (Ministry of Science and ICT), Korea, under the SW Starlab (IITP-2015-0-00209) supervised by the IITP (Institute for Information & Communications Technology Promotion) and partly supported by Next-Generation Information Computing Development Program through the National Research Foundation of Korea (NRF) funded by the MSIT (2017M3C4A7065925, On-the-fly Machine Learning and Its Specialized Real-time/Security System SW for Evolving Intelligent CPS).

References

1. Akesson, B., Goossens, K.: Architectures and modeling of predictable memory controllers for improved system integration. In: 2011 Design, Automation Test in Europe. pp. 1–6, March 2011. https://doi.org/10.1109/DATE.2011.5763145
2. Burns, A., Davis, R.: Mixed criticality systems-a review. Department of Computer Science, University of York, Technical Reports (2013)
3. Ecco, L., Tobuschat, S., Saidi, S., Ernst, R.: A mixed critical memory controller using bank privatization and fixed priority scheduling. In: 2014 IEEE 20th International Conference on Embedded and Real-Time Computing Systems and Applications, pp. 1–10, August 2014. https://doi.org/10.1109/RTCSA.2014.6910550

4. Goossens, S., Kuijsten, J., Akesson, B., Goossens, K.: A reconfigurable real-time sdram controller for mixed time-criticality systems. In: 2013 International Conference on Hardware/Software Codesign and System Synthesis (CODES+ISSS), pp. 1–10, September 2013. https://doi.org/10.1109/CODES-ISSS.2013.6658989

5. Henning, J.L.: SPEC CPU2006 benchmark descriptions. SIGARCH Comput. Archit. News **34**(4), 1–17 (2006). https://doi.org/10.1145/1186736.1186737

6. Jacob, B., Ng, S., Wang, D.: Memory Systems: Cache, DRAM, Disk. Morgan Kaufmann Publishers Inc., San Francisco (2007)

7. Kim, H., Broman, D., Lee, E.A., Zimmer, M., Shrivastava, A., Oh, J.: A predictable and command-level priority-based dram controller for mixed-criticality systems. In: 21st IEEE Real-Time and Embedded Technology and Applications Symposium, pp. 317–326, April 2015. https://doi.org/10.1109/RTAS.2015.7108455

8. Kim, H., de Niz, D., Andersson, B., Klein, M., Mutlu, O., Rajkumar, R.: Bounding memory interference delay in cots-based multi-core systems. In: 2014 IEEE 19th Real-Time and Embedded Technology and Applications Symposium (RTAS), pp. 145–154, April 2014. https://doi.org/10.1109/RTAS.2014.6925998

9. Kim, Y., Papamichael, M., Mutlu, O., Harchol-Balter, M.: Thread cluster memory scheduling: exploiting differences in memory access behavior. In: 2010 43rd Annual IEEE/ACM International Symposium on Microarchitecture, pp. 65–76, December 2010. https://doi.org/10.1109/MICRO.2010.51

10. Liu, L., Cui, Z., Li, Y., Bao, Y., Chen, M., Wu, C.: BPM/BPM+: software-based dynamic memory partitioning mechanisms for mitigating dram bank-/channel-level interferences in multicore systems. ACM Trans. Archit. Code Optim. (TACO) **11**(1), 5 (2014)

11. Liu, L., Cui, Z., Xing, M., Bao, Y., Chen, M., Wu, C.: A software memory partition approach for eliminating bank-level interference in multicore systems. In: Proceedings of the 21st International Conference on Parallel Architectures and Compilation Techniques, pp. 367–376. ACM (2012)

12. Mancuso, R., Pellizzoni, R., Caccamo, M., Sha, L., Yun, H.: WCET(m) estimation in multi-core systems using single core equivalence. In: 2015 27th Euromicro Conference on Real-Time Systems, pp. 174–183, July 2015. https://doi.org/10.1109/ECRTS.2015.23

13. Mutlu, O., Moscibroda, T.: Parallelism-aware batch scheduling: enhancing both performance and fairness of shared dram systems. In: Proceedings of the 35th Annual International Symposium on Computer Architecture, ISCA 2008, pp. 63–74. IEEE Computer Society, Washington (2008). https://doi.org/10.1109/ISCA.2008.7

14. Reineke, J., Liu, I., Patel, H.D., Kim, S., Lee, E.A.: Pret dram controller: bank privatization for predictability and temporal isolation. In: 2011 Proceedings of the Ninth IEEE/ACM/IFIP International Conference on Hardware/Software Codesign and System Synthesis (CODES+ISSS), pp. 99–108, October 2011. https://doi.org/10.1145/2039370.2039388

15. Rixner, S.: Memory controller optimizations for web servers. In: Proceedings of the 37th Annual IEEE/ACM International Symposium on Microarchitecture, MICRO 37, pp. 355–366. IEEE Computer Society, Washington (2004). https://doi.org/10.1109/MICRO.2004.22

16. Rixner, S., Dally, W.J., Kapasi, U.J., Mattson, P., Owens, J.D.: Memory access scheduling. In: Proceedings of the 27th Annual International Symposium on Computer Architecture, ISCA 2000, pp. 128–138. ACM, New York (2000). https://doi.org/10.1145/339647.339668

17. Snavely, A., Tullsen, D.M.: Symbiotic jobscheduling for a simultaneous multi-threaded processor. In: Proceedings of the Ninth International Conference on Architectural Support for Programming Languages and Operating Systems, ASP-LOS IX, pp. 234–244. ACM, New York (2000). https://doi.org/10.1145/378993.379244

18. Xie, M., Tong, D., Huang, K., Cheng, X.: Improving system throughput and fairness simultaneously in shared memory cmp systems via dynamic bank partitioning. In: 2014 IEEE 20th International Symposium on High Performance Computer Architecture (HPCA), pp. 344–355, February 2014. https://doi.org/10.1109/HPCA.2014.6835945

19. Yun, H., Mancuso, R., Wu, Z.P., Pellizzoni, R.: PALLOC: DRAM bank-aware memory allocator for performance isolation on multicore platforms. In: 2014 IEEE 19th Real-Time and Embedded Technology and Applications Symposium (RTAS), pp. 155–166, April 2014. https://doi.org/10.1109/RTAS.2014.6925999

20. Yun, H., Pellizzon, R., Valsan, P.K.: Parallelism-aware memory interference delay analysis for cots multicore systems. In: 2015 27th Euromicro Conference on Real-Time Systems, pp. 184–195, July 2015. https://doi.org/10.1109/ECRTS.2015.24

21. Zhou, Y., Wentzlaff, D.: MITTS: memory inter-arrival time traffic shaping. In: Proceedings of the 43rd International Symposium on Computer Architecture, ISCA 2016, pp. 532–544. IEEE Press, Piscataway (2016). https://doi.org/10.1109/ISCA.2016.53

Increasing Safety by Combining Multiple Declarative Rules in Robotic Perception Systems

Johann Thor Mogensen Ingibergsson, Dirk Kraft, and Ulrik Pagh Schultz[✉]

Mærsk Mc-Kinney Møller Institute, University of Southern Denmark,
Campusvej 55, 5230 Odense M, Denmark
{jomo,kraft,ups}@mmmi.sdu.dk

Abstract. Advanced cyber-physical systems such as mobile, networked robots are increasingly finding use in everyday society. A critical aspect of mobile robotics is the ability to react to a dynamically changing environment, which imposes significant requirements on the robot perception system. The perception system is key to maintaining safe navigation and operation for the robot and is often considered a safety-critical aspect of the system as a whole. To allow the system to operate in a public area the perception system thus has to be certified. The key issue that we address is how to have safety-compliant systems while keeping implementation transparency high and complexity low. In this paper we present an evaluation of different methods for modelling combinations of simple explicit computer vision rules designed to increase the trustworthiness of the perception system. We utilise the best-performing method, focusing on keeping the models of the perception pipeline transparent and understandable. We find that it is possible to improve the safety of the system with some performance cost, depending on the acceptable risk level.

Keywords: Safety · Computer vision · Robotics · Functional safety

1 Introduction

The significant growth of highly interconnected Cyber-Physical Systems (CPS) is currently imposing complex conglomerates of software and hardware on personal life and many sectors of industry. While the high degree of integration between software, mechanical, and electrical engineering is well-known and visible in sectors such as automotive or aviation, more "traditional" sectors such as agriculture and consumer electronics also benefit from the opportunities provided by the latest information and communications technology concepts and solutions. Driven by this trend, the domain of robotics is continuously expanding from large industrial machines in cages to free-moving consumer products. This expansion is reflected by the current market and projected increase in the future [11,22].

© Springer Nature Switzerland AG 2019
R. Chamberlain et al. (Eds.): CyPhy 2017, LNCS 11267, pp. 43–60, 2019.
https://doi.org/10.1007/978-3-030-17910-6_4

Computer vision is a key point for robotics—and thus CPS in general—to be able to act in a dynamic world [7]. The task for a computer vision system is to understand what exists, where a mobile robotic system is located, and if obstacles require an immediate action. These goals are functional requirements of the system and should be addressed with an explicit focus on safety when dealing with mobile robots. Indeed, a requirement for introducing autonomy in established domains is safety, which is done through compliance with functional safety standards that rely on code and documentation reviews. To support the use of vision in safety-critical systems, we propose to use simple and explicit computer vision rules as a means to determine specific problems in input images and the perception system as a whole [15]. Increasing the readability of the code and the perception rules can increase the overall trustworthiness of the system [13], facilitating the certification process [15]. Such simple and explicit computer vision rules can be implemented in a domain specific programming languages (DSL), supporting safe implementation of computer vision for safety-critical systems [14].

In this paper, we investigate how to combine such simple and explicit rules in an understandable way in order to judge the current operational safety of the robots perception system during autonomous operation. The safety system consists of code generated using the Vision Safety Language (ViSaL; [14]), where the developer specifies rules to safeguard the system from malfunctions. Our investigations build on the combination of explicitly written rules and address the issue of how this combination should be modelled, in particular, whether it can be done manually or automatically. The tested methods have a clear focus on being explicit and thereby easy to understand to facilitate clear communication to functional safety certifiers, such that the intent of the code and the system can be deducted. Concretely, we compare three manual programmatic methods with an automatic method based on decision trees. The decision tree method is deemed most appropriate in this comparison and is then assessed on a robot as an added safety layer for the You Only Look Once (YOLO) neural network (NN) [26] to investigate the performance and cost for the system. Compared to our earlier work where rules were evaluated independently [13–15], we here design, implement, and test combinations of rules and evaluate these combinations as a safety layer for a state-of-the-art NN.

The rest of this paper is structured as follows. In Sect. 2 we discuss safety in the context of robotics and related industries, followed by an overview of our initial work on safety and computer vision in connection to learning methods. In Sect. 3 we present different methods that can be used for modelling a safety layer for a computer vision system based on declarative rules, along with two datasets used for experimentally investigating the methods. The performance evaluation and comparison of the different methods will be conducted in Sect. 4, where they are tested on the datasets. The best-performing method is experimentally evaluated in Sect. 5, by introducing the safety method in a robotic system as a means to improve the safety of a NN. We end with an overall conclusion and an outline of future work in Sect. 6.

2   Fundamentals and Related Work

2.1   Safety in Robotics

While robotics is a thriving research area within academia, the penetration into industry has mostly been limited to replacing manual labour in factories. The intent of commercialising robots and selling them on a mass market puts certi-fication as a central requirement as increasingly complex autonomous systems are introduced [27]. Certification allows products to comply with international standards, and thus lowers liability concerns [30]. A critical requirement for cer-tification is that the software controlling the robot has been reviewed and paired with textual requirements, meaning that a clear interpretation of the intent is needed. Safety can be defined as, e.g., *"freedom from unacceptable risk"* [37]. Certification can consume more than 50% of the resources required to develop new safety-critical systems in related domains [1]; development of safety-critical software is expensive.

Safety is discussed in many settings and is often mentioned in papers, e.g., for computer vision, however without explicitly dealing with the challenges that arise [12]. As a result, safety is an obstacle for robots to operate autonomously in the public domain, while various ad-hoc safety measures have been designed, often focused on a specific risk such as collision, certification is not undertaken. It follows that there is a need for generalised methods for facilitating compliance and certification [20]. In the industrial domain developers rely on functional safety, which is defined as: *"part of the overall safety relating to the [equipment under control] EUC and the EUC control system that depends on the correct functioning of the [electrical and/or electronic and/or programmable electronic] E/E/PE safety-related systems and other risk reduction measures"* [37].

2.2   Perception Systems

The safety issue is partially at odds with how robotic autonomy is normally developed today. Researchers often rely on machine learning and Artificial Intel-ligence (AI) to achieve required performance and safety, however, the safety aspect is difficult for humans to interpret. This tension is described in *Defence Science Board 2016 Summer Study on Autonomy* which argues that it is hard for humans to understand and predict AI systems [6]. In computer vision, the focus is on performance [12], and the improved safety is often claimed despite introducing ever more complex algorithms. That *"in spite of their complexity, they fail frequently. "* moreover, *"in part **due to** their complexity, they fail in seemingly inexplicable ways."* [2].

Robots rely on perception systems to navigate the world, as such the systems require both safety certification and a minimal performance. Safety certification could be done by adapting IEC 61496 [36] for outdoors use. Despite the scope of the standard being for machines in an industrial setting, it is noted that additional requirements can be applied to the system if it is intended for outdoor applications, which means that the developer has to argue for the safety in the system and thus can disregard the cages. Regarding performance, drafts exist of standards for outdoor robotics, e.g., ISO/DIS 18497 [35] and ISO/DIS 17757 [34]. The standards quantify detection performance, the tests have however been criticised [33]. The criticism is that the test object can be robustly detected in varying conditions using a NN, while not being able to detect humans.

The concept of safe states, i.e., fall-back behaviour, are important for perception systems since sensors, in general, have a risk of failing [3]. These failures require that the sensors are robust, without robustness the robot may "hallucinate" and respond inappropriately [23]. The failures are not limited to hardware, but also software and NNs *"need serious design effort, pre-planning and proved to be fragile in face of sensor errors in practice"* [38]. It is therefore important for functional safety to look at software safety verification of the input sensor data, and thereby to give assurance about the hardware by verifying inputs and outputs.

There are many requirements to a computer vision system [5]. Precision for vision algorithms is an issue in general, as a result it can be beneficial to create multiple classification regions. Multiple regions allow the system to deal with images that can be difficult to classify. Mekki-Mokhtar et al. proposed a concept called multiclass classification, as seen in other safety-critical systems [21]. The multiclass classification allows a system to have more than a boolean decision, e.g., "bad", "warning" and "good". This will enable a decision system to decide the trustworthiness of different sensors, and thereby decide if the robot needs to stop or just slow down. A benefit of using multiclass classification is tolerance towards the issue that sensors are in some way disturbed by noise, and thus the data may be unreliable. A common approach is to employ redundancy [10]. The multiclass classification can allow different sensors to use voting similar to sensor fusion [10].

A standard measure for evaluating algorithm performance within computer vision is Precision-Recall (PR). PR curves are used to identify the performance of classifiers. Other methods exists such as the well-known Receiver Operating Characteristics (ROC), however we choose PR curves over ROC because if a curve dominates in the PR-space, it will also dominate in the ROC space [4]. Furthermore, ROC does not take the baseline into account, and since categories for annotated data can be unbalanced, the PR-curves are a better statistical measure. An issue with the use of statistical measures is the notion of an acceptable risk, this is however not specified in functional safety standards. Therefore it is up to the developer to decide when the systems performance is good enough, with respect to acceptable risk. To evaluate the PR-curves we utilise Area Under the Curve (AUC). An approximation is however needed, such as trapezoidal approximation, to evaluate the AUC of the resulting PR curves and find an "optimum". This is because linear approximation is insufficient for PR [4]. The use of AUC in combination with PR instead of ROC is further supported by Saito et al. *"The PRC [Precision-ReCall] plot is more informative than ROC, CROC [Concentrated ROC], and CC [Cost Curve] plots when evaluating binary classifiers on imbalanced datasets"* [29]. With the hope of using these methods in connection with argumentation for functional safety, a perfect score would be desirable, however not a plausible result to aim for. This leaves the developer to rely on upcoming performance standards [34,35] and to assume an acceptable risk level for the system.

An issue with PR is however that one has two values that are being improved (precision and recall). To remedy this an optimum point is chosen based on the F_β score. The F_β score is a statistical measure that can be used to evaluate the classification performance. The β is a number reflecting a weight on either recall or precision. We have chosen 1 which results in the harmonic mean of precision and recall. The F_1 score is a weighted average where the best value is at 1 and the worst is 0.

2.3   Learning and Computer Vision

"Software developers have a history of adding security to their products after the fact rather than integrating it into the development phase [...] Now, he warned, the machine learning community is poised to make the same mistake." [17]. We note that NNs have received significant attention in the computer vision community, beating other methods in performance on many tasks. Nevertheless, safety certification of neural networks remains an open issue [18]. NNs should ideally be understandable and readable by humans, while still allowing for individual, meaningful rules [18]. Many industries have looked into the use of NNs [31], investigating the use of NNs since the 1980s [31].

Gupta et al. propose verification and validation of adaptive NNs [8], although with a focus on control systems. Specifically the absence of analytical certification methods restricts NNs to advisory roles in safety-related systems [19]. Moreover, we note that deep NN and similar recently popular methods share the same issue of being hard to assess in terms of safety. There do exist probabilistic measures for failure detection [40]. The issue with these methods is however that it is difficult to prove that the underlying distributions cover the entire normal behaviour. The difficulty is illustrated by the spurious behaviour learning methods can exhibit, where the neural network wrongly makes different classifications of images indistinguishable for humans [25]. The key problem is that classifiers and learning are complex tasks that are hard to prove reliable for humans, in particular through reviews. This shows that safety certification of NNs remains an open issue [9,19]. Because of functional safety and the requirement for code reviews, we do not believe that online trained or adaptive NNs are certifiable, despite recent advances [8].

To comply with functional safety the NN would have to be transparent. In the case of pre-trained NN the learning method and learned models would be available for the reviewer. The resulting NNs are however still "black boxes", moreover the computations can be time consuming [9]. This makes NN infeasible for safety-critical systems; however other learning methods exists that are more intuitive to understand, such as decision trees [24]. A decision tree is *"a hierarchical model composed of discriminant functions, or decision rules, that are applied recursively to partition the feature space of a dataset into pure, single-class subspaces*" [39]. A decision tree T consists of branches T_t where t is the number of branches. Decision trees can be explicitly depicted to give reviewers an intuitive understanding of the data flow. When using decision trees there is an inherent issue of over-fitting, which is addressed using pruning. Pruning refers to replacing branch nodes with leaves, thereby decreasing complexity and simplifying the tree. Trees can be trained with a stopping criterion, but it is generally accepted that it is better to overgrow a decision tree and then prune back [24]. "*Pruning a branch T_t from a tree T consists of deleting all descendants of t. Denote the pruned tree as $T - T_t$.*" [28]. There are multiple algorithms for pruning decision trees [28].

The NN for which we will introduce a safety layer in this paper is YOLO. From a software point of view, the safety check consists of executing code from ViSaL for assessing the input images for the YOLO algorithm, specifically we use YOLOv2 [26]. In this paper, we refer to YOLOv2 as YOLO. The algorithm finds anchor boxes of proposed predictions for the image, which are then thresholded based on a probability criteria. The predictions are then found using non-max suppression. Our reason for using YOLO is not the algorithm components, but its performance and speed, i.e., high precision and 45 frames per second [26].

Introducing a safety system could have a potential negative impact on the overall performance of the system, because some images categorised as good could be distrusted by the system. In a nutshell, a safety system that distrusts all images ensures that a NN will never make any miscategorisations, but is not useful. We use the term *uptime cost* to refer to the overhead of using a safety system, in terms of how many useful images are incorrectly discarded. Concretely, we measure the uptime cost by assessing how many images are removed from the highest category, i.e., the most usable images, to estimate the cost of introducing a safety layer to a perception system.

2.4   Programming Safe Perception Systems

Initial steps towards establishing a safe implementation of perception systems have been demonstrated using explicit declarative rules to address specific issues in a perception pipeline [14,15]. The rules are focused on different particularities of an image such as pixel distributions, pixel changes, and frequency. The simple rules use multiclass classification, because of the uncertainties in specifying precise thresholds for classifying images using the rules, thereby establishing a margin of reliability in the classifications. The many categories however also make the classification problem harder and thereby the performance of the algorithm deteriorates. As a result the concept of soft-boundaries was introduced to evaluate multiclass classification systems without penalizing the system performance excessively [15]. The computer vision rules have been implemented in the Vision Safety Language (ViSaL) DSL for automatic generation of their implementation [14] and an initial assessment has been performed with respect to readability with the goal of facilitating certification [13]. An excerpt of a ViSaL program is shown in Fig. 1, the rule FB detects images with abnormal distribution of pixels in a colour histogram, which for example detects underexposed or overexposed images unsuitable for further processing in a perception pipeline.

The declarative rules in ViSaL function independently, which means that ViSaL outputs individual scores for each rule, i.e., ok, warn or bad. The set of problems and symptoms that can result in problematic issues in a perception pipeline, are covered by a subset of the defined rules in ViSaL, therefore the entire rule set overlaps the problem space. This paper is focused on combining the rules, as this allows for a clear decision on the system integrity and can increase safety.

The focus of the combination of the rules is a means to give a clear statement on the integrity of the system, and as such the sum of rules does not in itself increase safety. Nevertheless, certain standards allow for combinations of safety-functions to increase safety. An example is ISO 26262 [16], where there exists a concept called decomposition, which allows for lower-rated safety function to safeguard high levels by combining safety-functions. In this paper the method of combining the rules is addressed, serving as an experimental continuation of the initial steps made in previously published papers [13–15].

```
1  ...
2  Image(height=752, width=480) monoLeft = Bayer2Mono (source =
           camera.left.image);
3  Histogram h = histogram ( source = monoLeft, bins = 16 );
4  ...
5  rule FB { // Filled Bins ratio of a histogram.
6  //The field "binSizes" contains a set of the sizes of all bins
           in the histogram. Set, then extracts
7  //a subset from "binSizes" and size evaluates the resulting
           number of bins.
8    case size(set(uint x in h.binSizes: x>100)) / size(h) {
9      [0.9, 1] yield ok;
10     [0.7, 0.9[ yield warn;
11     [0, 0.7[ yield bad;
12   }
13 }
```

Fig. 1. Excerpt of ViSaL implementation of image analysis rules for verifying the data integrity of images [14].

3 Methods

3.1 Datasets

In our experiments, we use datasets consisting of images labelled using a usability category, where five is a usable image and one is unusable, i.e., unusable to make reliable safety decisions. Datasets consist of RGB and depth information and are processed by the rules ("raw data"), based on which thresholds are found in the data using precision-recall curves ("threshold data") [15]. We use two datasets: "agriculture", from an outdoor setting [15]; and "turtlebot" from an indoor setting. Both datasets consist of 406 images labelled using the usability category.

3.2 Decision Trees

We employ decision trees because we view them as a valid method in the context of functional safety, since the trees are an intuitively understandable visualization of a decision process. This means that the learned model can be verified and understood by tracing the propagation of images through the tree, and thereby iterate over an understandable model. Two decision trees are created using Matlab, where the trees are based on the raw data and on the threshold data respectively. We employ pruning on the automatically generated decision trees. For pruning we use cross-validation, meaning that the training data is split into train, test, and validation, to evaluate the model, i.e., the level of pruning for the decision tree.

3.3 Manual Programming

The manual programming approach utilises pre-defined thresholds for simple declarative rules, as to explicitly combine the rule evaluations, i.e., "bad", "warning" and "good" [15]. The use of a manual programming approach should allow the derived rules to be intuitively understood. Ultimately an extension of the ViSaL DSL would be used for this, but in this paper, we investigate the feasibility of such an approach, rather than the design of the language. For this reason, we use a mathematical notation to express the programmed rule combinations, leaving a concrete DSL syntax for rule combinations for future work. In this paper we consider three different manual programming approaches: "top-down","bottom-up", and "inferred learning".

The "top-down" approach refers to the idea that the combination of the rules are based on intuitive ideas by the developer, e.g., if all rules dealing with exposure or bin distributions are "good", then the image is assumed "good". The second approach,"bottom-up", relies on fitting a rule to the underlying data of the training set, e.g., the existing rule combinations. Last the "inferred learning" approach is based on creating rules using a combination of the two above approaches and by utilising insights manually inferred from an automatically generated decision tree.

The mathematical notation used to support the combination of rules can be seen in Fig. 2. It describes an overall evaluation of an image based on all rules R. The notation is based on a sequence S of compound rules P defined as propositions that combine rule evaluations $\alpha^r(x)$ using a weighting.

$$
\begin{array}{l}
R \text{ set of all rules, } r \in R, I \text{ set of all images, } x \in I \\[8pt]
\alpha^r(x) : \begin{cases} \mathbf{b}, & r(x) < t_r^{\mathrm{error}} \\ \mathbf{g}, & r(x) > t_r^{\mathrm{warn}} \\ \mathbf{w}, & \text{Otherwise} \end{cases} \\[20pt]
\alpha_0^*(x) : \begin{cases} \mathbf{b}, & \exists r \in R : \alpha^r(x) = \mathbf{b} \\ \mathbf{g}, & \forall r \in R : \alpha^r(x) = \mathbf{g} \\ \mathbf{w}, & \text{Otherwise} \end{cases} \hspace{2cm} (1)
\end{array}
$$

$$
S \equiv \{(o_1, P_1), ..., (o_n, P_n)\}, \text{ where } o_i \in \{\mathbf{g}, \mathbf{w}, \mathbf{b}\} \hspace{1cm} (2)
$$

$$
\beta^S(x) : \begin{cases} o_m, & m = \min_{j \in \mathbb{N}} : P_j(x) \\ \alpha_0^*(x), & \forall m \in \mathbb{N} : \neg P_m(x) \end{cases}
$$

Fig. 2. Mathematical representation of the combination of rules, where the thresholds t_r are assumed to always be an upper limit. The function $\alpha^r(x)$ corresponds to the evaluation of individual rules, where **b** corresponds to an image being categorised as "bad", **w** as "warning", and finally **g** as "good". The $\alpha_0^*(x)$ function is defined such that if one rule for a given image evaluates to "bad" then the combined result would be "bad", whereas if one image is "warn" and none are "bad", then the combined result is "warn". In all other cases, the result is "good", meaning that the rules have an equal weighting. The rule in Eq. 1 can be adapted for different scenarios. The use of the compound rules is done using a sequence S, consisting of an output and a compound rule, as described by Eq. 2. The sequence S of propositions is evaluated using $\beta^S(x)$, meaning that the first-occurring satisfied compound rule of an image will result in the images evaluating to the corresponding output value. If no compound rule is true then the result defaults to $\alpha_0^*(x)$.

Top-Down. The top-down approach relies on first combining the rules by using the dominant state of the rule results as in Eq. 1. Equation 1 implies an equal weighting of the rules. The combination of rules is created as compound rules, meaning that they are designed as propositions P combined in a sequence S, and evaluated using $\beta^S(x)$.

Bottom-Up. The bottom-up approach uses the same initial combination approach (Eq. 1). The compound rules for this task are found by investigating the data, e.g., using a loop for testing all possible rule combinations and their performance. The best-performing combinations are then introduced, and the process can be iterated. An alternative approach used is to investigate the existing rule combinations in the data. The new rules are therefore found based on the chosen training data.

Inferred Learning. Because of the risk of over-fitting the inferred learning approach utilizes pruned decision trees. Using decision trees as heuristics for creating manual rules could possibly benefit the creation. The key benefit of using
the heuristics is however that the decision tree and in particular the predictor
importance allows for improving the weights in $\alpha_0^*(x)$ (Eq. 1) because there is
an understanding of the rule's impact based on the available data.

4   Combining Declarative Rules

4.1   Combination of Rules

We benchmark the three manual approaches (top-down, bottom-up, and inferred
learning) and the two decision trees (non-pruned and pruned). A key issue is
that manual rules are only created once per split, meaning that the statistical
properties such as the mean and the standard deviation are impacted since some
training data will be present in the test data. We however believe that it is still
interesting to see the statistical results as a means to evaluate the prediction
methods with respect to the decision trees.

For functional safety the optimal process for conveying information would
be to create manual rules based on expert knowledge, as to argue for the logic
behind the choices, which allows for explicitly pairing the safety goals to the
implementation, thereby making a clear reference for the reviewer. As an example
we show an extract of the rules defined as a result of the top-down (TD) analysis,
where the three ViSaL rules $CAbot$, $CAtop$, and BF are used. These rules deal
with connected components in the image ($CAbot$ and $CAtop$) whereas BF finds
the largest bin and its corresponding fill level.

$$P_{g_1}^{TD}(x) \equiv \exists r' \in R \setminus \{CAbot, CAtop, BF\} :$$

$$\alpha^{CAbot}(x) = \alpha^{CAtop}(x) = \alpha^{BF}(x) = \alpha^{r'}(x) = \mathbf{g} \tag{3}$$

$$P_{b_1}^{TD}(x) \equiv \alpha^{CAbot}(x) = \alpha^{CAtop}(x) = \mathbf{w} \tag{4}$$

$$P_{b_2}^{TD}(x) \equiv \alpha^{FR}(x) = \mathbf{w} \wedge \left(\alpha^{CAbot}(x) = \mathbf{w} \vee \alpha^{CAtop}(x) = \mathbf{w}\right) \tag{5}$$

$$P_{b_3}^{TD}(x) \equiv \exists r' \neq r'' \neq r''' \neq r'''' \in R :$$

$$\alpha^{r'}(x) = \alpha^{r''}(x) = \alpha^{r'''}(x) = \alpha^{r''''}(x) = \mathbf{w} \tag{6}$$

The propositions P shown in Eqs. 3 to 6 are examples of the rules found
using the top-down analysis. The top-down manual rules were found by first
combining the rules individual results with $\alpha_0^*(x)$. This results in the combination
represented as a sequence S shown in Eq. 7.

$$S_{TD} \equiv \{(\mathbf{b}, P_{b_3}^{TD}), (\mathbf{b}, P_{b_2}^{TD}), (\mathbf{b}, P_{b_1}^{TD}), (\mathbf{g}, P_{g_1}^{TD})\} \tag{7}$$

The performance of the manual approaches top-down and bottom-up can be
seen in Table 1, where it is evident that they are not feasible. The inferred learning approach which uses the decision tree as heuristics for creating the manual

Table 1. The mean, μ, and the standard deviation, σ, of the individual results of the pruned decision tree training for the two datasets, on the raw and threshold results on the 200 random splits (see also Sect. 3.1).

Decision trees	Turtlebot test pruned	Agriculture test pruned
	threshold μ 0.40 σ 0.32	threshold μ 0.33 σ 0.07
	raw μ 0.95 σ 0.01	raw μ 0.80 σ 0.02

Manual programmatic	Top-down		Bottom-up		Inferred learning	
	μ	σ	μ	σ	μ	σ
Agriculture	0.80	0.03	0.80	0.03	0.80	0.03
Turtlebot	0.83	0.02	0.78	0.03	0.91	0.02

rules has better performance and the combination of rules was also done faster by the human programmer. Nevertheless, the results of the decision trees still outperformed the manually programmed rules. It should not be concluded that manually programmed rules can be disregarded, but rather that the overall performance can be improved using decision trees. Intuitive rules can still be created to express specific safety goals, assuming the performance is good enough. The methods should, therefore, be viewed as complementary with respect to complying with safety standards. Nevertheless the decision trees significantly outperformed the manually programmed rules, as can be seen in Table 1, where it is evident that the "raw" results outperform the "threshold" results.

5 Experimental Evaluation

5.1 Robot Platform

For our experimental evaluation, we utilise a robot from Conpleks Innovation ApS, shown in Fig. 3. The robot runs ROS Kinetic on Ubuntu 16.04, and the system navigates autonomously using an RTK-GPS and perception sensors. The software for the robot runs on two embedded platforms. First, the controller for the motors is a Conpleks robotech controller 501 based on an Aaeon GENE-QM77, which is an embedded single-board computer consisting of a 3rd generation Intel i5 processor. Second, the sensor fusion platform is based on a GeForce GTX 1080 interfaced to an Intel i7-6700K, which enables real-time processing of the sensor data. This robot is equipped with a sensor kit consisting of a thermal camera, a stereo camera, and a 360 degrees lidar. The current sensor fusion platform is built using consumer-grade electronics and is as such not usable for an industrial setting. For data collection, the robot was controlled manually and only the stereo camera was used.

Fig. 3. Conpleks' robot created for collecting golf balls autonomously [32].

5.2 Test Setup

The recordings are used to evaluate the combination of the YOLO algorithm and the safety layer. The evaluation is thus not performed on-line during operation of the robot, but at a later time using recorded images. We implemented YOLO on industrial-grade embedded boards, namely NVidia Jetson TX2 boards. The Jetson TX2 board was used as the test setup and is running ROS Kinetic on Ubuntu 16.04, making it suitable future for deployment on our robotic platform.

5.3 Data Acquisition

The recordings of the dataset were done in Odense Airport 21st-22nd of August 2017. The recording session consisted of an operator remote controlling the robot while between zero and two persons moved around in front of the robot. In addition, a second part of the recordings consisted of stressing the camera by exposing it to potential hazards for the image: over- and under-exposure was simulated by emitting light into the lens and covering it up; frozen image was simulated by covering the lens; dirty lens was simulated using grass, dirt, and water. Frozen image normally means that the same image is emitted several times, i.e., it would not be limited to black images. This means that the experiment is a special case. Nevertheless, the general example would be caught by rules using optical flow and/or lack of pixel changes, both of which are examples of rules which we use [15]. In addition, the focus was changed by adding different levels of water and plastic in front of the lens to distort the scene.

5.4 Dataset

The recordings consisted of 4471 images which are manually labelled based on the usability category. One researcher (the first author) did the labelling manually. Randomised images for the five usability categories were then extracted with an equal weighting for all categories for the data analysis. The equal weighting allows us to create three datasets: training; test; and validation, where each set consists of 545 images, which were split evenly into the five categories, i.e., 109 images per category.

The dataset is further annotated based on the YOLO algorithms performance, this is done after the usability categorisation, as to not have an impact

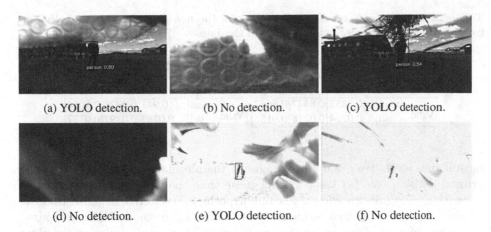

| (a) YOLO detection. | (b) No detection. | (c) YOLO detection. |

| (d) No detection. | (e) YOLO detection. | (f) No detection. |

Fig. 4. Image examples from the dataset evaluated by the YOLO algorithm, where the bounding boxes indicate if the YOLO algorithm made a detection. Images a–d had their brightness increased similarly to help the reader see the structures in the images, whereas images e and f retain their original brightness.

on the results. The YOLO labels are 1 if there is at least one human present, and 0 if no persons are present in the image. The detection precision of YOLO is also labelled by 1 and 0.

5.5 Initial Data Exploration

To investigate if the labelling was acceptable we examine it using the YOLO detections as a baseline. From the entire dataset of 4471 images, there are 1942 good images with people in the scene. Out of these, the YOLO detected at least one human in 1922. Resulting in a failure percentage of 1.04%. Second, we look at the bad images consisting of 607 images with people in the scene. YOLO was able to detect a human in 405 images. Resulting in a failure percentage of 33.28%. We use these results as an indication that the usability labelling of the images seems to be correct. Despite YOLO detecting correctly in 66.7% of the bad images, they can still be interpreted as bad, referring to Fig. 4. This means that a correct detection is not the same as stating the image is usable.

5.6 Usability

The results are extracted based on 192 random splits used for both the pruned and non-pruned decision trees. The results for the precision, recall, and F1-scores for the decision trees can be seen in Table 2.

We test the impact of the pruning using the F1-score via a paired t-test. We do this for both the test and validation splits where we test the null hypothesis that the pairwise difference between data vectors of the pruned decision tree (x) and non-pruned decision tree (y) has a mean equal to zero at the 1%

Table 2. The precision, recall and F1 scores for the *non-pruned* and *pruned* decision trees evaluated on the 192 random splits in the dataset.

Non-pruned		Precision	Recall	F1	Pruned		Precision	Recall	F1
test	mean	0.8911	0.8384	0.8636	test	mean	0.9429	0.8741	0.907
	std	0.0165	0.027	0.0134		std	0.0211	0.0224	0.0176
Valid	mean	0.8852	0.8447	0.8642	Valid	mean	0.941	0.8728	0.9054
	std	0.0264	0.0218	0.0186		std	0.0263	0.0197	0.0177

significance level. We evaluate this against the alternative hypothesis that the pruned decision tree (x) has a greater mean than the non-pruned decision tree (y) with a 1% significance level. The null hypothesis is rejected, meaning that the pruned decision trees have a higher performance on unknown data, compared to the non-pruned. Comparing the results with the manual results on the older datasets in Table 1, it is evident that the new decision trees perform better. We use these comparisons to conclude that the decision trees are applicable.

5.7   Assessment

The decision trees based on the ViSaL rules are now used to analyse the images before the YOLO algorithm is applied. The goal of the system is to signal to a decision system whether or not the data is trustworthy. This means that if the image is not usable or if there is a human in the image, the robot should be stopped. We, therefore, conduct three analyses for comparison. The three different analyses are: using only the YOLO algorithm without any impact from the ViSaL rules; using YOLO and ViSaL based decision trees, not trusting bad images; and finally YOLO and ViSaL based decision trees only trusting good images. These assessments are done for both the pruned decision tree and can be seen in Table 3.

In Table 3 the rows represent the results based on 192 iterations. The first row "Total Images" corresponds to the number of images that is checked in every iteration. The second row "Trusted Images" refers to the images that YOLO is exposed to, the range is a result of the random sampling for the 192 iterations. The "Humans Missed" row refers to the humans that are visible in the image and that were not detected by YOLO. "Mean Percentage Detection" refers to the detection performance of the YOLO algorithm on "Trusted Images", where if at least one human was detected it was a correct detection. The "Uptime Cost" row is based on the usable images in the fifth category and how many of those have been removed by the ViSaL decision trees. The cost is only based on the fifth category because we are using the soft boundary method [15], which means that the fourth category can be moved into the warning region. Finally, the last two rows give the F1 scores of the YOLO detections and the safety layer. For the YOLO detections it is calculated based on: a true positive is a correct detection of all humans in the image; a false positive is a wrong detection in the image; false negative is if YOLO misses a detection in the image; and true negative is if

Table 3. The table illustrates the performance impact of using ViSaL-based pruned decision trees in connection with YOLO, see text for details.

	YOLO no safety		YOLO, distrust "warn" and "bad"		YOLO, distrust only "bad"	
	mean	std	mean	std	mean	std
Total images	545	0	545	0	545	0
Trusted images	545	0	112.56	9.34	328.63	9.10
Humans missed	62.25	7	2.63	1.62	11.38	3.11
Percentage detection	88.58%	0.0128	97.67%	0.0139	96.54%	0.0096
Uptime cost	0%	0	28.78%	0.0521	4.99%	0.0225
F1 for detections	0.82	0.0136	0.87	0.0337	0.88	0.0154
F1 of safety layer	N/A	N/A	0.88	0.0380	0.92	0.0159

no humans are present and there are no detections. Furthermore, it is important to note that although the number of images removed seems excessive, the two worst categories consist of 218 images. This means that when the system only distrusts bad images, the trusted images column will decrease with around 218 images, as can be seen on the right side of the table. For the middle column, the number of removed images increases because there potentially are 327 warning images due to the soft boundaries, where the warning region is incorporated.

From Table 3 it can be seen that the removed images correspond to the intuition from earlier. In addition, it is evident that the introduction of the safety layer drastically reduces the number of missed persons. This means that the choice of the aggressiveness of the safety layer, i.e., the reduction of accepted images, has to be evaluated as to what is an acceptable and an unacceptable risk.

6   Conclusion and Future Work

In this paper, we investigated how to model the combination of declarative rules as a means to improve a vision pipeline with respect to performance and safety. The modelling choices focused on a standard approach to learning within computer vision. The data is recorded using a robot platform and analysed on an industrial-grade embedded board to have a feeling for real-time performance. We found that introducing the safety layer into a vision system can improve the performance, with some uptime cost. The definition of acceptable risk is, therefore, a critical issue for fielding autonomous systems that rely on approaches where human operators are not in the decision loop.

To use decision trees in functional safety it is critical to understand the intent and to generate code for embedded platforms, we believe that such an approach can improve the communication with certification authorities [39]. This means that understandability and readability are equally critical for the software. While readability for ViSaL has been investigated [13], further studies are needed. Finally, a more detailed analysis of specific faults is needed to understand which specific hazards are currently detected robustly and which need more rules.

References

1. Baheti, R., Gill, H.: Cyber-physical systems. Impact Control Technol. **12**, 161–166 (2011)
2. Bansal, A., Farhadi, A., Parikh, D.: Towards transparent systems: semantic characterization of failure modes. In: Fleet, D., Pajdla, T., Schiele, B., Tuytelaars, T. (eds.) ECCV 2014. LNCS, vol. 8694, pp. 366–381. Springer, Cham (2014). https://doi.org/10.1007/978-3-319-10599-4_24
3. Daigle, M.J., Koutsoukos, X.D., Biswas, G.: Distributed diagnosis in formations of mobile robots. IEEE Trans. Robo. **23**(2), 353–369 (2007)
4. Davis, J., Goadrich, M.: The relationship between precision-recall and roc curves. In: Proceedings of the 23rd International Conference on Machine Learning, pp. 233–240 (2006)
5. De Cabrol, A., Garcia, T., Bonnin, P., Chetto, M.: A concept of dynamically reconfigurable real-time vision system for autonomous mobile robotics. Int. J. Autom. Comput. **5**(2), 174–184 (2008)
6. Fields, C., David, R., Nielsen, P.: Defense science board 2016 summer study on autonomy. Defense Science Board (2016)
7. Frese, U., Hirschmüller, H.: Special issue on robot vision: what is robot vision? J. Real-Time Image Process. **10**(4), 597–598 (2015)
8. Gupta, P., Loparo, K., Mackall, D., Schumann, J., Soares, F.: Verification and validation methodology of real-time adaptive neural networks for aerospace applications. In: International Conference on Computational Intelligence for Modeling, Control, and Automation (2004)
9. Hauge, A., Tonnesen, A.: Use of artificial neural networks in safety critical systems. Faculty of Computer Sciences (2004)
10. Heckemann, K., Gesell, M., Pfister, T., Berns, K., Schneider, K., Trapp, M.: Safe automotive software. In: König, A., Dengel, A., Hinkelmann, K., Kise, K., Howlett, R.J., Jain, L.C. (eds.) KES 2011. LNCS (LNAI), vol. 6884, pp. 167–176. Springer, Heidelberg (2011). https://doi.org/10.1007/978-3-642-23866-6_18
11. IFR: World Robotics 2014 Industrial Robots (2014)
12. Ingibergsson, J.T.M., Schultz, U.P., Kuhrmann, M.: On the use of safety certification practices in autonomous field robot software development: a systematic mapping study. In: Abrahamsson, P., Corral, L., Oivo, M., Russo, B. (eds.) PROFES 2015. LNCS, vol. 9459, pp. 335–352. Springer, Cham (2015). https://doi.org/10.1007/978-3-319-26844-6_25
13. Ingibergsson, J.T.M., Hanenberg, S., Sunshine, J., Schultz, U.P.: Readability study of a domain specific language: process and outcome. In: Accepted for the 33rd ACM/SIGAPP Symposium on Applied Computing (SAC-18) (2018)
14. Ingibergsson, J.T.M., Kraft, D., Schultz, U.P.: Declarative rule-based safety for robotic perception systems. J. Software Eng. Rob. (JOSER) **8**(1), 17–31 (2017)
15. Ingibergsson, J.T.M., Kraft, D., Schultz, U.P.: Explicit image quality detection rules for functional safety in computer vision. In: 12th International Conference on Computer Vision Theory and Applications (VISAPP), p. 12, Marts 2017

16. ISO TC22/SC3/WG16. ISO/IEC 26262:2011: Road vehicles - Functional safety. Technical report, International Organization for Standardization (2011)
17. Klarreich, E.: Learning securely. Commun. ACM **59**(11), 12–14 (2016)
18. Kurd, Z., Kelly, T.: Establishing safety criteria for artificial neural networks. In: Palade, V., Howlett, R.J., Jain, L. (eds.) KES 2003. LNCS (LNAI), vol. 2773, pp. 163–169. Springer, Heidelberg (2003). https://doi.org/10.1007/978-3-540-45224-9_24
19. Kurd, Z., Kelly, T., Austin, J.: Safety criteria and safety lifecycle for artificial neural networks. In: Proceedings of Eunite, vol. 2003 (2003)
20. Machin, M., Dufossé, F., Blanquart, J.-P., Guiochet, J., Powell, D., Waeselynck, H.: Specifying safety monitors for autonomous systems using model-checking. In: Bondavalli, A., Di Giandomenico, F. (eds.) SAFECOMP 2014. LNCS, vol. 8666, pp. 262–277. Springer, Cham (2014). https://doi.org/10.1007/978-3-319-10506-2_18
21. Mekki-Mokhtar, A., Blanquart, J.-P., Guiochet, J., Powell, D., Roy, M.: Safety trigger conditions for critical autonomous systems. In: 18th Pacific Rim International Symposium on Dependable Computing, pp. 61–69. IEEE (2012)
22. METI: Trends in the Market for the Robot Industry in 2012, July 2013
23. Murphy, R.R., Hershberger, D.: Handling sensing failures in autonomous mobile robots. Int. J. Robot. Res. **18**(4), 382–400 (1999)
24. Myles, A.J., Feudale, R.N., Liu, Y., Woody, N.A., Brown, S.D.: An introduction to decision tree modeling. J. Chemom. **18**(6), 275–285 (2004)
25. Nguyen, A., Yosinski, J., Clune, J.: Deep neural networks are easily fooled: High confidence predictions for unrecognizable images. In: Conference on Computer Vision and Pattern Recognition (CVPR), pp. 427–436. IEEE (2015)
26. Redmon, J., Farhadi, A.: YOLO9000: Better, faster, stronger. arXiv preprint arXiv:1612.08242 (2016)
27. Reichardt, M., Föhst, T., Berns, K.: On software quality-motivated design of a real-time framework for complex robot control systems. In: International Workshop on Software Quality and Maintainability (2013)
28. Safavian, S.R., Landgrebe, D.: A survey of decision tree classifier methodology. IEEE Trans. Syst. Man Cybern. **21**(3), 660–674 (1991)
29. Saito, T., Rehmsmeier, M.: The precision-recall plot is more informative than the ROC plot when evaluating binary classifiers on imbalanced datasets. In: PLoS ONE, pp. 1–21 (2015)
30. Santosuosso, A., Boscarato, C., Caroleo, F., Labruto, R., Leroux, C.: Robots, market and civil liability: a european perspective. In: RO-MAN, pp. 1051–1058. IEEE (2012)
31. Schumann, J., Gupta, P., Liu, Y.: Application of neural networks in high assurance systems: a survey. In: Schumann, J., Liu, Y. (eds.) Applications of Neural Networks in High Assurance Systems, pp. 1–19. Springer, Heidelberg (2010). https://doi.org/10.1007/978-3-642-10690-3_1
32. SDU: Marken er mejet af en robot (2017)
33. Steen, K.A., Christiansen, P., Karstoft, H., Jørgensen, R.N.: Using deep learning to challenge safety standard for highly autonomous machines in agriculture. J. Imaging **2**(1), 6 (2016)
34. TC 127: Earth-moving machinery - autonomous machine system safety. In: International Standard ISO 17757–2015, International Organization for Standardization (2015)
35. TC 23: Agricultural machinery and tractors - Safety of highly automated machinery. International Standard ISO/DIS 18497, International Organization for Standardization (2014)

36. TC 44: Safety of machinery - electro-sensitive protective equipment. International Standard IEC 61496–2012, International Electronical Commission (2012)
37. TC 65: Safety of machinery - electro-sensitive protective equipment. International Standard IEC 61508–2011, International Electronical Commission (2011)
38. Veres, S.M., Lincoln, N.K., Molnar, L.: Control engineering of autonomous cognitive vehicles-a practical tutorial. Technical report, Faculty of Engineering and the Environment, University of Southampton, Technical report (2011)
39. Yang, Y., Keller, P., Livnat, Y., Liggesmeyer, P.: Improving safety-critical systems by visual analysis. In: OASIcs-OpenAccess Series in Informatics, vol. 27. Schloss Dagstuhl-Leibniz-Zentrum fuer Informatik (2012)
40. Zhang, P., Wang, J., Farhadi, A., Hebert, M., Parikh, D.: Predicting failures of vision systems. In: Proceedings of the IEEE Conference on Computer Vision and Pattern Recognition, pp. 3566–3573 (2014)

Simulation

Template-Based Monte-Carlo Test Generation for Simulink Models

Takashi Tomita[1(✉)], Daisuke Ishii[2], Toru Murakami[3], Shigeki Takeuchi[3], and Toshiaki Aoki[1]

[1] Japan Advanced Institute of Science and Technology, Nomi, Japan
{tomita,toshiaki}@jaist.ac.jp
[2] University of Fukui, Fukui, Japan
dsksh@u-fukui.ac.jp
[3] Gaio Technology Co., Ltd., Tokyo, Japan
{murakami.t,takeuchi.s}@gaio.co.jp

Abstract. In this paper, we propose a Monte-Carlo test generation method that is able to conduct decision, condition and MC/DC coverage testing for practical Simulink models. To generate a test suite efficiently for models with dozens of thousands blocks, we introduce several techniques. Firstly, we propose using *templates* of input signals, which characterize shapes of entire waveforms of the signals with a few parameters. By using templates, we can easily generate candidate test cases and reduce a search space to plausible one. Secondly, we propose *biased sampling framework* to get efficiently test cases meeting uncovered objectives. In the framework, a biased distribution generating new candidate test cases is iteratively refined based on *fitness values* of the previous candidates. We performed two experiments for each of the techniques and confirmed that they are effective enough for Simulink models which cannot be dealt with a de-facto standard tool SLDV.

1 Introduction

1.1 Background

A modern automobile involves hundreds of electric control units (ECUs), which manage engine, brake, steering, etc., mainly by feedback control. It is strongly required that these physical/mechanical modules are controlled safely and reliably. *Model-based development* (MBD) is widely employed for developing highly safe and reliable software on ECUs. For this purpose, $MATLAB^1$/$Simulink^2$ provide numeric computation, modeling, and simulation environment and is used as the de-facto standard MBD tool in many fields.

In most cases, *testing* is a feasible and reasonable method to guarantee the quality of practical models. This is because industrial models are very large and

---

[1] https://www.mathworks.com/products/matlab.html
[2] https://www.mathworks.com/products/simulink.html

© Springer Nature Switzerland AG 2019
R. Chamberlain et al. (Eds.): CyPhy 2017, LNCS 11267, pp. 63–78, 2019.
https://doi.org/10.1007/978-3-030-17910-6_5

complex, and therefore formal verification takes very high costs, or is undecidable at the worst case. When testing Simulink models, we first build a *test suite* that consists of *test cases*, which are groups of input signals, and then simulate and check behaviors of the model for the test suite. Several *test criteria* are introduced to guarantee an acceptable quality, e.g., *decision coverage, condition coverage,* and *modified condition/decision coverage* (MC/DC coverage). It is typically required to test a model by using a high-coverage test suite. Actually, ISO 26262 ("Road vehicles – Functional safety") requires to conduct an MC/DC coverage test. MATLAB/Simulink has toolboxes for this purpose: *Simulink Design Verifier*[3] (SLDV) and *Simulink Verification and Validation*[4] (V&V).

1.2 Issues

Scalability and Complexity: A practical model often consists of hundreds of inputs and dozens of thousands blocks, and represents a complex function combined with logical/linear/non-linear operations, adaptive digital filters, etc. Unfortunately, formal analysis does not scale against such models, and becomes undecidable because of the non-linearity. Test case generation of SLDV is mainly based on formal analysis and thus it cannot deal with most of practical models. To overcome the issue on scalability and complexity, *Monte-Carlo approach* is often employed, which generates test cases sequentially and randomly. A test suite is constructed by a contributable subset of them.

Difficulty on Monte-Carlo Approach: It is not rare that a model has objectives which are difficult to cover with Monte-Carlo methods due to the large search space of time-series data with numerical domain. Objectives in some type of circuit (e.g., a narrow-band digital filter) is covered only by a signal with a specific waveform (e.g. a sine wave with a certain frequency); then it becomes difficult to generate such signal without a useful guide.

1.3 Objectives and Approach

In this paper, our objectives is to propose a feasible Monte-Carlo method to generate high decision, condition and MC/DC coverage test suites for practical Simulink models.

Firstly, we introduce *template-based approach*. In our experience, it is frequently sufficient to consider several simple types of input signals, e.g., *constant, linear, step* and *sine-wave*, in a test case/suite generation. By using *templates* of such input signals characterized with a few parameters, we can simplify a process of generating test cases, and the search space is reduced to plausible one effectively. Secondly, we propose *biased sampling framework* to get more

---

[3] https://www.mathworks.com/products/sldesignverifier.html
[4] https://www.mathworks.com/products/simverification.html

efficiently test cases meeting uncovered objectives. For each objective, we provide a *fitness function*, which gives a higher value as a test case inducing a behavior of the model closer to a target objective. A new candidate test case is generated based on a biased probability distribution considering the fitness values of previous candidate test cases. We show that these techniques are effective enough for Simulink models which cannot be dealt with by SLDV.

1.4 Related Work

Random testing is a well-known technique to find software bugs. On testing for codes, various methods were introduced, e.g., directed random testing [1,2], adaptive random testing [3], to obtain a higher coverage test suite. In this paper, we focus on testing for models.

SLDV is a MATLAB/Simulink toolbox for design error detection, test case generation, model slicing, etc. The design error detector tries to find dead logic (i.e., unexercisable) objects of the model. The test case generator tries to construct test cases which cover as much objectives as possible for given coverage criteria, e.g., decision, condition, MC/DC and relational boundary. Since SLDV is mainly based on static analysis, it cannot treat most practical models.

As we have seen so far, randomized techniques are promising for test suite/case generation for practical models. Reactis[5] [4] is another MBD tool consisting of simulator, tester and validator, which supports Simulink models and several coverage criteria, e.g., state, branch, and MC/DC. The tester generates test cases based on a Monte Carlo method and *guided simulation* technique. Guided simulation tries to choose a contributable test case, based on a backward data-flow analysis for simulations of previous test cases. As another technique, Satpathy et al. introduced a *randomized directed testing* (REDIRECT) approach [5], which combines randomization, directed, backtracking and feedback-based testing. These techniques try to make new contributable test cases by refining suffixes of previous test cases. In contrast, our method randomly make entirely new candidates from templates (based on those of previous test cases with high fitness values).

We focus on decision, condition and MC/DC coverage criteria, while Matinnejad et al. proposed a randomized test suite generation method that focuses on the *output diversity* criterion [6], in which a more desirable test suite derives a greater variety of behaviors of the models. Their method attempts to refine a test suite based on an evolutionary algorithm (EA) with a fitness function focusing on various behavioral features of a target model.

---

[5] http://www.reactive-systems.com/.

2   Preliminaries

2.1   Simulink Models

A Simulink model is constructed with various types of *blocks*, e.g., *input/output*, *mathematical operator*, *logical/relational operator*, *(multiport) switch*, and *delay*; blocks are connected with *lines* which transfer Boolean, integer or floating/fixed point data among them. Simulink supports hierarchical structure by *subsystems*. A subsystem consists of some blocks and lines; input/output ports of the subsystem are associated with their low-level *input/output* blocks. Additional ports, e.g., *enable* and *trigger* ports, may be equipped with a subsystem for selective activation/inactivation by external signals. Temporal behavior of a block is either based on continuous-time or discrete-time.

The type of a block b_1 is denoted by $\mathsf{BlockType}(b_1)$, and the line connected to the i-th input port of b_1 by $\mathsf{InputLine}(b_1, i)$. $\mathsf{PredBlock}(l)$ denotes a pair $\langle b_2, j \rangle$ of a block b_2 and the index j of output port connected to the line l. In a simulation, the time-series signal flowing on a line l is denoted by $\mathsf{Signal}(l)$, i.e., $\mathsf{Signal}(l)(t)$ represents the value of the signal at time t. The data type of the signal is denoted by $\mathsf{DataType}(l)$. For a *(multi-port) switch* block b_3, $\mathsf{DataPorts}(b_3)$ denotes a set of port indices of input signals possible to pass. For a discrete-time *delay* block b_4, $\mathsf{Delay}(b_4)$ and $\mathsf{InitialValue}(b_4)$ denotes a number k of delay steps and the initial value within the first k steps, respectively. For an *input* block b_5, $\mathsf{InputPort}(b_5)$ denotes a pair $\langle b_6, m \rangle$ of an *subsystem* block b_6 and the index m of its input port associated with b_5. $\mathsf{OutputBlock}(b_6, n)$ denotes an *output* block associated with the n-th output port of b_6.

2.2   Testing for Simulink Models

Typically, we use a harness model for testing a given target model. A harness model consists of a subsystem copied from the target model and a *signal builder* block providing a group of input signals for the subsystem (Fig. 1). SLDV has a function to construct such harness model. Then, we simulate behavior of the model for the group, and compare back-to-back it with that of another model (e.g., more abstracted or concretized one) for the same group. That is, the group is a test case in this back-to-back testing.

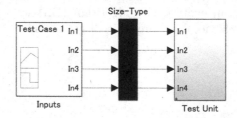

Fig. 1. Exapmle of a harness model. A signal builder block, named "Inputs," provides test cases for "Test Unit" subsystem copied from a target model

Definition 1 (Test Case/Suite). *A test case is a group of input signals. A test suite is a set of test cases.* □

Given a test case, the *model coverage* is a measure of how exhaustively the model objects are exercised. The model coverage for a test suite is an accumulation of that of every test case in the test suite. In decision, condition and MC/DC model coverage criteria, a *measured object* is a block whose activity changes logical characteristics (i.e., data flow pattern) of the model. In the case of Simulink, they are, e.g., *logical/relational operator blocks, (multi-port) switch blocks* and *subsystems with active-control ports*. For a measured block b, Formula(b, o) denotes the logical formula mechanically derived from settings of b, which holds only if an outcome of its decision is o. A *outcome* of a decision is `true` or `false` for a logical/relational operator block and for a subsystem[6] with active-control ports, and the index of a passing input for a (multi-port) switch[7]. Formula(b, o) has the following form[8]:

$$\text{Formula: } \varphi ::= c \mid \varphi \vee \varphi \mid \varphi \wedge \varphi, \tag{1}$$

$$\text{Condition: } c ::= \text{prop}(i) \mid \neg\text{prop}(i) \mid \text{rel}(i, \sim, j) \mid \text{rel\_const}(i, \sim, a), \tag{2}$$

where i is the index of an input port of b, $\sim$ is a relational operator, and a is a constant. Intuitively, $\text{prop}(i)$ (resp., $\neg\text{prop}(i)$) means the propositional condition "the i-th Boolean input signal of b is `true` (resp., `false`)." $\text{rel}(i, \sim, j)$ means the relational condition "a relation $\sim$ holds between the i-th and j-th input signals of b." $\text{rel\_const}(i, \sim, a)$ means the relational condition "a relation $\sim$ holds between the i-th input signal of b and the constant a." That is, *outcomes o' of the conditions are trivially Boolean values.* Without loss of generality, we can assume that Formula(b, o) has the *disjunctive* or *conjunctive normal form* (DNF or CNF).

Definition 2 (Objectives). *A* decision objective *is a pair $\langle b, o \rangle$ of a measured block b and its outcome o. A* condition objective *is a pair $\langle b, \langle c, o' \rangle \rangle$ of b and a pair $\langle c, o' \rangle$ of a condition c affecting the decision of b (defined by Equation (2)) and its outcome o'. An* MC/DC objective *is a pair $\langle b, \{\langle c_1, o_1 \rangle, \ldots, \langle c_n, o_n \rangle\} \rangle$ of b and a set of pairs $\langle c_m, o_m \rangle$ of its conditions c_m and their corresponding outcomes o_m.*

Note that a condition objective $\langle b, \langle \text{prop}(i), \text{true} \rangle \rangle$ (resp., $\langle b, \langle \text{rel}(i, \sim, j), \text{true} \rangle \rangle$, $\langle b, \langle \text{rel}(i, <, j), \text{true} \rangle \rangle$, etc.) is equivalent to $\langle b, \langle \neg\text{prop}(i), \text{false} \rangle \rangle$ (resp., $\langle b, \langle \text{rel}(i, \not\sim, j), \text{false} \rangle \rangle$, $\langle b, \langle \text{rel}(j, >, i), \text{true} \rangle \rangle$, etc.).

Definition 3 (Coverage). *A test suite is* full decision coverage *if, for each measured block b, each possible outcome o of b is observed at some time step by a test case in the test suite. A test suite is* full condition coverage *if, for each condition c of every b, each possible outcome o' of c is observed at some time*

---

[6] `true` ane `false` mean activated and inactivated, respectively.

[7] That is, the outcome is in DataPorts(b) for a (multi-port) switch block b.

[8] For simplicity, we omit trigger conditions in this paper.

step by a test case in the test suite. A test suite is full MC/DC coverage *if, for each b whose decision depends on multiple conditions* $c_1, \ldots, c_n$, *the test suite includes test cases which show each* c_m *independently affects its decision.*   □

For these criteria, we can measure and report coverage for a given model by using built-in functions of V&V.

3   Template-Based Monte-Carlo Test Suite Generation

3.1   Signal Templates

As previous mentioned, a test cases is characterized as a group of input signals. Each signal may have an arbitrary shape of a waveform. However, input signals are provided by other electric modules which are likely well-controlled, or by physical objects which are dominated by physical laws. So it may be unnecessary to consider arbitrary signals. Additionally, in our experience, it is frequently sufficient to consider several simple types of input signals, which can be characterized with a few parameters, for achieving high decision, condition and MC/DC coverage. The types are, e.g., *constant, linear, step, sine-wave*, etc. Actually, a signal builder block provides a group of signals with such types. Behavior of a model for the group is relatively easy to understand for a design engineer. Thus it is helpful for refining the given model.

Therefore, we provide *templates* for input signals, and search test cases within the subset of instances of the templates.

Definition 4 (Signal Templates). *A template is a subset of signals, which is characterized a fixed number of parameters.*   □

Example 1. A template Step$(\cdot, \cdot, \cdot)$ of step signals is represented by 3 parameters, step time, initial value and *final value*. That is, an instantiated signal Step(x, y, z) is given as Eq. (3) for time t.   □

$$\mathsf{Step}(x, y, z)(t) = \begin{cases} y & \text{if } t < x, \\ z & \text{otherwise.} \end{cases} \tag{3}$$

Example 2. A template Sine$(\cdot, \cdot, \cdot, \cdot)$ of sine-wave signals is represented by 4 parameters, *frequency, amplitude, phase* and *bias*. That is, an instantiated signal Sine(w, x, y, z) is given as Eq. (4) for time t.   □

$$\mathsf{Sine}(w, x, y, z)(t) = x \cdot \sin(w \cdot t + y) + z. \tag{4}$$

3.2   Overview

A naive algorithm for test suite generation is shown in Algorithm 1. (i) We generate *randomly* an entire candidate test case (i.e., a group of input signals) based on templates (at Line 4). The details of how to randomly generate the candidate will be presented in Sect. 3.3. (ii) Then we simulate the model for the candidate and measure its coverage (at Lines 5–6). Note that the simulation and measurement can be performed by cvsim function in V&V. (iii) If the candidate is contributable to the coverage, we add it to the test suite (at Lines 7–10). Also note that the contributability can be easily checked by referring coverage data returned from cvsim function. The steps (i)–(iii) are repeated until the test suite achieves full coverage.

An advantage of this approach is easy to be parallelized because iterations (at Line 3–11) are almost independent from each other. That is, it is very hopeful to handle a very large model.

Algorithm 1. Template-based test suite generation

Inputs: Simulink model mdl
Outputs: Test suite ts
1: ts := ∅;
2: tsc := null_coverage;
3: **repeat**
4:     cand := generateTestCaseFromTemplates(mdl);
5:     sd := simulate(mdl, cand);
6:     candc := measureCoverage(mdl, sd);
7:     **if** a covering area of candc is not subset of that of tsc **then**
8:         ts := ts ∪ {cand};
9:         tsc := accumulateCoverage(tsc, candc);
10:    **end if**
11: **until** tsc achieves full coverage
12: **return** ts;

3.3   Template-Based Test Case Generation

By using templates, we can easily generate randomly an entire candidate test case (at Line 4 in Algorithm 1). The generation can be divided into 2 parts. One is for choosing a combination of templates for input signals. The other is for instantiating signals from chosen templates, i.e., determining arguments of parameters of the templates.

We indicate naive methods for them, based on *uniform distributions*.

Choosing Templates: For simplicity, we assume a number of available templates is bounded. For each input block, we uniformly-randomly and independently sample a template considering the data type of the block.

Example 3. If the data type of the input block is Boolean, *constant* and *step* are available, however, neither *linear* or *sine-wave* is selected.   □

Remark 1. We can use any probabilistic distribution for choosing templates. Additionally, some templates can be manually unselectable for each input block in advance because implausible templates are often known.   □

Determining Arguments: For each parameter of every templates, we uniformly-randomly and independently sample an argument value from the sample space corresponding to the discretized argument range for the parameter.

Example 4. The range for *step time* parameter of step signal is $(0, t_{\max})$, where $t_{\max}$ is the simulation stop time.   □

Example 5. The range for *amplitude* parameter of sine-wave signal with `uint8` (unsigned 8-bit integer) data type is $(0, 127]$, and that of *bias* parameter is $[w - 128, 127 + w]$ where w is an sampled argument value for *amplitude* parameter.   □

Remark 2. We can also use any probabilistic distribution for determining arguments. Additionally, it is possible to narrow manually the ranges of arguments in advance because an actual range is often limited and known.   □

4   Template-Based Biased Sampling Framework

In this section, we illustrate *biased sampling framework* for template-based test case generation to get more efficiently test cases meeting uncovered objectives.

In general, Monte-Carlo methods may fail to achieve a complete solution (i.e., full coverage test suite in this study) due to its randomness. Algorithm 1 presents a method to collect contributable test cases haphazardly, without focusing uncovered objectives. However, for obtaining a test case meeting one of them, it is efficient to adapt specifically a sampling method (at Line in 4 in Algorithm 1) to the one. Thus we propose biased sampling for uncovered objectives. To adapt a sampling method for a target objective, we provide a *fitness function* assigning a fitness value in $(0, 1]$ for a test case. The fitness function gives 1 for a desired test case (i.e., one meeting the objective), and a higher value for a more desirable test case, i.e., a test case makes a state of the model closer to the target objective at some time step. Then, a new candidate test case is generated based on a biased probability distribution considering fitness values of previous candidate test cases. By biased sampling, we try to find efficiently a test case for each of uncovered objectives one by one.

4.1   Overview

An algorithm of template-based test case generation with biased sampling is shown in Algorithm 2. (i) Firstly, a probabilistic distribution for sampling is initialized, e.g., as the uniform distribution (at Line 2). Of cause we can employ another distribution. (ii) An entire candidate test case is generated based on the current distribution (at Line 4). (iii) Then we simulate and log a behavior of the model for the candidate by `sim` function in standard MATLAB/Simulink, and evaluate the fitness of the candidate for the target objective, based on the logged signals (at Lines 5–6). (iv-a) If the fitness value is 1, the candidate is returned as a desired test case (at Line 8). (iv-b) If the fitness value is less than

1, a pair of the candidate and the fitness value is added to a history, and the probabilistic distribution is refined based on the history (at Lines 10–11). The steps (ii)–(iv) are repeated until the candidate meets the target objective. The probability distribution is iteratively refined, and thus it is expected to generate candidates gradually closer to a desired test case.

The problems are how to determine a fitness function for a target objective, and how to refine a probabilistic distribution from a history of candidates and its fitness values.

Algorithm 2. Monte-Carlo Targeted Test Case Generation

Inputs: Simulink model `mdl`,
    fitness function `fitnessFunction` for a given target objective, and
    distribution refinement method `refineDistribution` for biased sampling
Outputs: Test case `tc`
 1: `hist := empty_history;`
 2: `dist := uniform_distribution;`
 3: **loop**
 4:    `tc := generateTestCaseFromTemplates_Biased(mdl, dist);`
 5:    `sd := simulate(mdl, tc);`
 6:    `fv := fitnessFunction(sd);`
 7:    **if** `fv == 1` **then**
 8:      **return** `tc;`
 9:    **else**
10:      `hist := addHistory(hist, tc, fv);`
11:      `dist := refineDistribution(hist);`
12:    **end if**
13: **end loop**

4.2 Fitness Functions

In decision, condition and MC/DC coverage criteria, each objective to be covered by a test suite consists of a measured block and outcome(s) of its decision/condition(s). The outcomes of the decision/conditions change over time, so the fitness function (`fitnessFunction` in Algorithm 2) can be defined as one that gives the maximum value of fitness value $F_{\mathrm{obj}}^{t}(\mathbf{sd})$ at time t for a target objective *obj*.

$$\texttt{fitnessFunction}(\mathbf{sd}) = \max_{0 \leq t \leq t_{\max}} \{F_{obj}^{\mathbf{sd}}(t)\}, \tag{5}$$

where $t_{\max}$ is the simulation stop time. Note that (1) the outcome of the decision is derived from those of the conditions, (2) the conditions are derived from input signals of the measured block, (3) the input signals are provided from predecessor blocks of the measured block and depends on decisions of the predecessor blocks, and (4) All signal data $\mathbf{sd}$ (i.e., $\{\mathrm{Signal}(l) \mid l$ is a line in the target model$\}$) can be obtained by logging the behavior of the model for the test case. In this paper, we give a naive inductive definition for $F_{obj}^{sd}(t)$. However, for simplicity, we omit description on how to deal with subsystems with active-control ports[9].

For a decision objective $\langle b, o \rangle$, a fitness value at time t is given as follows:

$$
F_{\langle b, o \rangle}^{sd}(t) = \begin{cases}
\epsilon + (1 - \epsilon) \cdot \max_i \left\{ \prod_j F_{\langle c_{ij}, \text{true} \rangle}^{sd}(t) \right\} \\
\quad \text{if Formula}(b, o) \text{ is a DNF formula } \bigvee_i \bigwedge_j c_{ij}, \\
\epsilon + (1 - \epsilon) \cdot \prod_i \max_j \left\{ F_{\langle c_{ij}, \text{true} \rangle}^{sd}(t) \right\} \\
\quad \text{if Formula}(b, o) \text{ is a CNF formula } \bigwedge_i \bigvee_j c_{ij},
\end{cases}
\tag{6}
$$

where ϵ is a certain small positive value less than 1.

Remark 3. Equation (6) (and also Eqs. (8) and (14) described later) is based on numerical *max/product* evaluations for logical disjunction/conjunction operations. We can employ another one, e.g., *max/min*.   □

For a propositional condition objective $\langle b, \langle c, o \rangle \rangle$ such that c is $\text{prop}(i)$ or $\neg\text{prop}(i)$, a fitness value at time t is given as follows:

$$
F_{\langle b, \langle c, o \rangle \rangle}^{sd}(t) = \begin{cases}
f_{\langle \text{InputLine}(b,i), o \rangle}^{sd}(t) & \text{if } c \text{ is } \text{prop}(i) \\
f_{\langle \text{InputLine}(b,i), \neg o \rangle}^{sd}(t) & \text{if } c \text{ is } \neg\text{prop}(i),
\end{cases}
\tag{7}
$$

where $f_{\langle l, o \rangle}^{sd}(t)$ is a function that gives a fitness of a Boolean signal flowing on line l at time t for desirable outcome o. For $\langle b', j \rangle = \text{PredBlock}(l)$, it is given as follows:

$$
f_{\langle l, o \rangle}^{sd}(t) = \begin{cases}
F_{\langle b', o \rangle}^{sd}(t) & \text{if BlockType}(b') \text{ is } logical/relational\ operator, \\
\epsilon + (1 - \epsilon) \cdot \max_{m \in \text{DataPorts}(b')} \{ F_{\langle b', m \rangle}^{sd}(t) \cdot f_{\langle \text{InputLine}(b', m), o \rangle}^{sd}(t) \} \\
\quad \text{if BlockType}(b') \text{ is (multi-port) } switch, \\
f_{\langle \text{InputLine}(b', 1), o \rangle}^{sd}(t - \text{Delay}(b')) \\
\quad \text{if BlockType}(b') \text{ is } delay \text{ and } t \geq \text{Delay}(b'), \\
\max\{ \mathbf{1}_{\text{InitialValue}(b') \leftrightarrow o}, \epsilon \} & \text{if BlockType}(b') \text{ is } delay \text{ and } t < \text{Delay}(b'), \\
f_{\langle \text{InputLine}(\text{OutputBlock}(b', j), 1), o \rangle}^{sd}(t) & \text{if BlockType}(b') \text{ is } subsystem, \\
f_{\langle \text{InputLine}(\text{InputPort}(b')), o \rangle}^{sd}(t) & \text{if BlockType}(b') \text{ is low-level } input, \\
\max\{ \mathbf{1}_{\text{Signal}(l)(t) \leftrightarrow o}, \epsilon \} & \text{if BlockType}(b') \text{ is top-level } input,
\end{cases}
\tag{8}
$$

where $\mathbf{1}_v$ is a characteristic function, i.e, it gives 1 if v holds, otherwise 0.

Remark 4. The above definition for a (multi-port) switch block b' is based on the fact that an output signal of b' corresponds with a disjunction of conjunctive clauses of Formula(b', m) and signals flowing on InputLine(b', m).   □

---

[9] Additionally, blocks in a subsystem with active-control ports are exercised only if the subsystem is activated. Therefore, we also need to correct a fitness for an objective related to the blocks.

For a relational condition objective $\langle b, \langle c, o \rangle \rangle$ such that c is $\mathsf{rel}(i, \sim, j)$ or $\mathsf{rel\_const}(i, \sim, a)$, a fitness value at time t is given as follows:

$$F^{\mathsf{sd}}_{\langle b, \langle c, o \rangle \rangle}(t) = \begin{cases} 1 & \text{if } \mathsf{Signal}(l_1)(t) \sim s(t) \Leftrightarrow o, \\ e^{-\alpha \cdot |\mathsf{Signal}(l_1)(t) - s(t)| + \beta} & \text{otherwise,} \end{cases} \tag{9}$$

$$l_1 = \mathsf{InputLine}(b, i), \tag{10}$$

$$s(t) = \begin{cases} \mathsf{Signal}(\mathsf{InputLine}(b, j))(t) & \text{if } c \text{ is } \mathsf{rel}(i, \sim, j), \\ a & \text{if } c \text{ is } \mathsf{rel\_const}(i, \sim, a), \end{cases} \tag{11}$$

$$\alpha = \frac{\log(1 - \epsilon) - \log(\epsilon)}{\max \mathsf{Range}(\mathsf{DataType}(l_1)) - \min \mathsf{Range}(\mathsf{DataType}(l_1))}, \tag{12}$$

$$\beta = \log(1 - \epsilon), \tag{13}$$

where $\mathsf{Range}(T)$ is the range of values of the data type T.

Remark 5. Equation (9) is given based on a negative exponential function for the difference between the signals. By scaling with α and β, the function gives a value in $[1 - \epsilon, \epsilon]$ when missing the objective. However, we can employ any function *decreasing monotonically* for the difference. Additionally, it is possible to narrow manually the data range for a line $\mathsf{InputLine}(b, i)$ in advance because an actually-used region of the data range is often limited and known.   □

An MC/DC objective $\langle b, \{ \langle c_1, o_1, \rangle, \ldots, \langle c_n, o_n \rangle \} \rangle$ is just a conjunction of its condition sub objectives. So a fitness value at time t for the MC/DC objective is given as follows:

$$F^{\mathsf{sd}}_{\langle b, \{ \langle c_1, o_1, \rangle, \ldots, \langle c_n, o_n \rangle \} \rangle}(t) = \epsilon + (1 - \epsilon) \cdot \prod_{1 \leq m \leq n} F^{\mathsf{sd}}_{\langle b, \langle c_m, o_m \rangle \rangle}(t) \tag{14}$$

4.3 Distribution Refinement

As previously mentioned in Sect. 3.3, a refined distribution for sampling templated test cases can be divided into 2 parts. Note that we can employ any construction method for the refined distribution.

Choosing Templates: One of the simplest approach for refining probabilistic distribution of a combination of templates is based on (i) the occurrence numbers and (ii) fitness values of test cases with each combination of templates in the history. That is, a combination of templates providing more test cases with higher fitness values in the history is chosen with a higher probability.

In this paper, we give a refined distribution for choosing templates as one regularized by averages (of top 5%) of fitness values of test cases belonging to combinations of templates. That is, for a set of possible template assignments $a_1, \ldots, a_n$ for a group of input signals, each probability p_i of choosing a_i is given as follows.

$$p_i = \frac{w_i + \epsilon}{\sum_{1 \leq j \leq n} (w_j + \epsilon)}, \tag{15}$$

where w_j is the average (of top 5%) of fitness values of test cases belonging to a_j and ϵ is a certain small positive value (e.g., $1/n$) less than 1.

Determining Arguments: One of the simplest approach for refining distribution of arguments[10] of the chosen templates is based on a (multi-dimensional) truncated normal distribution centering arguments of a test case which is a pivot selected with a certain policy within the same combination of templates. To intensively search hopeful test cases, it may be effective to use annealing, i.e., to decrease gradually a variance of a normal distribution.

In this paper, we employ a Markov chain Monte-Carlo (MCMC) policy, i.e., to change probabilistically a pivot test case tc_{crnt}, when a new candidate test case tc_{cand} is added to the history, to the candidate as the new pivot. The probability p_{chng} of changing the pivot is given as follows:

$$p_{\mathrm{chng}} = \begin{cases} 1 & \text{if } v_{\mathrm{cand}} > v_{\mathrm{crnt}}, \\ v_{\mathrm{cand}}/v_{\mathrm{crnt}} & \text{otherwise}, \end{cases} \tag{16}$$

where v_{crnt} and v_{cand} are fitness values of tc_{crnt} and tc_{cand}, respectively.

Remark 6. We can employ any methods for choosing templates and determining arguments. For example, the simplest policy for selecting a pivot test case on determining arguments is the *greedy* one, i.e., to select a test case with the highest fitness value as a pivot.   □

5   Experiments

We implemented prototype tools for Algorithms 1 and 2 by MATLAB script, and conducted experiments. The prototype receives a harness model constructed from a given target model by SLDV, and generates a test suite/case by editing its *signal builder* block. V&V is used for measuring coverage. In this section, we report results of the experiments to show the effectiveness of proposed techniques.

The experiments performed on a PC with Windows 10 Enterprise 64-bit OS, Intel Core i5-4300U 1.9 GHz CPU and 4 GB LPDDR4 1,600 MHz RAM. The version of MATLAB/Simulink (including SLDV and V&V) is 2017a.

---

[10] For a Boolean argument, its range is treated as $[0, 1]$, and a value greater (resp., less) than a half is interpreted as `true` (resp., `false`).

5.1   Descriptions

Experiment 1: To confirm the effectiveness of our template-based method in Sect. 3, we prepared a middle-sized controller model actually-used in industry (Fig. 2). The target model has: 4 top-level inputs, 23 subsystems (7 of them have enable/trigger ports), 453 blocks which includes 34 switches, 16 relational operator blocks, 7 logical operator blocks, etc. The number of decision, condition and MC/DC objectives are total 200, and 2 of them are dead (i.e., unexercisable), which are detected by SLDV design error detection.

We observed and compared 10 runs of our prototype tool for Algorithm 1, and 1 run of SLDV test case generator. Time out for the runs is 3,600 seconds. Timer optimization option of SLDV is enabled. The following assumptions are given: The ranges for "target" signal and "HU/HV/HW" triplex signals are given because they are limited and known. A template of an input signal "target" is Step. A template of triplex input signals "HU/HV/HW" is Sine because an predecessor subsystem provides triplex signals with sine-like waves. The range for *frequency* parameter of the template is given. An argument for *bias* parameter of the template is fixed to 0 because it is known the sine-line waves are unbiased.

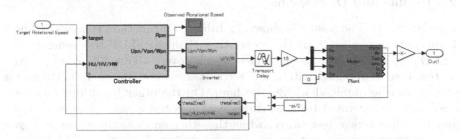

Fig. 2. Overview of a practical controller-plant system. A target model for Experiment 1 is the light-green controller module.

Experiment 2: To confirm the effectiveness of our template-based method in Sect. 4, we prepared a toy model combined with a 4th-order elliptic band-pass filter and forgetful integrator (Fig. 3) and assumed that a target objective is "the decision of the downmost logical operator b_{dm} is true." SLDV cannot generate a test case for the objective by reproducible internal errors.

For the objective, we used a fitness function following Eqs. (6), (7), (9) and (14), given in Sect. 4.2. We implement two modules for distribution refinement (Sect. 4.3). One module employs the normal distribution method with the MCMC policy for determining arguments of templates. The other module employs that with the greedy policy. Variances of normal distributions are fixed to an eighth of the size of the range of the input signals.

We observed 100 runs for each module, and compared with 100 runs for uniform random searching. The runs were aborted when numbers of candidates reached 3,000. The following assumption is given: The range for both "In1" and

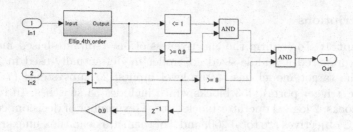

Fig. 3. A target model (in Experiment 2) combined with a 4th-order elliptic band-pass filter and forgetful integrator.

"In2" signals is $[-1, 1]$. A template of an input signal "In1" is Sine. The range for *frequency* parameter of template is given. An argument for *amplitude*, *phase* and *bias* parameters of Sine template are fixed to 1, 0 and 0, respectively. A template of an input signal "In2" is Step. The ranges of output signals of "Ellip_4th_order" subsystem and "ADD" operator block are $[-1, 1]$ and $[-10, 10]$, respectively.

5.2   Results and Discussions

Experiment 1: The results is shown in Table 1. Our method generated almost full coverage test suites in much shorter time than the SLDV test generator.

SLDV generated only one test case which covers about 80% of objectives. The test case is obtained within few seconds, however, no other contributable test case can be obtained within one hour. On the other hand, our template-based method generated ten test suites with 6–8 test cases. 9 out of 10 trials provided full coverage test suites, while the other one was timed-out and gave a test suite which does not cover only one decision objective. Table 2 shows accumulations of coverages for first 10 candidates in Experiment 1. The results suggest that our template-based method is hopeful for sorting out difficult-to-be-covered objectives.

Table 1. Experimental results for Experiment 1

	Template-based method (10 trials)			SLDV
	Best	Average	Worst	
Processing time (sec)	386.7	1056.0	>3600	>3600
Size of test suite	6	6.6	8	1
Number of candidates	6	15.5	55	–
Decision coverage	121/121	120.9/121	120/121	87/121
Condition coverage	64/64	64/64	64/64	61/64
MC/DC coverage	13/13	13/13	13/13	9/13

Table 2. Accumulations of coverages for first 10 candidates in Experiment 1

	Template-based method (10 trials)		
	Best	Average	Worst
Decision coverage	121/121	119.8/121	116/121
Condition coverage	64/64	64/64	64/64
MC/DC coverage	13/13	12.2/13	9/13

Experiment 2: The results and its summary are shown in Fig. 4 and Table 3. For the target model in Experiment 2, our method with MCMC policy was about triple as efficient as the uniform random searching.

This is not guaranteed for a general case, so we may need to construct a fitness function adaptively for a target model and objective. The greedy policy was as efficient as the MCMC policy in many cases. Although, the greedy policy required a large number of candidates in some cases, and 7 runs were aborted by exceeding the limit number of candidates. This suggests that the greedy policy has still a common risk to be trapped by local optima.

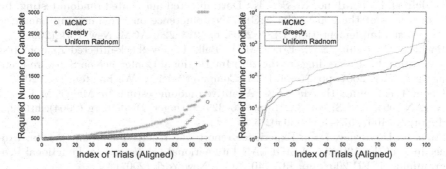

Fig. 4. Distribution of required number of candidates for Experiment 2. The left and right ones are normal and logarithm scales, respectively.

Table 3. Summary of the results for Experiment 2

	Average number of candidates			Total processing time (sec)
	Top 20%	Middle 60%	Bottom 20%	
MCMC policy	20.5	84.2	240.3	3473.6
Greedy policy	17.0	84.4	1365.0	11346.8
Uniform random	28.5	240.4	833.0	10404.6

6   Conclusions and Future Work

We proposed a template-based Monte-Carlo test generation method to deal with practical (i.e, large and complex) Simulink models. By using templates of input signals, we can simplify a process of generating test cases and reduce a search space to plausible one. Additionally, we introduced a biased sampling framework to get more efficiently test cases meeting uncovered objectives. The experimental results suggests our template-based method works well to produce efficiently a desired test case/suite for models which cannot be dealt with by SLDV.

A future direction is to combine the techniques with other ones. Static analysis is effective for narrowing the search space. Our techniques are based on randomized search, and thus it is possible to apply non-conservative approximation on static analysis. Genetic algorithms are also effective on targeted test case generation with biased sampling. Our fitness function can be adapted directly to them. Another direction is to implement a practical tool, based on feedback of trial use of the prototype in industries.

References

1. Godefroid, P., Klarlund, N., Sen, K.: Dart: directed automated random testing. In: Proceedings of the 2005 ACM SIGPLAN Conference on Programming Language Design and Implementation, PLDI 2005, pp. 213–223. ACM, New York (2005)
2. Pacheco, C., Lahiri, S.K., Ernst, M.D., Ball, T.: Feedback-directed random test generation. In: Proceedings of the 29th International Conference on Software Engineering, ICSE 2007, pp. 75–84. IEEE Computer Society, Washington, DC (2007)
3. Chen, T.Y., Leung, H., Mak, I.K.: Adaptive random testing. In: Maher, M.J. (ed.) ASIAN 2004. LNCS, vol. 3321, pp. 320–329. Springer, Heidelberg (2004). https://doi.org/10.1007/978-3-540-30502-6_23
4. Sims, S., DuVarney, D.C.: Experience report: the reactis validation tool. In: Proceedings of the 12th ACM SIGPLAN International Conference on Functional Programming, ICFP 2007, pp. 137–140. ACM, New York (2007)
5. Satpathy, M., Yeolekar, A., Ramesh, S.: Randomized directed testing (REDIRECT) for Simulink/Stateflow models. In: Proceedings of the 8th ACM International Conference on Embedded Software, EMSOFT 2008, pp. 217–226. ACM, New York (2008)
6. Matinnejad, R., Nejati, S., Briand, L.C., Bruckmann, T.: Automated test suite generation for time-continuous Simulink models. In: Proceedings of the 38th International Conference on Software Engineering, ICSE 2016, pp. 595–606. ACM, New York (2016)

Reliable Simulation and Monitoring of Hybrid Systems Based on Interval Analysis

(Extended Abstract)

Daisuke Ishii[1]([✉]), Alexandre Goldsztejn[2], and Naoki Yonezaki[3]

[1] University of Fukui, Fukui, Japan
dsksh@acm.org
[2] CNRS/LS2N, Nantes, France
alexandre.goldsztejn@gmail.com
[3] Tokyo Denki University, Tokyo, Japan
yonezaki@mail.dendai.ac.jp

Hybrid systems serve as a high-level model of cyber-physical systems. Formal methods for hybrid systems have been studied energetically for around three decades and various methods for reachability analysis and approximation of continuous states/behaviors have been proposed (e.g., [1,8]). Another line of technology, e.g., MATLAB/Simulink[1] and Modelica[2], has been developed in the simulation of hybrid systems and has driven the rise of model-based development in the industry. While reachability analysis methods aim to analyze whole behaviors of a given system with carefully taking care of numerical computation errors, the latter technology focuses on efficient simulation of an approximated trajectory of a practical model.

We present two methods for the simulation and analysis of hybrid systems using interval analysis. First, we have developed a rigorous numerical simulation method that, given a (closed) hybrid system with a specific initial value, computes an interval enclosure of the state for each simulation step [9]. Second, we have proposed a monitoring method that checks whether a system satisfies or not a given temporal property, within a bounded time horizon, by cooperating with the interval-based simulator [12,13]. Both methods intensively utilize techniques of interval analysis: a numerical computation framework that replaces floating-point numbers with (machine representable) intervals. We consider our work can be positioned in between the reachability methods and the numerical simulation methods.

Simulation Method. Our interval-based method computes an overapproximation of a bounded trajectory (or a set of trajectories) that is composed of *boxes* (i.e., closed interval vectors) and *parallelotopes* (i.e., linear transformed intervals) [9]. The computation can be regarded as reachability analysis; it allows a

---

[1] https://www.mathworks.com/products/matlab.html.
[2] https://www.modelica.org/.

© Springer Nature Switzerland AG 2019
R. Chamberlain et al. (Eds.): CyPhy 2017, LNCS 11267, pp. 79–82, 2019.
https://doi.org/10.1007/978-3-030-17910-6_6

model to involve an interval as an initial value in the specification. Several interval methods, e.g., [2–4,6,7,10,14,17–20], have been proposed recently in parallel to our work. Our method is characterized by the following two aspects when compared with other reachability analysis tools.

First, the simulation process carefully reduces the wrapping effect that occurs in a computation of hybrid trajectories. In general, results of the wrapping effect accumulate as several overapproximation processes are concatenated during a simulation. To reduce the number of overapproximation processes and to improve the accuracy, we formalize a trajectory $\omega(x, t)$ of a hybrid system, which evolves from an initial value x and exhibits a discrete jump at $\tau(x)$, as a composite function as follows:

$$\omega(x, t) := \psi(\delta(\varphi(x, \tau(x))), t - \tau(x)),$$

where δ represents the discrete jump and φ and ψ represent the continuous trajectories before and after the jump. Then, we consider a *parallelotope extension* $\langle \omega \rangle$ of the trajectory function ω. Let $\langle \boldsymbol{x} \rangle$ be a parallelotope representing a set of initial values:

$$\langle \boldsymbol{x} \rangle := \langle A, \boldsymbol{u}, \tilde{x} \rangle = \{\tilde{x} + Au \mid u \in \boldsymbol{u}\},$$

where $A \in \mathbb{R}^{n \times n}$, $\boldsymbol{u} \in \mathbb{IR}^n$, $\tilde{x} \in \mathbb{R}^n$. Our method computes a parallelotope enclosure

$$\langle \boldsymbol{\omega} \rangle(\langle \boldsymbol{x} \rangle, t) := \langle B, \boldsymbol{v}, \tilde{y} \rangle,$$

such that $\forall x \in \langle \boldsymbol{x} \rangle$, $\omega(x, t) \in \langle \boldsymbol{\omega} \rangle(\langle \boldsymbol{x} \rangle, t)$, with the following steps:

1. Compute $\tilde{y}$ as an approximated value of $\omega(\tilde{x}, t)$ obtained by a numerical computation.
2. Compute B that should well capture a linear characteristic of the map ω. An efficient choice of B is (mid $\boldsymbol{J}$)A, where $\boldsymbol{J}$ is an interval enclosure of $\frac{\partial \omega}{\partial x}$.
3. Compute $\boldsymbol{v}$ such that $\boldsymbol{v} \supseteq B^{-1}(\omega(\langle \boldsymbol{x} \rangle, t) - \tilde{y})$ by computing an interval enclosure of the right-hand side (with a mean-value form).

The derivative $\frac{\partial \omega}{\partial x}$ is obtained by the chain rule and functions involved, e.g., φ and τ, are implemented as numerical solving processes. In the experiments, our method is able to simulate a system for a greater number of steps than other overapproximation-based tools; e.g., it can simulate a periodic bouncing ball for more than a thousand steps.

Second, our method relies on the soundness of interval computation so that the resulting overapproximation is verified to contain a theoretical trajectory. Interval-based integration processes for ODEs can verify a unique existence of a solution trajectory φ within an enclosure, i.e., $\forall x \in \boldsymbol{x}$, $\exists! y \in \boldsymbol{\varphi}(\boldsymbol{x}, t)$, $y = \varphi(x, t)$ is verified. Likewise, when solving a guard equation $h(\varphi(x, \tau(x))) = 0$, we can compute an interval enclosure of $\tau(x)$ that is verified to contain a unique solution of the equation using an interval Newton method. Accordingly, our method is able to verify:

$$\forall x \in \boldsymbol{x}, \ \exists! y \in \langle \boldsymbol{\omega} \rangle(\boldsymbol{x}, t), \ y = \omega(x, t).$$

This verification may fail, e.g., when an ODE is *stiff* or when a trajectory and a guard are close to tangent, resulting in an enclosure too large to enable any inference. Due to this *quasi-complete* manner, the simulation process performs efficiently whenever a numerically manageable model is given.

Monitoring Method. Verification of temporal logic properties plays a crucial role in proving the desired behaviors of hybrid systems. Thus, we proposed an interval method that verifies the properties described by a signal temporal logic (STL) [15]. We relax the problem so that if the verification process cannot succeed at the prescribed precision, it outputs an inconclusive result. The problem is solved by an efficient and rigorous interval analysis [13]. Given an STL formula f, our method first performs a simulation with the parallelotope method and detects a set of time intervals in which the evaluation of an atomic proposition within f switches. For a time interval $[s, t]$ in a simulation timeline, within which an atomic proposition holds, our method computes the interval enclosures s and t that are verified to contain a unique boundary; therefore, both inner- and overapproximations of $[s, t]$ will be obtained. Next, the method validates the property by propagating the time intervals. Our method is also able to compute a *robustness* signal [5] for the property with an algorithm that manipulates the interval enclosures of a trajectory, which are handled segment-wise over the timeline.

Conclusion. Our methods are implemented in a tool HySIA [11]. As a future work, more detailed analysis and explanation of the inconclusive results will be needed. Further development of the proposed methods can be planned to incorporate into e.g. statistical model checking [21,22] and testing [16] of hybrid systems.

Acknowledgments. This work was partially funded by JSPS (KAKENHI 25880008, 15K15968, and 26280024).

References

1. Alur, R., et al.: The algorithmic analysis of hybrid systems. Theor. Comput. Sci. **138**(1), 3–34 (1995)
2. Bouissou, O., Mimram, S., Chapoutot, A.: HySon: set-based simulation of hybrid systems. In: 23rd IEEE International Symposium on Rapid System Prototyping (RSP), pp. 79–85 (2012)
3. Chen, X., Abraham, E., Sankaranarayanan, S.: Taylor model flowpipe construction for non-linear hybrid systems. In: IEEE Real-Time Systems Symposium, pp. 183–192 (2012)
4. Collins, P., Goldsztejn, A.: The reach-and-evolve algorithm for reachability analysis of nonlinear dynamical systems. Electron. Notes Theor. Comput. Sci. **223**(639), 87–102 (2008)

5. Donzé, A., Maler, O.: Robust satisfaction of temporal logic over real-valued signals. In: Chatterjee, K., Henzinger, T.A. (eds.) FORMATS 2010. LNCS, vol. 6246, pp. 92–106. Springer, Heidelberg (2010). https://doi.org/10.1007/978-3-642-15297-9_9
6. Duracz, A., Bartha, F.A., Taha, W.: Accurate rigorous simulation should be possible for good designs. In: Workshop on Symbolic and Numerical Methods for Reachability Analysis (SNR), pp. 1–10 (2016)
7. Eggers, A., Fränzle, M., Herde, C.: SAT modulo ODE: a direct SAT approach to hybrid systems. In: Cha, S.S., Choi, J.-Y., Kim, M., Lee, I., Viswanathan, M. (eds.) ATVA 2008. LNCS, vol. 5311, pp. 171–185. Springer, Heidelberg (2008). https://doi.org/10.1007/978-3-540-88387-6_14
8. Frehse, G., et al.: SpaceEx: scalable verification of hybrid systems. In: Gopalakrishnan, G., Qadeer, S. (eds.) CAV 2011. LNCS, vol. 6806, pp. 379–395. Springer, Heidelberg (2011). https://doi.org/10.1007/978-3-642-22110-1_30
9. Goldsztejn, A., Ishii, D.: A parallelotope method for hybrid system simulation. Reliable Comput. 23, 163–185 (2016)
10. Goubault, E., Mullier, O., Kieffer, M.: Inner approximated reachability analysis. In: HSCC, pp. 163–172 (2014)
11. Ishii, D., Goldsztejn, A.: HySIA: tool for simulating and monitoring hybrid automata based on interval analysis. In: Lahiri, S., Reger, G. (eds.) RV 2017. LNCS, vol. 10548, pp. 370–379. Springer, Cham (2017). https://doi.org/10.1007/978-3-319-67531-2_23
12. Ishii, D., Yonezaki, N., Goldsztejn, A.: Monitoring bounded LTL properties using interval analysis. In: 8th International Workshop on Numerical Software Verification (NSV). ENTCS 317, pp. 85–100 (2015)
13. Ishii, D., Yonezaki, N., Goldsztejn, A.: Monitoring temporal properties using interval analysis. In: IEICE Transactions on Fundamentals of Electronics, Communications and Computer Sciences E99-A (2016)
14. Kong, S., Gao, S., Chen, W., Clarke, E.: dReach: δ-reachability analysis for hybrid systems. In: Baier, C., Tinelli, C. (eds.) TACAS 2015. LNCS, vol. 9035, pp. 200–205. Springer, Heidelberg (2015). https://doi.org/10.1007/978-3-662-46681-0_15
15. Maler, O., Nickovic, D.: Monitoring temporal properties of continuous signals. In: Lakhnech, Y., Yovine, S. (eds.) FORMATS/FTRTFT - 2004. LNCS, vol. 3253, pp. 152–166. Springer, Heidelberg (2004). https://doi.org/10.1007/978-3-540-30206-3_12
16. Mohaqeqi, M., Mousavi, M.R., Taha, W.: Conformance testing of cyber-physical systems: a comparative study. In: 14th International Workshop on Automated Verification of Critical Systems (AVOCS) (2014)
17. Ramdani, N., Meslem, N., Candau, Y.: A hybrid bounding method for computing an over-approximation for the reachable set of uncertain nonlinear systems. IEEE Trans. Autom. Control 54(10), 2352–2364 (2009)
18. Ramdani, N., Nedialkov, N.S.: Computing reachable sets for uncertain nonlinear hybrid systems using interval constraint-propagation techniques. Nonlinear Anal. Hybrid Syst. 5(2), 149–162 (2011)
19. Ratschan, S.: Safety verification of non-linear hybrid systems is quasi-decidable. Formal Methods Syst. Des. 44(1), 71–90 (2014)
20. Sandretto, J.A.D., Chapoutot, A.: Validated explicit and implicit runge-kutta methods. Reliable Comput. 22, 78–103 (2016)
21. Shmarov, F., Zuliani, P.: ProbReach: Verified probabilistic delta-reachability for stochastic hybrid systems. In: HSCC, pp. 134–139 (2015)
22. Wang, Q., Zuliani, P., Kong, S., Gao, S., Clarke, E.M.: SReach: A Bounded Model Checker for Stochastic Hybrid Systems. CoRR abs/1404.7206 (2015)

An Integrated Simulation Tool for Computer Architecture and Cyber-Physical Systems

Hokeun Kim[1]([⊠]), Armin Wasicek[2], and Edward A. Lee[1]

[1] University of California, Berkeley, USA
{hokeunkim,eal}@eecs.berkeley.edu
[2] Technical University Vienna, Vienna, Austria
armin@vmars.tuwien.ac.at

Abstract. Simulating computer architecture as a cyber-physical system has many potential use cases including simulation of side channels and software-in-the-loop modeling and simulation. This paper presents an integrated simulation tool using a computer architecture simulator, gem5 and Ptolemy II. As a case study of this tool, we build a power and thermal model for a DRAM using the proposed tool integration approach where architectural aspects are modeled in gem5 and physical aspects are modeled in Ptolemy II. We also demonstrate simulation results of power and temperature of a DRAM with software benchmarks.

Keywords: Tool integration · Architectural simulation ·
Cyber-physical systems · DRAM thermal modeling

1 Introduction

Ptolemy II [17] is a powerful framework, where multiple models of computation can be explored for actor-based design of cyber-physical systems [8]. For many applications, it is important to model details of the computer architecture for a candidate design. Consequently, the Ptolemy II framework can significantly benefit from the integration of architecture models. In this paper, we propose a tool integration of the gem5 computer architecture simulator [2] and Ptolemy II. For a specific computer architecture, gem5 generates execution information that is used to build a more fine-grained system model in Ptolemy II.

This integration supports many usage scenarios including:

– Simulation of side channels: Side-channel attacks target primarily the physical implementation of a computer system. Unlike traditional computer systems, embedded systems are particularly vulnerable to this class of attacks, because they are often accessible in untrusted environments [11]. An example of a side channel attack is a cold boot attack on DRAM memories [10], where an attacker obtains a memory dump after a cold restart to read out sensitive information like cryptographic keys.

© Springer Nature Switzerland AG 2019
R. Chamberlain et al. (Eds.): CyPhy 2017, LNCS 11267, pp. 83–93, 2019.
https://doi.org/10.1007/978-3-030-17910-6_7

– Software-in-the-Loop modeling and simulation: In this scenario the embedded processor, sensors, and actuators are modeled with gem5 and the physical environment is modeled in Ptolemy II. This could support, for example, automated grading of embedded systems lab exercises in massively online open courses (MOOCs) [18]. For example, this would be useful for the EECS149.1x cyber-physical systems [13] course at UC Berkeley. In the labs of this class, students develop programs for an iRobot.

We demonstrate the integration of both tools by modeling power and temperature of a DRAM in a computer architecture. To simulate behavior of the processor including memory accesses, we use the gem5 simulator. A Ptolemy II model performs power and thermal modeling, using discrete-event and continuous time models. Experimental results show how a computer architecture and workloads affect power and the temperature of a DRAM.

2   Related Work

Currently, Ptolemy II offers the inclusion of an execution environment's characteristics through a modeling method called Aspect-Oriented Modeling (AOM) [1]. For instance, an execution aspect can model execution times of a processor [5]. Metro II [7] provides an environment for platform-based design, where functional aspects and architectural aspects are modeled separately. Kim *et al.* [12] propose a tool integration approach where execution times on given architectures are modeled in SystemC, and integrated into Ptolemy II using Metro II. This approach has more flexibility in architectures, whereas our approach provides higher accuracy in architectural models.

The gem5 architecture simulator [2] is one of the most popular and widely used architecture simulators in academia and industry. It started as a merger of the General Execution-driven Multiprocessor Simulator (GEMS) [16] and the M5 simulator [3]. The gem5 simulator takes advantage of memory systems simulation features from GEMS, while it benefits from multiple ISAs and diverse CPU models supported by M5.

The gem5 simulator is object-oriented and based on the discrete-event model of computation. It also provides modular and interchangeable computer architecture components such as CPUs, memories, buses and interconnects. This architectural simulator is also flexible in terms of accuracy and simulation time providing multiple levels of accuracy, such as more accurate but slower simulation models and faster but less accurate simulation models [4].

A variety of approaches have been studied for power and thermal modeling of DRAMs. Lin *et al.* [14] suggest a model to compute power and the temperature of a DRAM based on throughput information, while Liu *et al.* [15] propose a power and thermal model based on RC circuit models. In this paper, we choose the model used by Lin *et al.* [14] Heat dissipation from DRAM devices is based on a device's power which is almost proportional to memory throughput. Thus, knowing a memory's read and write throughput (in GB/s), the temperature can

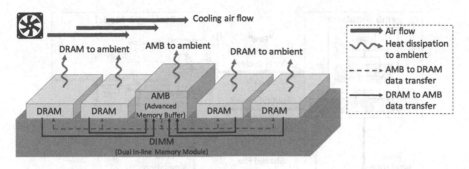

Fig. 1. Heat dissipation of DIMM. (Redrawn from the figure given by Lin *et al.* [14] and included here by permission of the publisher.)

be derived. In addition to the current flowing through the DRAM, its temperature is also affected by cooling air flow and the physical structure of DIMM (Dual In-line Memory Module). Figure 1 depicts their model of DIMM structure and the temperature. The Advanced Memory Buffer (AMB) stores and transfers data between the different DRAM channels. The AMB is also a major source of heat in their model, therefore, they also consider the data throughput across DRAM channels. An ambient temperature refers to the temperature of the device's environment and is in the most cases the room temperature.

There have been some approaches including DRAMPower [6] for simulating power and energy of a DRAM on a specific computer architecture. However, to the best of our knowledge, our case study is the first attempt to simulate heat and temperature of a DRAM by integrating a thermal model with a real-time computer architecture simulator, gem5.

3   Approach

In this section, we illustrate the integrated simulator design and the power and thermal model of a DRAM. For accessibility of our tool, we made all the working source code and experimental models available on-line. Configurations for the gem5 simulator and benchmark programs can be found at our GitHub repository (https://github.com/gem5-ptolemy/gem5-ptolemy/) and Ptolemy II can be downloaded from its homepage (http://ptolemy.org). An experimental model is included under "ptolemy/actor/lib/gem5/demo/DramThermalModel", in Ptolemy II Version 11.0 (developer's version).

3.1   Configuring the gem5 Simulator

To integrate gem5 into Ptolemy II, we modify some configurations and source code of the latest stable version of the gem5 simulator. We modify some components so that they can generate information we need. We also configure the execution flow of the simulator so that it can run interactively by stopping and

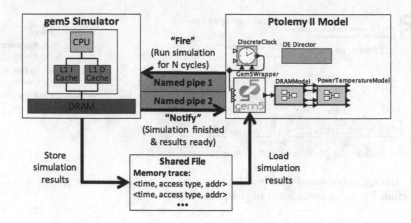

Fig. 2. An overview of gem5 and Ptolemy II integration

resuming the simulation when we want. In gem5, the main components such as CPUs and memory models are implemented in C++ for high performance, while connection between components and execution of components are implemented in Python so that the configurations are easily changed.

For power and thermal modeling, we modify C++ source codes associated with the DRAM memory controller model in gem5 to generate memory access traces. We obtain extra information for power and thermal modeling by adding debug print functions defined in the gem5 simulator (*DPRINTF*) for recording memory access commands. For interactive simulation, we modify python scripts to call *Simulate* function iteratively with specified execution cycles.

3.2   Communication Between gem5 and Ptolemy II

Figure 2 illustrates an overview of gem5 and Ptolemy II integration. The gem5 simulator and a *Gem5Wrapper* actor in a Ptolemy II model interact with each other. The *Gem5Wrapper* actor is a Java actor in Ptolemy II model. It communicates with gem5 through named pipes and a shared file. When the Gem5Wrapper is initialized in the Ptolemy II, it fires the gem5 simulator by writing on the named pipe where the gem5 simulator is blocked on read. The Gem5Wrapper actor also gets blocked on read on another named pipe in its *fire()* method. The gem5 simulator runs for the specified number of cycles. While running, the gem5 simulator records execution information such as a memory trace on the shared file. When the simulation is finished, gem5 notifies Gem5Wrapper by writing on another named pipe where Gem5Wrapper is blocked. Then, Gem5Wrapper resumes in its *fire()* and reads execution information from the shared file. Gem5Wrapper fires gem5 again in its *postfire()* and this pattern is repeated.

Simulation results are transferred to Gem5Wrapper through the shared file and used for DRAM power and thermal modeling. The results include DRAM memory access events. Each access events is composed of the time when the event occurred, an access type (e.g. read/write) and a memory address (e.g. bank and channel numbers).

3.3 DRAM Behavioral Model in Ptolemy II

The Ptolemy II model for the overall system consists of two main parts. DRAM's behavior is modeled in the first part, and power and the temperature of the DRAM is modeled in the second part. In the Ptolemy II model, Gem5Wrapper is triggered periodically by a DiscreteClock actor. When Gem5Wrapper receives simulation results from gem5, it stores result data as an array type defined in Ptolemy II. Then, Gem5Wrapper sends the data array to a composite actor called *DRAMModel* shown in the middle of Fig. 3.

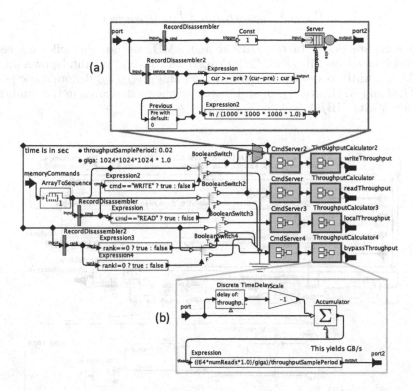

Fig. 3. Ptolemy II DRAM model overview (*DRAMModel*). (a) command server actor (*CmdServer*) (b) throughput calculator (*ThroughputCalculator*)

The data array is decomposed into a sequence of memory access events inside the *DRAMModel*, and a sequence of memory access events are sent to the *Cmd-Server* actor in Fig. 3(a). Each memory access event becomes a discrete event in *CmdServer* and is sent to the *ThroughputCalculator* actor in Fig. 3(b), where the throughput results are computed. The types of throughput results include *read*, *write*, *local* (to a local DRAM channel) and *bypass* (to non-local DRAM channels). The throughput results are used for AMB/DRAM power estimation in the section below.

3.4   Memory Power and Thermal Modeling in Ptolemy II

Power and the temperature of a DRAM is modeled in the second part of the Ptolemy II model within a composite actor called *PowerTemperatureModel* described in Fig. 4. This actor runs in the continuous-time domain, sampling throughput information from input ports. Power models for CMOS devices usually combine the static power of the device with its dynamic power. Static power is the power when transistors are not in the process of switching. Dynamic power occurs during switching operations:

$$P_{device} = P_{DRAM\_static} + P_{DRAM\_dynamic} \tag{1}$$

To compute power in the DRAM and AMB, we use the following equations introduced by Lin *et al.* [14] P_{DRAM} and P_{AMB} are total power in the DRAM and AMB, respectively. P_{DRAM_static} and P_{AMB_idle} denote static power of DRAM and AMB. α_1, α_2, β, and γ are coefficients measured in [14], and their units are Watt/(GB/s).

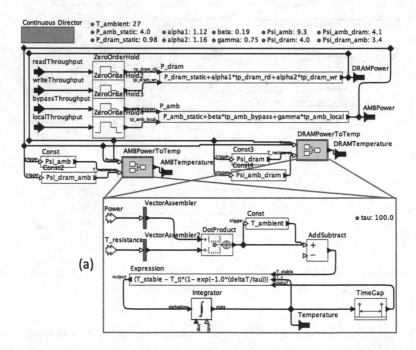

Fig. 4. Ptolemy II DRAM power and thermal model overview (*PowerTemperature-Model* actor). (a) *AMB/DRAMPowerToTemp actor* that estimates the temperature of an AMB/DRAM based on its power

$$P_{DRAM} = P_{DRAM\_static} + \alpha_1 \times Throughput_{read} + \alpha_2 \times Throughput_{write} \quad (2)$$

$$P_{AMB} = P_{AMB\_idle} + \beta \times Throughput_{Bypass} + \gamma \times Throughput_{Local} \quad (3)$$

The power computed above is used to estimate temperatures in the AMB and DRAM. The composite actor shown in Fig. 4(a) implements this thermal estimation. We use following equations introduced by Lin *et al.* [14] to calculate temperatures of the AMB and DRAM. T_{AMB} and T_{DRAM} are stable temperatures of the AMB and DRAM, respectively. T_A stands for the ambient temperature explained in Sect. 2. Parameters Ψ_{AMB} and Ψ_{DRAM} denote the thermal resistances of the AMB and DRAM. The thermal resistances are measured as the ratio of the change of the stable temperature over the change of power. The thermal resistances from AMB to DRAM and from DRAM to AMB are denoted as Ψ_{AMB_DRAM} and Ψ_{DRAM_AMB}, respectively.

$$T_{AMB} = T_A + P_{AMB} \times \Psi_{AMB} + P_{DRAM} \times \Psi_{DRAM\_AMB} \quad (4)$$

$$T_{DRAM} = T_A + P_{AMB} \times \Psi_{AMB\_DRAM} + P_{DRAM} \times \Psi_{DRAM} \quad (5)$$

The equation expressing the relation between the stable temperature and the actual temperature is as follows. $T(t)$ is the actual temperature at t and Δt denotes each time step. We use the τ value, which is the time for the temperature difference to be reduced to $1/e$, as measured in [14]. This equation is realized with the Integrator actor in Ptolemy II as illustrated in Fig. 4(a).

$$T(t + \Delta t) - T(t) = (T_{stable} - T(t))(1 - e^{-\frac{\Delta t}{\tau}}) \quad (6)$$

4   Experiments and Results

4.1   Experimental Setup

The architectural configurations used for experiments are as follows. The CPU was based on ARM ISA, and the type of the CPU was *TimingSimpleCPU* defined in the gem5 simulator, which stalls on every load memory access. The clock rate of both the CPU and the overall system was 1 GHz. The type of off-chip DRAM memory was DDR3 SDRAM with a data rate of 1600 MHz and a bus width of 16 bits. We assumed the program and data exist in the DRAM before starting the execution. The size of cache blocks was 64 bytes.

We chose MiBench [9] as the benchmark for our experiments. Among MiBench programs executable in the gem5, top 5 programs with the highest memory intensity were chosen for our experiments. We defined the memory intensity as the number of memory accesses per instruction, and the memory intensity was computed by running each program for one million cycles in gem5. The benchmark programs used for our experiments are listed in Table 1.

4.2   Power and Temperature Results

Table 2 shows average power and the peak temperature of the DRAM and AMB for different cache configurations. The results were obtained by running the gem5 simulator and Ptolemy II DRAM power and thermal model together for 0.1 s in simulated time (100 million cycles). For this experiment, *cjpeg_large* in MiBench was used as a software workload. The temperature is expressed in the difference between the highest temperature and the ambient temperature. We assumed the processor has two level-1 (L1) caches, each for instructions and data. Bigger caches led to less cache misses, and thus less DRAM accesses.

Table 1. List of benchmark programs used for example workloads

MiBench programs	Writes	Reads	Total instructions executed	Memory intensity (%)
consumer/cjpeg_large	6,183	74,966	1,000,000	8.11
security/rijndael_large	2,558	68,458	1,000,000	7.10
consumer/typeset_small	12,843	55,963	1,000,000	6.88
network/dijkstra_large	4,942	59,198	1,000,000	6.41
network/patricia_large	4,255	49,198	1,000,000	5.35

Table 2. Power and temperature results for different cache configurations for the workload *cjpeg_large*

Cache size options (KB)		Average power (mW)		Maximum temperature increase (10^{-6} °C)	
L1	L2	DRAM	AMB	DRAM	AMB
16	N/A	1,057	4,027	2.67	6.05
32	N/A	1,023	4,011	2.63	5.93
64	N/A	1,000	4,008	2.46	5.51
32	128	996	4,006	2.17	4.86
32	256	995	4,006	1.99	4.47

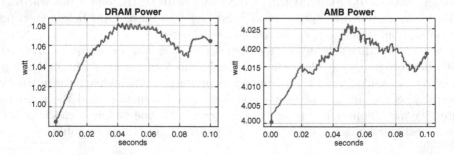

Fig. 5. DRAM and AMB power results in graphs for *cjpeg_large* with 16 KB L1 caches

Since the level-2 (L2) cache absorbed off-chip traffic from L1 caches, they reduced DRAM memory accesses. Therefore, we could see decrease in DRAM power and the peak temperature in the results shown in Table 2.

Figure 5 illustrates DRAM and AMB power graphs for the workload *cjpeg_large* with 16 KB L1 caches. *cjpeg_large* loads a 786 KB Portable Pixel Map (PPM) file for a raw image and compresses it to a JPEG format. We could see DRAM power was affected by total read/write throughput while AMB power was related to cross-channel accesses. The power consumption for both DRAM and AMB steadily increases as the benchmark program initializes until around 0.02 s. The program shows heavy power consumption between 0.02 and 0.063 s while actively loading and compressing the raw image, followed by a slight decrease in power consumption after 0.063 s as the program wraps up. The total simulation time for 100 million cycles (0.1 s in simulated time) was ranging from 89 s (*cjpeg_large*) to 320 s (*patricia_large*) on a MacBook Pro laptop with 2.2 GHz Intel Core i7 and 16 GB DRAM.

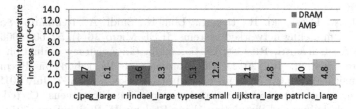

Fig. 6. Temperature results for different software workloads

Different workloads also led to change in the peak DRAM temperatures as illustrated in Fig. 6. For this experiment, we used 16 KB L1 caches without an L2 cache. The results suggest that other aspects of workloads as well as the memory intensity can affect thermal behaviors of DRAMs. Specifically, *rijndael_large* and *typeset_small* had higher peak temperatures although they had lower memory intensity than *cjpeg_large*. This was because they had higher bypass throughput, which caused higher power in the AMB, thus resulting in higher peak temperatures both in the AMB and DRAM. Moreover, *typeset_small* showed the highest write throughput, also leading to the highest peak temperatures.

5   Conclusions

In this paper, we integrate the widely used gem5 architecture simulator into Ptolemy II to have a more accurate architectural model in Ptolemy II. Effectiveness and usefulness of this integration is demonstrated by constructing a power and thermal model of a DRAM in computer architecture. Execution information such as memory accesses on given architectures are modeled in gem5 whereas the power and temperature of a DRAM are modeled in the continuous time domain in Ptolemy II. The constructed model is used for experiments of simulating different architectural configurations and software workloads.

As future work, we can apply the proposed approach to more applications, for example, the two use cases suggested in Sect. 1. Another possible extension is to use gem5 for aspect-oriented modeling in Ptolemy II. Specifically, execution aspect parameters such as execution time can be obtained dynamically through gem5 simulation for higher accuracy.

Acknowledgments. This work was supported in part by the TerraSwarm Research Center, one of six centers supported by the STARnet phase of the Focus Center Research Program (FCRP) a Semiconductor Research Corporation program sponsored by MARCO and DARPA.

References

1. Akkaya, I., Derler, P., Emoto, S., Lee, E.A.: Systems engineering for industrial cyber-physical systems using aspects. Proc. IEEE **104**(5), 997–1012 (2016)
2. Binkert, N., et al.: The gem5 simulator. SIGARCH Comput. Archit. News **39**(2), 1–7 (2011)
3. Binkert, N., Dreslinski, R., Hsu, L., Lim, K., Saidi, A., Reinhardt, S.: The M5 simulator: modeling networked systems. IEEE Micro **26**(4), 52–60 (2006)
4. Butko, A., Garibotti, R., Ost, L., Sassatelli, G.: Accuracy evaluation of GEM5 simulator system. In: 2012 7th International Workshop on Reconfigurable Communication-centric Systems-on-Chip (ReCoSoC), pp. 1–7, July 2012
5. Cardoso, J., et al.: Modeling timed systems. In: Ptolemaeus, C. (ed.) System Design, Modeling, and Simulation Using Ptolemy II. Ptolemy.org (2014)
6. Chandrasekar, K., et al.: DRAMPower: open-source DRAM power & energy estimation tool (2012). http://www.drampower.info
7. Davare, A., et al.: Metro II: a design environment for cyber-physical systems. ACM Trans. Embed. Comput. Syst. **12**(1s), 49:1–49:31 (2013)
8. Derler, P., Lee, E.A., Vincentelli, A.S.: Modeling cyber-physical systems. Proc. IEEE **100**(1), 13–28 (2012)
9. Guthaus, M., Ringenberg, J., Ernst, D., Austin, T., Mudge, T., Brown, R.: MiBench: a free, commercially representative embedded benchmark suite. In: IEEE International Workshop on Workload Characterization, WWC-4, pp. 3–14, December 2001
10. Halderman, J.A., et al.: Lest we remember: cold-boot attacks on encryption keys. Commun. ACM **52**(5), 91–98 (2009)
11. Hwang, D.D., Schaumont, P., Tiri, K., Verbauwhede, I.: Securing embedded systems. IEEE Computer Society (2006)
12. Kim, H., Guo, L., Lee, E.A., Sangiovanni-Vincentelli, A.: A tool integration approach for architectural exploration of aircraft electric power systems. In: 2013 IEEE 1st International Conference on Cyber-Physical Systems, Networks, and Applications (CPSNA), pp. 38–43, August 2013
13. Lee, E.A., Seshia, S., Jensen, J.: EECS149.1x, Cyber-Physical Systems. EECS, University of California, Berkeley, May 2014. https://www.edx.org/course/cyber-physical-systems-uc-berkeleyx-eecs149-1x
14. Lin, J., Zheng, H., Zhu, Z., David, H., Zhang, Z.: Thermal modeling and management of DRAM memory systems. In: Proceedings of the 34th Annual International Symposium on Computer Architecture, ISCA 2007, pp. 312–322. ACM, New York (2007)

15. Liu, S., Leung, B., Neckar, A., Memik, S., Memik, G., Hardavellas, N.: Hardware/software techniques for DRAM thermal management. In: IEEE 17th International Symposium on High Performance Computer Architecture (HPCA), pp. 515–525, February 2011
16. Martin, M.M.K., et al.: Multifacet's general execution-driven multiprocessor simulator (GEMS) toolset. SIGARCH Comput. Archit. News **33**(4), 92–99 (2005)
17. Ptolemaeus, C. (ed.): System Design, Modeling, and Simulation using Ptolemy II. Ptolemy.org (2014). http://ptolemy.org/books/Systems
18. Skiba, D.J.: Disruption in higher education: Massively Open Online Courses (MOOCs). Nurs. Educ. Perspect. **33**(6), 416–417 (2012)

Safe At Any Speed: A Simulation-Based Test Harness for Autonomous Vehicles

Houssam Abbas, Matthew O'Kelly, Alena Rodionova$^{(\boxtimes)}$, and Rahul Mangharam

University of Pennsylvania, Philadelphia, PA 19104, USA
{habbas,mokelly,alena.rodionova,rahulm}@seas.upenn.edu

Abstract. The testing of Autonomous Vehicles (AVs) requires driving the AV billions of miles under varied scenarios in order to find bugs, accidents and otherwise inappropriate behavior. Because driving a real AV that many miles is too slow and costly, this motivates the use of sophisticated 'world simulators', which present the AV's perception pipeline with realistic input scenes, and present the AV's control stack with realistic traffic and physics to which to react. Thus the simulator is a crucial piece of any CAD toolchain for AV testing. In this work, we build a test harness for driving an arbitrary AV's code in a simulated world. We demonstrate this harness by using the game Grand Theft Auto V (GTA) as world simulator for AV testing. Namely, our AV code, for both perception and control, interacts in real-time with the game engine to drive our AV in the GTA world, and we search for weather conditions and AV operating conditions that lead to dangerous situations. This goes beyond the current state-of-the-art where AVs are tested under ideal weather conditions, and lays the ground work for a more comprehensive testing effort. We also propose and demonstrate necessary analyses to validate the simulation results relative to the real world. The results of such analyses allow the designers and verification engineers to weigh the results of simulation-based testing.

1 Introduction: Testing AVs in Simulated Worlds

The development of Autonomous Vehicles (AVs) has seen a remarkable acceleration in the last decade, as technological advances like Deep Learning have allowed breakthroughs in processing visual information, and regulators have come to appreciate the potential of AVs to reduce accidents. While the first wave of AV development focused on improving the performance of individual components, like the Computer Vision (CV) pipeline or the behavioral controller, there is a growing need for whole-AV testing. This is testing of the *integrated AV as a whole*, where perception, control and environment conditions interact in unforeseen and complicated ways. This is an essential step towards building technical, regulatory, and public confidence in AVs as the solution to some of our transportation problems.

© Springer Nature Switzerland AG 2019
R. Chamberlain et al. (Eds.): CyPhy 2017, LNCS 11267, pp. 94–106, 2019.
https://doi.org/10.1007/978-3-030-17910-6_8

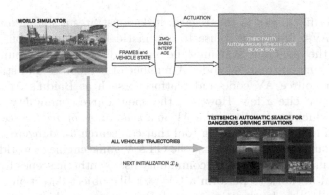

Fig. 1. The test harness.

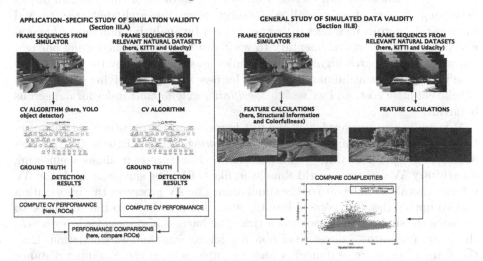

Fig. 2. Analyzes of test results on synthetic data.

Testing the real AV on real roads is a necessary part of this effort, but is woefully insufficient: a recent statistical study by the RAND Corporation (a U.S.-based policy think tank) found that AVs would have to drive "hundreds of millions of miles and, under some scenarios, hundreds of billions of miles to create enough data to clearly demonstrate their safety". According to the same report, "it would take existing fleets of autonomous vehicles tens and even hundreds of years to log sufficient miles" to demonstrate their safety when compared to human-driven vehicles. This constitutes a definitive argument for building *world simulators*, that the AV can be driven in. A world simulator provides the AV with perceptual inputs (like video and range data), traffic conditions (like other cars and pedestrians), varied weather conditions, and moves the AV in the simulated world in response to the AV's computed actuation commands. Simulation is many orders of magnitude cheaper and faster than real-world testing (Fig. 1).

This paper fills a gap in this regard: it demonstrates a *simulation-based test harness* for AVs, illustrates it use to automatically find dangerous situations, and clarifies the questions that must be answered when using simulation-based results for debugging real AV code. A number of companies and startups have released open-source AV code and platforms, such as Baidu's Apollo [3] and Autoware [8], to cite a few. However, the open-source community still lacks a simulator in which to test *the whole AV* in a *wide range of driving scenarios*, and a corresponding automatic testing tool that can search for dangerous scenarios. To illustrate our test harness, we use the GTA V game engine as world simulator. Recent work in the deep learning community uses synthetic scenes from GTA to *train* a neural network to perform a CV task like object detection [7] or image segmentation [12] or depth estimation [4]. By contrast, in this paper, we explore the use of synthetic scenes to *test* a *given pre-trained* algorithm (like an object detector), as part of an overall AV testing effort. Research that tries to find the most dangerous instances of *human driving* by analyzing millions of *human-driven* miles [15] is complementary to what can be accomplished using our test harness. That research highlights what miles *must* be driven by the AV to make sure it doesn't repeat human errors; our harness allows the driving of *any* kinds of miles at little cost, and we search *specifically autonomous miles* for dangerous behavior.

Figure 2 gives an overview of the test harness and the questions we answer in this paper, and which are detailed in the following sections. Briefly, the test harness consists of a real-time communication architecture that allows connecting an arbitrary AV code to a world simulator, like GTA. The simulator feeds the AV information about the state of the simulation. The AV processes this information and computes the next control inputs, which are sent back to the simulator to advance the simulation by one clock tick. The harness also includes a *testbench*: the latter computes a measure of how dangerous was the last simulation. E.g., the simplest measure of danger, which we implement, is the minimum distance between the AV and other traffic participants. Based on this value, the testbench decides on how to *initialize* the next simulation, including at what time of day it should take place. The ability to control the time of day, and thus the lighting conditions, in a simulator is a very powerful feature, since it allows us to stress the perception algorithms and the speed of reaction of the AV. Section 2 describes sample testing results that we obtain.

Using a simulator to test the AV raises questions on the applicability of the results to the real world. This can be broken down into two questions: the relation between the perception algorithms' performance in the simulated vs. the real world, and the validity of the simulated AV dynamical model vs. the real dynamics of the vehicle. In Sect. 3 of this paper, we explain the types of analyzes that are needed to answer the first of these two questions, and which are implemented by the test harness, as shown in Fig. 2. Briefly, they are statistical analysis of the performance of specific algorithms (Sect. 3.1) and a more general study of the visual complexity of scenes in the simulator vs. in the real world (Sect. 3.2). Section 4 concludes the paper.

2 Searching the World for Non-robust Behavior

A world simulator for testing AVs must have at least the following features:

- it must provide sufficiently realistic graphics so the perception pipeline is adequately tested.
- it must provide sufficiently realistic dynamics for the AV and other cars so that the AV controller's commands are implemented appropriately, and the other cars' reactions are realistic.
- it must create a variety of short-term traffic conditions for the AV to navigate (e.g., traffic at a T-junction).
- it must vary the weather conditions, since it is known that the environmental conditions can affect perception algorithms like objet detectors and image segmentors.

The test harness, which connects the AV to this simulated world, must have the following features:

- it must allow us to plug-in third-party AV code (both the perception and control components), so the AV can drive in this simulated world, and to collect all relevant data from an execution, like distance to obstacles and time-to-collision.
- it must support the plugging of general-purpose optimization algorithms, that can then be used to search for dangerous driving situations.
- it must support real-time simulation or faster.
- it must support replay of particular driving scenarios so the designers can debug the dangerous scenarios and improve the design.

We have developed a test harness that allows us to drive an AV in a simulated world, and which possesses the features described above. The harness, and the analyses it provides, are illustrated in Fig. 2, and described in the following sections. As a particular example of using this harness, we use GTA as a world simulator. We should stress that the harness can be used with any specialized simulator that supports the required, generic interface described in the next section.

2.1 Game-in-the-loop Test Harness

Figure 2 shows the architecture of the software used to test our AV code inside GTA. Most AVs use machine learning algorithms in their perception pipeline, typically some form of deep neural network which performs inference on images obtained by the vehicle's cameras. In the AV domain timing is critical: for many perception tasks, an algorithm that takes more than 100 ms to execute is practically useless because both the AV's and the environment's state may change significantly in that time. As a result, most machine learning frameworks utilize GPUs in order to perform perception tasks quickly enough; the majority of such frameworks are compiled for UNIX machines. Thus, it is important that the AV code must run on a Linux machine even if the game engine does not. Moreover, separating the computational hosts enables modularity: an updated AV software stack or improved simulation engine can be swapped during the design cycle. This enables continuous comparison of software releases without changing the internal workings of the simulation engine.

A typical simulation runs as follows: The *test harness* selects an initial state of the AV (e.g., initial position, velocity, jitter, etc). It also selects initial environment conditions: number of cars, their initial positions and velocities, and time of day. The time of day is a way to control the lighting conditions: from bright and clear skies in the morning, to dark and cloudy skies later in the day. As explained in the Introduction, this is particularly important for stressing the perception pipeline. This initialization is then sent to the simulator. The testbench samples the simulation once every second: every second, the simulator sends back to the testbench the current states of all traffic participants, including the AV, and the current "video" frame. The testbench stores the state for later computation of performance objectives. The AV's perception pipeline processes the frame (e.g., to detect objects' positions and velocities), and the controller then computes the next actuation (steering angle and acceleration). The control commands are passed back to the simulator, and this loop continues until the end of simulation. In the experiments the perception pipeline consists of the YOLO object detector, but there is no inherent restriction on using other sensors' models.

Our test harness allows this to run in real-time (so 10 s of simulated time require about 10 s of wallclock time). Given that we visualize the simulation *as it runs*, faster than real-time is not possible. Another simulator, that can run without the graphics, could run faster than real-time. The bottleneck of the current setup is the GTA simulator, not the testbench.

2.2   Search Algorithm

The test harness can be used to test the AV code as follows. First, pick a location in GTA's map. Next, define the AV state vector $x \in \mathcal{R}^5$, consisting of AV 2D position, 2D velocity and longitudinal jitter (second derivative of longitudinal velocity). The AV state can be initialized, in a given simulation, to any value in a pre-determined set X, e.g. $X = [-1,1]^2 \times [5,15]^2 \times [-5,5]$. We also define a time-of-day variable tod, measured in minutes, and which can be initialized to $D = \{0,1,\ldots,60 \times 24\}$. E.g. $tod = 0$ is midnight and $tod = 60 \times 8$ is 8 a.m. Finally, we define an environment vector $y \in \mathcal{R}^{4N}$, consisting of the positions and velocities of N other traffic participants. This can also be initialized to a set Y. Collectively, we refer to $z = (x, tod, y)$ as the *world state*, and it can be initialized to $Z = X \times D \times Y$. If the testbench initializes the test harness with a given $z \in Z$, the harness will simulate the resulting driving situation as explained in Sect. 2.1. The objective of the search is to find a value of z in Z such that the resulting simulation exposes dangerous driving situations, be they due to the AV's errors of control or perception, or because of unfortunate circumstances that might not have occurred to the AV designers. Indeed, even accidents that are not due to the AV's fault are informative, as they might cause the designers to equip the AV with better sensors or make it more conservative.

For illustration purposes in this paper, we define a 'dangerous driving situation' to be a state where the minimum distance between the AV and other cars or pedestrians is smaller than a nominal value. Therefore, we can now run an *optimization*: the objective function is $f : Z \to [0, \infty)$ where $f(z)$ is the minimum distance between the AV and other cars or pedestrians, in the simulation initialized at z. Our goal is to minimize f over Z: find the most dangerous situation, where the AV gets closest to moving obstacles. Of course, if $f(z_*) = 0$, then z_* actually witnesses an accident. All dangerous situations are then returned to designers to examine: did the object detector miss the obstacle? Did it detect it but too late? Did the obstacle come from behind a blind corner, if so, do we need to annotate the AV map with blind intersections? Or was the controller tuned too aggressively and an accident followed?

The AV code and simulator are treated as black boxes both due to their complexity and in order to provide a methodology which works to examine proprietary software without jeopardizing trade secrets or IP. Therefore we need to use a gradient-free optimization heuristic. While a simple uniform random sampling is always possible, in the experiments we use Simulated Annealing [5], a popular optimization algorithm that offers asymptotic guarantees (namely, as the number of simulations goes to infinity, the probability of being more than ϵ away from the global minimum goes to $0.$[1]). Simulated Annealing and its variations have been successfully used in a very wide array of applications in the last 60 years. Other heuristics can be used, of course. The next section presents some illustrative results obtained by this test harness.

2.3 Optimization Results

We selected a T-junction in Los Santos, the fictional city that is the setting for GTA. The objective of the AV is to make a safe right turn, and obey the Stop Sign. The simulation continues until either the objective is achieved, or a timeout (set to 20 s) occurs.

The search automatically found an accident between the AV and another car in under 100 simulations. (The search space X was described in the previous section.) We can examine the exact conditions that led to the accident to understand what happened. First, let's describe the accident: the AV approaches the T-junction, and starts the right turn. Another car approaches from the left. Neither car is able to stop on time, even though they both eventually 'saw' each other. In this case, two factors contributed to the accident: first, the scenario takes place at twilight. While the YOLO object detector correctly classified the stop sign there is some delay. This delay was nevertheless enough to allow the AV to edge further into the intersection before stopping. Secondly, the other car

---

[1] Since a countable infinite set always has measure 0 in a continuous search space, uniform random sampling cannot offer such a guarantee. That said, currently known bounds on the convergence rate of Simulated Annealing are too loose in our context.

was traveling at a speed similar to the AV's. Any faster, and it would've passed the AV before it started the right turn. Any slower, and the ego-vehicle would've been able to stop on time. In addition, the other vehicle is initially occluded and subsequently missed in several frames just as the ego vehicle makes a decision to turn.

This is an example of a non-trivial accident, where just the right conditions of timing and vehicle behavior must be present to cause the accident.

The automatic search enabled by our harness thus found environment conditions (lighting) and traffic conditions (speed of one other car) that produced an accident. Another accident, captured from 3 different camera angles, can be found at this anonymous Dropbox link: http://bit.ly/2fe2tZq.

3   Fake World, Real News: On the Validity of Using Synthetic Environments for Testing AVs

The described test harness allows us to test orders of magnitude more scenarios than we could in the real world, and dangerous situations (so-called 'counter-examples') that are exposed in simulation can help improve the design and flush out bugs. The natural question we need to answer is: do accidents discovered in simulation tell us something about real-world accidents? Without actually running the AV in the real world and correlating real-world results to the simulated results, it is impossible to obtain a direct empirical answer to this question. However, there are two 'big' questions that one can answer instead, and which go a long way toward establishing confidence in the simulated results. They are:

1. What is the relation between the *perception algorithms' performance* on synthetic driving scenes rendered by the graphics engine and their performance on natural ('real') driving scenes?
2. What is the relation between *the effect of AV controller's actions* in the simulator and their effect in the real world?

If we have confidence in our answers to these two questions, then we have more confidence that the whole-AV test enabled by our test harness is useful.

In this paper, we study the first question above. For the second question, it suffices to note that any dynamical model used in the automotive industry will be thoroughly validated by the automotive engineers, and the test harness we propose can accommodate any world simulator as explained earlier.

We answer the first question on two levels: first, in Sect. 3.1, we do a direct comparison between the performance of a perception algorithm (e.g., object detection) on synthetic and natural scenes. This gives an application-specific evaluation of the suitability of synthetic scenes for our purposes. The same study can be done on any CV algorithm. Secondly, in Sect. 3.2, we study the *visual complexity* of synthetic and natural scenes. Such a study is *application-independent*, and gives us a broader understanding of the differences and similarities between synthetic and natural scenes. While such a broader understanding is, at first, harder to apply than an application-specific comparison, it has a benefit: by understanding the ways in which synthetic scenes (as an ensemble) differ from natural scenes, we can better weigh the results of simulation-based testing and their relevance to real-world testing, *accross a range of peception algorithms*. E.g., visual complexity plays an important role in many computer vision algorithms, like edge detection and motion from structure. If the complexity of synthetic scenes is, say, poorer than that of natural scenes, we know that these algorithms will perform better on them, which allows us to weigh the evidence obtained from simulations.

Note that these questions are not only relevant for the case where the world simulator uses synthetic scenes, such as GTA. They apply equally to the case where natural scenes are used (e.g., when driving through Google Street View): as we show, the dataset of images encountered by the AV does have an effect on its performance, and any simulation-based testing must first evaluate the validity of test environment using multiple measures.

(a) KITTI

(b) Udacity

(c) Darmstadt

(d) Michigan

Fig. 3. Examples of images from the datasets.

The Datasets. We use the KITTI [6] and Udacity datasets [13] as sources of natural scenes. **KITTI** is extensively used in the Computer Vision and Image Processing communities to test their algorithms. We use its test set of 7481 images of urban and rural driving in and around a mid-size German city (Karlsruhe). **Udacity** is made of 15,000 images obtained by driving over Highway 92 in California during daylight conditions. For synthetic scenes, we use two sets of frames obtained from GTA: the **Darmstadt** [12] set of 25,000 frames and the **Michigan** set of 15,000 frames [7]. They were collected from the game using two plugins, Script Hook V and Script Hook V.NET [2]. The images in the datasets are highly variable in their content and layout. A range of different times of day and weather typees are captured: day, night, morning and dusk, and sun, fog, rain and haze. The Michigan dataset is annotated with the true bounding boxes for the objects in it and so can be used for profiling object detection algorithms. See Fig. 3 for example frames from these 4 datasets.

3.1   Object Detection on Synthetic and Natural Scenes

An object detection algorithm takes in an image and returns a set of bounding boxes, one box around each object it has detected in the image. See Fig. 4. It also returns the type of each detected object, e.g., 'car', 'person', or 'stop sign'. In order to evaluate the performance of a given object detection algorithm, we use the three following standard metrics [1]: precision, recall and false alarm rate (FAR). These three measures belong to the interval $[0, 1]$ and are calculated using the number $\#TP$ of true positives, number $\#FN$ of false negatives FN, and the number $\#FP$ of false positives over the given data set. A *true positive* (TP) is a detected object that is indeed in the image. A *false positive* (FP) is a detected object that isn't in the image, i.e. a mis-detection. A *false negative* (FN) is an object in the image that was not detected by the algorithm. A threshold $\alpha \in (0,1)$ is used to compute $\#TP, \#FP$ and $\#FN$. Roughly, if a detected object's bounding box overlaps with the bounding box of a true object (of the same object type) by more than α, then this is considered to be a TP, otherwise, it's a FP. α is chosen during the network's validation phase and is fixed when running the network, therefore it is fixed in the following experiments.

We can now define the detection performance metrics: *precision* measures the fraction of detected objects that are correct: Precision $:= \#TP/(\#TP + \#FP)$. A higher precision is better. *Recall* measures the fraction of true objects that

Fig. 4. GTA frame with red bounding boxes around cars detected by YOLO, and green boxes around true cars. Note the red box around the bush on the left, indicating a YOLO false positive, and the lack of red box around the faraway car on the right, indicating a YOLO false negative. The red box in the middle is a true positive. (Color figure online)

were correctly detected: Recall := $\#TP/(\#TP+\#FN)$. Higher recall is better. The *False Alarm Rate* (FAR) measures the fraction of all detected objects that are not correct: FAR := $\#FP/(\#FP+\#TP)$. *Lower* FAR is better. Note that Precision, Recall and FAR are all in the range $[0,1]$.

Results. We measured the performance of YOLO9000 [10,11], a popular real-time object detection algorithm, on the KITTI, Udacity and Michigan datasets, for which we have ground truth data, i.e., the bounding boxes of true objects. (We don't have ground truth for Darmstadt). Because the values of Precision, Recall and FAR depend on the threshold α, the appropriate way to compare YOLO's performance on different datasets is to vary the threshold and plot Receiver Operating Curves (ROCs). To avoid bias due to the content of the images ('content bias'), we performed this analysis on 50 randomly selected subsets of the data, each subset containing 80% of the images in the dataset. The ROCs and conclusions presented below hold accross the random selections.

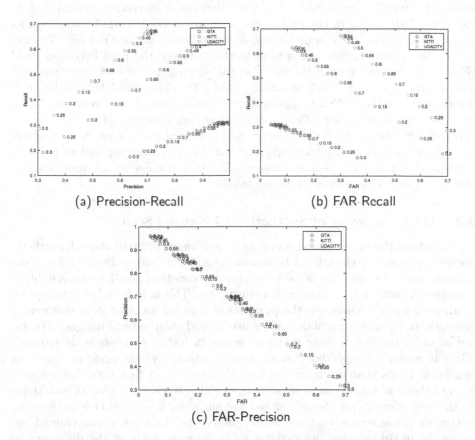

(a) Precision-Recall   (b) FAR-Recall

(c) FAR-Precision

Fig. 5. YOLO ROCs for three performance measures, plotted pair-wise, for 3 datasets. Every ROC contains 13 points, one per value of the overlap threshold α. The α value is indicated next to the point.

Figure 5 shows the results. The three performance measures are plotted against each other, two at a time. It can be seen that there is a measurable difference between YOLO on synthetic scenes (Michigan dataset) and real scenes. Indeed, there is a measurable difference *between natural datasets*. Both of these are confirmed by 2-sample Kolmogorov-Smirnov tests, which confirm that the performance numbers of different datasets come from different distributions. Thus, even if the world simulator used only natural scenes (e.g. if Google Street View is used to provide the visual input), *the question of how applicable testing results are must still be answered.*

The way to interpret and make use of these ROCs is as follows: suppose we will enforce a Precision of 0.7 during real AV operation (by selecting the right α). The Precision-Recall curve (Fig. 5a) tells us that at Precision = 0.7, GTA YOLO performance is a *lower bound* on YOLO performance in the real world (i.e., on natural images). That is, the KITTI and Udacity Recall values, for a Precision of 0.7, are both higher than the Michigan Recall value. *Thus, simulation results cannot mislead us*, since they are conservative. Similarly, if we enforce a FAR of 0.3 in the real world, then again GTA YOLO Recall results are a conservative lower bound on real-scenes Recall values (Fig. 5b). We will have more to say on this in the next section. Finally, the FAR-Precision ROC (Fig. 5c) reveals the noteworthy fact that the performance of YOLO on synthetic and natural scenes are nearly identical. Thus if Precision and FAR are the more important aspects of YOLO performance, simulations give a very good idea of real-world performance. *Thus a complex picture emerges, where the relation between performance in the simulator and in the real world depends on multiple factors, including on the trade-offs that the AV designers are willing to make between different performance measures.* The test harness we are presenting in this paper serves to analyze these trade-offs.

3.2 The Complexity of Synthetic and Natural Scenes

The results of the previous section might be surprising at first: after all, synthetic scenes are generally thought to be somewhat simpler, informally speaking, than natural scenes, because the latter have a greater variety of detail, texture, lighting changes, distortion and compression effects, etc. This is indirectly confirmed by studies such as [7] where, for the purposes of *training* an objet detection neural network, many more synthetic images are needed than natural images. (We are not aware of studies on using synthetic scenes in *testing* perception algorithms.) Thus it might be expected that an object detector would perform *better* on synthetic scenes than on natural scenes. However, let us first note that we used YOLO that was trained on natural scenes - which is what the real AV would use in the real world. This should temper the surprise, since YOLO is performing better on those scenes that are more 'similar' to the ones it was trained on. Secondly, in this section, we make a more rigorous study of the difference in complexity between natural and synthetic scenes.

An important property of a scene is its *visual complexity*, in terms of the density and distribution of edges, textures, colorfullness and contrast variations accross the image. A more complex scene, a priori, presents a greater challenge to any Computer Vision (CV) algorithm, because it makes it harder to extract features. E.g., a texture-rich image presents serious difficulties to an edge detector since textures can be confused for edges. In this section, we characterize the complexity of the datasets using the two complexity measures proposed in [14]: Spatial information (SI) and Colorfullness (CF). These are established measures of complexity in the Image Processing community (e.g., see their use in [9]) and they are simple to compute. Due to lack of space, we refer the reader to [14] for their mathematical definitions. Here, we mention that SI measures the strength and amount of edges in an image; edges are a crucial element of information for many image processing algorithms. CF measures the variation and intensity of colors in the image.

Results. To avoid content bias, we measured SI and CF on 50 randomly selected subsets of the four datasets, each selection containing 80% of the images. The results and conclusions presented below hold accross the random selections. Figure 6 shows the scatterplots of complexities from one such selection. There are clear differences between synthetic and real, but also *between synthetic datasets, and between real datasets*. The first, striking feature is that the Darmstadt (GTA) dataset complexity lies *between* the complexities of Kitti and Udacity (both real). Thus saying that 'synthetic is less complex' is too simplistic. The second feature we note is that there is a large degree of overlap between Udacity and Michigan datasets. Both have a wide range of SI, and comparatively small range of CF, which is the opposite of KITTI and Darmstadt. The complexity results suggest that using a simulated world is a reasonable means to test an AV, given the intermediate complexity of synthetic scenes, and the overlap between synthetic and some real scenes. Computer vision algorithms that are affected by the complexity of the images, like object tracking, can thus be tested in this simulated world with relevance to the real world.

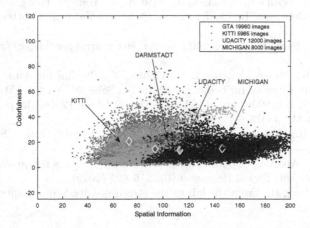

Fig. 6. Complexity of datasets. Diamonds show the centroids of the clusters. Red: KITTI, Black: Udacity (both natural) Blue: Darmstadt, Green: Michigan (both synthetic from GTA). Colors in digital version of paper. (Color figure online)

4   Conclusion

The test harness we have presented allows automatic testing of AV code in simulated worlds, and implements necessary analyses for understanding the similarities and differences between the simulated data and representative real-world data. The next step is to implement a more advanced notion of AV safety, which takes into account the driving context, and to automate the debugging process for the accidents we find.

References

1. Godil, A.A., et al.: Performance metrics for evaluating object and human detection and tracking systems, nIST Interagency/Internal Report (NISTIR) - 7972, July 2014
2. Alexander Blade, A.S.D.: Script hook v.net, September 2017. https://github.com/crosire/scripthookvdotnet
3. Baidu: Apollo platform, September 2017. apollo.auto
4. Chen, C., Seff, A., Kornhauser, A., Xiao, J.: Deepdriving: learning affordance for direct perception in autonomous driving. In: International Conference on Computer Vision (2015)
5. Chib, S., Greenberg, E.: Understanding the Metropolis-Hastings algorithm. Am. Stat. **49**(4), 327–335 (1995)
6. Geiger, A., Lenz, P., Stiller, C., Urtasun, R.: Vision meets robotics: the kitti dataset. Int. J. Robot. Res. **32**(11), 1231–1237 (2013)
7. Johnson-Roberson, M., Barto, C., Mehta, R., Sridhar, S.N., Rosaen, K., Vasudevan, R.: Driving in the matrix: can virtual worlds replace human-generated annotations for real world tasks? In: ICRA, May 2017
8. Kato, S.: Autoware, September 2017. https://github.com/CPFL/Autoware
9. Kundu, D.: Subjective and objective quality evaluation of synthetic and high dynamic range images, Ph.D. Dissertation, May 2016
10. Redmon, J., Divvala, S., Girshick, R., Farhadi, A.: You only look once: unified, real-time object detection. In: Conference on Computer Vision and Pattern Recognition (2016)
11. Redmon, J., Farhadi, A.: Yolo9000: better, faster, stronger. https://arxiv.org/abs/1612.08242
12. Richter, S.R., Vineet, V., Roth, S., Koltun, V.: Playing for data: ground truth from computer games. In: Leibe, B., Matas, J., Sebe, N., Welling, M. (eds.) ECCV 2016. LNCS, vol. 9906, pp. 102–118. Springer, Cham (2016). https://doi.org/10.1007/978-3-319-46475-6_7
13. Udacity, A.R.: Udacity self-driving car dataset, p. 2 (2017). http://bit.ly/udacity-annotations-autti
14. Winkler, S.: Analysis of public image and video databases for quality assessment. IEEE J. Sel. Top. Signal Process. **6**(6), 616–625 (2012)
15. Zhao, D., Peng, H.: From the lab to the street, m-City White Paper, May 2017

Formal Methods

Switching Delays and the Skorokhod Distance in Incrementally Stable Switched Systems

Kengo Kido[1,2], Sean Sedwards[3], and Ichiro Hasuo[4,5(✉)]

[1] University of Tokyo, Tokyo, Japan
[2] JSPS Research Fellow, Tokyo, Japan
[3] University of Waterloo, Waterloo, Canada
[4] National Institute of Informatics, Tokyo, Japan
i.hasuo@acm.org
[5] The Graduate University for Advanced Studies (SOKENDAI), Tokyo, Japan

Abstract. We introduce an approximate bisimulation-based framework that gives an upper bound of the Skorokhod metric between a switched system with delays and its delay-free model. To establish the approximate bisimulation relation, we rely on an incremental stability assumption. We showcase our framework using an example of a boost DC-DC converter. The obtained upper bound of the Skorokhod metric can be used to reduce the reachability analysis (or the safety controller synthesis) of the switched system with delays to that of the delay-free model.

1 Introduction

In cyber-physical systems (CPS), physical systems are controlled by digital controllers. A recent trend in CPS is *networked control systems (NCS)*, which means the physical plant and the controller are separated and connected via a network. One of the most important challenges in NCS is the *time delays*. Delays are inevitable due to data transfer via a network and also due to the computation of the controller. It is not easy to reduce the delay or estimate the exact length of the delay.

In this paper, we introduce an approximate bisimulation-based framework to find an overapproximation of the effect of the delays. Approximate bisimulation is a relaxation of the classical notion of bisimulation suitable for continuous state space. It was first introduced in [10]. One of the main applications of approximate bisimulation in the literature is the symbolic abstraction of continuous or hybrid systems. For switched systems with nonlinear continuous behavior, [12] constructed an approximate bisimulation between the actual system and its

The authors are supported by JST ERATO HASUO Metamathematics for Systems Design Project (No. JPMJER1603), and JSPS Grant-in-Aid No. 15KT0012. K.K. is supported by JSPS under JSPS Grants-in-Aid for JSPS Research Fellows No. 15J05580. The results of this paper are part of K.K.'s Ph.D. thesis [15].

R. Chamberlain et al. (Eds.): CyPhy 2017, LNCS 11267, pp. 109–126, 2019.
https://doi.org/10.1007/978-3-030-17910-6_9

symbolic model, under the assumption of incremental stability. Our target systems are the same as [12]—incrementally stable switched systems with possibly nonlinear continuous behavior—but we take time delays into account.

To construct an approximate bisimulation, we first define two transition systems from the delayed system and its delay-free model, and a cost function on the output set of them. The cost is designed to bound the *Skorokhod metric*. It is a metric defined between trajectories that allows certain timing mismatches. It has been studied in the area of conformance testing, and showed in [7] that it accommodates a transference result: it can be used for sound analysis of a variant of temporal logic specifications. Then, the cost is bounded by constructing an approximate bisimulation relation between the transition systems built from the delayed system and its delay-free model. This construction is based on an incremental stability assumption, namely δ-GUAS. Using this approximate bisimulation, we can find an upper bound of the Skorokhod metric between a trajectory of the delayed system and the corresponding trajectory of its delay-free model. The framework has combined with existing approximate bisimulation for symbolic abstraction [12] and applied to controller synthesis, as presented in Fig. 1.

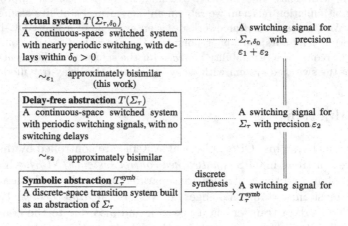

Fig. 1. A two-step control synthesis workflow for switched systems with delays. We separate two concerns: time delays and state-space discretization. The same stability assumption on Σ_τ can be used once for all, for establishing both $\sim_{\varepsilon_1}$ and $\sim_{\varepsilon_2}$.

Related Work. In our previous work [14], we constructed an approximate bisimulation between the delayed system and its delay-free model. The result was an upper bound of the *pointwise* metric that compares the states of the delayed and delay-free systems at the same time instant. A problem of the pointwise metric is that it sometimes returns large distances even if two systems are close in terms of, for example, reachability. See the example in Fig. 2. The pointwise distance gives the length of the black arrows at switchings. Once we obtain this distance (say ε), the reachability of the blue behavior is overapproximated by an expansion of the reachability of the red one by ε. However, the actual reachability of the two systems in red and blue is the same. The source of this unnecessarily large distance is that the pointwise metric does not allow any mismatches of the timing. The framework we propose in this paper compares the states at the corresponding switching times even if the switching times do not match exactly. As a result, we find an upper bound of the Skorokhod metric between the delayed and delay-free systems that allows certain timing mismatches. As one can see from the example in Sect. 7, a smaller bound is found that can still be used to reduce the safety controller synthesis of the delayed system to that of the delay-free model. As a result, more permissive safety controller is synthesized than [14].

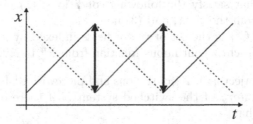

Fig. 2. The behavior of two systems are presented in red and blue. Solid and broken lines indicate two different modes. (Color figure online)

In [1,2], a metric called (τ, ϵ)-closeness is introduced. It also allows timing mismatches. In this paper we chose the Skorokhod metric because it is easier to bound in our setting.

In [5,19,21], approximate bisimulation-based frameworks for symbolic abstraction of systems with delays were studied. The goal of these works is to construct a comprehensive symbolic (discretized) model that encompasses all possible delays. One can make the proximity as small as desired, in a trade-off with the size of the symbolic model. One can apply various discrete techniques for analysis or controller synthesis to the obtained symbolic model. The biggest difference is that our framework aims at abstracting away the effect of delays. The generated delay-free model still includes continuous dynamics. Figure 1 shows its combination with controller synthesis by [12], but it is also possible to combine with existing hybrid system analysis tools such as SpaceEx [8]. It seems that ours has an advantage in complexity: collecting all the possible delays tends to result in a big number of transitions. One major drawback is that, in our results the proximity is fixed from the Lyapunov function.

[6,7,16,17] introduce algorithms to calculate the Skorokhod distance between trajectories. These methodologies can be applied to conformance testing. Our framework takes switched systems as inputs and analyzes them in a static manner, without making concrete trajectories. This is suitable for the purpose of static verification or controller synthesis.

Notations. The set of nonnegative real numbers is denoted by $\mathbb{R}^+$. We let $\|\_\|$ denote the usual Euclidean norm on $\mathbb{R}^n$.

2   Switched Systems

We assume that models are given as switched systems.

Definition 2.1 (switched system). A *switched system* is a quadruple $\Sigma = (\mathbb{R}^n, P, \mathbf{P}, F)$ that consists of:

- a *state space* $\mathbb{R}^n$;
- a finite set $P = \{1, 2, \ldots, m\}$ of *modes*;
- a set of *switching signals* $\mathbf{P} \subseteq \mathcal{S}(\mathbb{R}^+, P)$, where $\mathcal{S}(\mathbb{R}^+, P)$ is the set of functions from $\mathbb{R}^+$ to P that satisfy the following conditions: (1) piecewise constant, (2) continuous from the right, and (3) non-Zeno;
- $F = \{f_1, f_2, \ldots, f_m\}$ is the set of vector fields indexed by $p \in P$, where each f_p is a locally Lipschitz continuous function from $\mathbb{R}^n$ to $\mathbb{R}^n$.

Definition 2.2 (trajectory). A continuous and piecewise $\mathcal{C}^1$ function $\mathbf{x} : \mathbb{R}^+ \to \mathbb{R}^n$ is called a *trajectory* of the switched system Σ if there exists a switching signal $\mathbf{p} \in \mathbf{P}$ such that
$$\dot{\mathbf{x}}(t) = f_{\mathbf{p}(t)}(x(t))$$
holds at each time $t \in \mathbb{R}^+$ when the switching signal $\mathbf{p}$ is continuous. Note that the trajectory $\mathbf{x}$ is continuous, which means that we do not allow jumps of the continuous state even at switchings.

We let $\mathbf{x}(t, x, \mathbf{p})$ denote the point reached at time $t \in \mathbb{R}^+$, starting from the state $x \in \mathbb{R}^n$ (at $t = 0$), under the switching signal $\mathbf{p} \in \mathbf{P}$. In the special case where the switching signal is constant (i.e. $\mathbf{p}(s) = p$ for all $s \in \mathbb{R}^+$), the point reached at time $t \in \mathbb{R}^+$ starting from $x \in \mathbb{R}^n$ is denoted by $\mathbf{x}(t, x, p)$. The continuous subsystem of Σ with the constant switching signal $\mathbf{p}(s) = p$ for all $s \in \mathbb{R}^+$ is denoted by Σ_p. If P is a singleton $P = \{p\}$, the system $\Sigma = \Sigma_p$ is a continuous system without switching.

We focus on control systems with periodic[1] sensing. An ideal model without delays and the actual system with delays are modeled as switched systems using the following periodicity.

Definition 2.3 (periodicity, switching delay). Given a switching signal $\mathbf{p}$, those time instants $t \in \mathbb{R}^+$ where the switching signal $\mathbf{p}$ is discontinuous are called *switching times*. If a switching signal is continuous except at $k\tau$ (where $\tau > 0$ is a constant and $k \in \mathbb{N}$), it is called *τ-periodic*. A switched system is called *τ-periodic* if all the switching signals in $\mathbf{P}$ are τ-periodic. Given a τ-periodic

---

[1] The word "periodic" is usually used for a stronger condition that the same signal shape is repeated in every period. Our use of the word, which is weaker (Definition 2.3), follows some literature in the field such as [13].

switching signal, even though switching does not always occur at every $t = k\tau$, we denote the switching that occurs at $t = k\tau$ by *k-th switching*.

Let $\delta_0 \in \mathbb{R}^+$. A switching signal **p** is said to be *τ-periodic with switching delays within δ_0* if there exists a sequence $[t_k]_{k \in \mathbb{N}}$, such that $t_0 \in [0, \delta_0]$, $t_{k+1} \in [\max(t_k, (k+1)\tau), (k+1)\tau + \delta_0]$ and all the discontinuities of **p** can only occur at some t_k. For such a sequence, we call the switching that occurs at t_k *k-th switching*. A switched system $\Sigma = (\mathbb{R}^n, P, \mathbf{P}, F)$ is called *τ-periodic with switching delays within δ_0* if all the switching signals in **P** are τ-periodic with switching delays within δ_0. Note that the maximum delay δ_0, which was assumed to be smaller than the period τ in our previous work [14], can be larger than τ.

See Fig. 3 for illustration of periodic switching signals and those with delays.

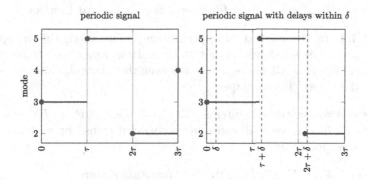

Fig. 3. Periodic switching signals, with and without delays

We focus on periodic switched systems with switching delays and their difference from those without switching delays. More specifically, we consider two switched systems

$$\begin{aligned}
\Sigma_{\tau, \delta_0} &= (\mathbb{R}^n, P, \mathbf{P}_{\tau, \delta_0}, F) \quad \text{τ-periodic with delays} \leq \delta_0 \\
\Sigma_\tau &= (\mathbb{R}^n, P, \mathbf{P}_\tau, F) \quad \text{τ-periodic}
\end{aligned} \tag{1}$$

that have a common state space $\mathbb{R}^n$, a common set P of modes and a common set F of vector fields. For the former system Σ_{τ, δ_0}, the set $\mathbf{P}_{\tau, \delta_0}$ consists of all τ-periodic signals with delays within δ_0; for the latter system Σ_τ the set $\mathbf{P}_\tau$ consists of all τ-periodic switching signals.

3   Transition Systems and Approximate Bisimulation

We formalize proximity between Σ_{τ, δ_0} and Σ_τ using the notion of approximate bisimulation [10,11]. Approximate bisimulations are defined between transitions systems.

Definition 3.1 (transition system). A *transition system* is a triple $T = (Q, L, \longrightarrow, O, H, I)$, where

- Q is a set of states;
- L is a set of labels;
- $\longrightarrow \subseteq Q \times L \times Q$ is a transition relation;
- O is a set of outputs;
- $H : Q \to O$ is an output function; and
- $I \subseteq Q$ is a set of initial states.

We let $q \overset{l}{\longrightarrow} q'$ denote the fact that $(q, l, q') \in \longrightarrow$.

In this paper, we assume that the set of outputs O is equipped with a function $d : O \times O \to \mathbb{R}^+ \cup \{\infty\}$ and the function d is called a *cost* function.

Remark 3.2. In the context of approximate bisimulation, this mapping d is usually a metric or some weaker notion of it. However, in our framework, the mapping d in Definition 3.4 does not satisfy even the triangular inequality. Therefore we call it "cost" in this paper.

For the two switched systems $\Sigma_{\tau, \delta_0} = (\mathbb{R}^n, P, \mathbf{P}_{\tau, \delta_0}, F)$ and $\Sigma_\tau = (\mathbb{R}^n, P, \mathbf{P}_\tau, F)$ in (1), we shall construct associated transition systems $T(\Sigma_{\tau, \delta_0})$ and $T(\Sigma_\tau)$, respectively.

Definition 3.3 $(T(\Sigma_{\tau, \delta_0}), T(\Sigma_\tau))$. The transition system

$$T(\Sigma_{\tau, \delta_0}) = (Q_{\tau, \delta_0}, L, \underset{\tau, \delta_0}{\longrightarrow}, O, H_{\tau, \delta_0}, I) \ ,$$

associated with the switched system Σ_{τ, δ_0} with delays in (1), is defined as follows:

- the set of states is $Q_{\tau, \delta_0} := \mathbb{R}^n \times \bigcup_{k \in \mathbb{N}} [k\tau, k\tau + \delta_0] \times P$;
- the set of labels L is the set of modes, i.e. $L := P$;
- the transition relation $\underset{\tau, \delta_0}{\longrightarrow} \subseteq Q_{\tau, \delta_0} \times L \times Q_{\tau, \delta_0}$ is defined by (x, t, p) $\underset{\tau, \delta_0}{\overset{p''}{\longrightarrow}} (x', t', p')$ if $p = p''$, $x' = \mathbf{x}(t' - t, x, p)$ and there exists $k \in \mathbb{N}$ such that $t \in [k\tau, k\tau + \delta_0]$ and $t' \in [(k+1)\tau, (k+1)\tau + \delta_0]$;
- the set of outputs is $O := \mathbb{R}^n \times \mathbb{R}^+ \times P$;
- the output function $H : Q_{\tau, \delta_0} \to O$ is the canonical embedding function $\mathbb{R}^n \times \bigcup_{k \in \mathbb{N}} [k\tau, k\tau + \delta_0] \times P \to \mathbb{R}^n \times \mathbb{R}^+ \times P$; and
- the set of initial states is $I := \mathbb{R}^n \times \{0\} \times P$.

Intuitively, each state (x, t, p) of $T(\Sigma_{\tau, \delta_0})$ marks switching in the system Σ_{τ, δ_0}: $x \in \mathbb{R}^n$ is the (continuous) state at switching; t is time of switching; and p is the next mode. Note that, by the assumption on Σ_{τ, δ_0}, t necessarily belongs to the interval $[k\tau, k\tau + \delta_0]$ for some $k \in \mathbb{N}$.

Similarly, the transition system

$$T(\Sigma_\tau) = (Q_\tau, L, \xrightarrow[\tau]{}, O, H_\tau, I) \ ,$$

associated with the switched system Σ_τ without delays in (1), is defined as follows:

- the set of states is $Q_\tau := \mathbb{R}^n \times \{0, \tau, 2\tau, \dots\} \times P$;
- the set of labels L is the set of modes, i.e. $L := P$;
- the transition relation $\xrightarrow[\tau]{} \subseteq Q_\tau \times L \times Q_\tau$ is defined by (x, t, p)
  $\xrightarrow[\tau]{p''} (x', t', p')$ if $p = p''$, $t' = t + \tau$ and $x' = \mathbf{x}(\tau, x, p)$;
- the set of outputs is $O := \mathbb{R}^n \times \mathbb{R}^+ \times P$;
- the output function $H \colon Q_{\tau, \delta_0} \to O$ is the canonical embedding function; and
- the set of initial states is $I := \mathbb{R}^n \times \{0\} \times P$.

Note that, in both of $T(\Sigma_{\tau, \delta_0})$ and $T(\Sigma_\tau)$, the label p'' for a transition is uniquely determined by the mode component p of the transition's source (x, t, p). Therefore, mathematically speaking, we do not need transition labels.

In [12], the state space Q of the transition system is defined to be $\mathbb{R}^n$ and is the same as the state space of the original switched system. In comparison, our definition has two additional components, namely time t and the current mode p. It is notable that moving a mode p from transition labels to state labels allows us to analyze what happens during switching delays, that is, when the system keeps operating under the mode p while it is not supposed to do so.

Now we define a cost function on the output set of these transition systems. It compares the states at the corresponding switching times even if the switching times do not match exactly.

Definition 3.4 (cost function). On the set of outputs $O = \mathbb{R}^n \times \mathbb{R}^+ \times P$ that is common to the two transition systems $T(\Sigma_{\tau, \delta_0})$ and $T(\Sigma_\tau)$, we define the following cost function d:

$$d((x, t, p), (x', t', p')) :=$$
$$\begin{cases} \|x - x'\| & \text{if } p = p', t' = k\tau \text{ and} \\ & \quad t \in [t', t' + \delta_0] \text{ for some } k \in \mathbb{N} \\ \infty & \text{otherwise.} \end{cases}$$

We review the notion of approximate bisimulation [10,11], a (co)inductive construct that guarantees henceforth proximity of behaviors of two states. The main results of this paper will be proved by constructing approximate bisimulation between the transition systems $T(\Sigma_{\tau, \delta_0})$ and $T(\Sigma_\tau)$.

Definition 3.5. Let $T_i = (Q_i, L, \xrightarrow[i]{}, O, H_i, I_i)$ $(i = 1, 2)$ be two transition systems with a cost function d; note that T_1 and T_2 share the same sets of actions L and outputs O. Let $\varepsilon \in \mathbb{R}^+$ be a positive number; we call it a *precision*. A relation $R \subseteq Q_1 \times Q_2$ is called an ε-*approximate bisimulation relation* between T_1 and T_2 if the following three conditions hold for all $(q_1, q_2) \in R$.

1. $d(H_1(q_1), H_2(q_2)) \leq \varepsilon$;
2. $\forall q_1 \xrightarrow{l}_1 q_1', \exists q_2 \xrightarrow{l}_2 q_2'$ such that $(q_1', q_2') \in R$; and
3. $\forall q_2 \xrightarrow{l}_2 q_2', \exists q_1 \xrightarrow{l}_1 q_1'$ such that $(q_1', q_2') \in R$.

The transition systems T_1 and T_2 are *approximately bisimilar with precision ε* if there exists an ε-approximate bisimulation relation R that satisfies the following conditions:

- $\forall q_1 \in I_1, \exists q_2 \in I_2$ such that $(q_1, q_2) \in R$;
- $\forall q_2 \in I_2, \exists q_1 \in I_1$ such that $(q_1, q_2) \in R$.

We let $T_1 \sim_\varepsilon T_2$ denote the fact that T_1 and T_2 are approximately bisimilar with precision ε.

4   Incremental Stability

After the pioneering work [18], a number of frameworks rely on the assumption of *incremental stability* for the construction of approximate bisimulations. Intuitively, a dynamical system is incrementally stable if, under any choice of an initial state, the resulting trajectory asymptotically converges to one reference trajectory.

In the subsequent definitions, we will be using the following classes of functions. A continuous function $\gamma : \mathbb{R}^+ \to \mathbb{R}^+$ is a *class $\mathcal{K}$ function* if it is strictly increasing and $\gamma(0) = 0$. A $\mathcal{K}$ function is a $\mathcal{K}_\infty$ *function* if $\gamma(x) \to \infty$ when $x \to \infty$. A continuous function $\beta : \mathbb{R}^+ \times \mathbb{R}^+ \to \mathbb{R}^+$ is a *class $\mathcal{KL}$ function* if (1) the function defined by $x \mapsto \beta(x, t)$ is a $\mathcal{K}_\infty$ function for any fixed t; and (2) for any fixed x, the function defined by $t \mapsto \beta(x, t)$ is strictly decreasing, and $\beta(x, t) \to 0$ when $t \to \infty$.

Definition 4.1 (δ-GAS system [3]). Let $\Sigma = (\mathbb{R}^n, P, \mathbf{P}, F)$ be a single-mode switched system where $P = \{p\}$ is a singleton (therefore there is actually no switching). The system Σ is *incrementally globally asymptotically stable (δ-GAS)* if there exists a $\mathcal{KL}$ function β such that

$$\|\mathbf{x}(t, x, p) - \mathbf{x}(t, y, p)\| \leq \beta(\|x - y\|, t)$$

for all $x, y \in \mathbb{R}^n$ and $t \in \mathbb{R}^+$.

The notion of δ-GAS is a well-known one among various notions of incremental stability. Directly establishing that a given system is δ-GAS is often hard. A usual technique in the field is to let a Lyapunov-type function play the role of witness for δ-GAS [3].

Definition 4.2. Let $\Sigma = (\mathbb{R}^n, P, \mathbf{P}, F)$ be a single-mode switched system with $P = \{p\}$. A smooth function $V : \mathbb{R}^n \times \mathbb{R}^n \to \mathbb{R}^+$ is a *δ-GAS Lyapunov function* *for* Σ *if there exist* $\mathcal{K}_\infty$ *functions* $\underline{\alpha}$, $\overline{\alpha}$ *and* $\kappa > 0$ *such that the following hold for all* $x, y \in \mathbb{R}^n$.

$$\underline{\alpha}(\|x - y\|) \leq V(x, y) \leq \overline{\alpha}(\|x - y\|) \tag{2}$$

$$\frac{\partial V}{\partial x}(x, y)f_p(x) + \frac{\partial V}{\partial y}(x, y)f_p(y) \leq -\kappa V(x, y) \tag{3}$$

Note that the left-hand side of (3) is much like the Lie derivative of V along the vector field f_p.

Theorem 4.3 ([3]). *Let* $\Sigma = (\mathbb{R}^n, P, \mathbf{P}, F)$ *be a single-mode switched system with* $P = \{p\}$. *The system* Σ *is* δ-*GAS if and only if it has a* δ-*GAS Lyapunov function.*   □

The notions so far are for systems without switching. Their extension to switched systems are introduced in [12].

Definition 4.4. Let $\Sigma = (\mathbb{R}^n, P, \mathbf{P}, F)$ be a switched system. Σ is said to be *incrementally globally uniformly asymptotically stable (*δ-GUAS*)* if there exists a $\mathcal{KL}$ function β such that the following holds for all $x, y \in \mathbb{R}^n$, $t \in \mathbb{R}^+$ and $\mathbf{p} \in \mathbf{P}$.

$$\|\mathbf{x}(t, x, \mathbf{p}) - \mathbf{x}(t, y, \mathbf{p})\| \leq \beta(\|x - y\|, t)$$

A sufficient condition for a switched system to be δ-GUAS is the existence of a common δ-GAS Lyapunov function.

Definition 4.5. Let $\Sigma = (\mathbb{R}^n, P, \mathbf{P}, F)$ be a switched system. A smooth function $V \colon \mathbb{R}^n \times \mathbb{R}^n \to \mathbb{R}^+$ is called a *common* δ-*GAS Lyapunov function for* Σ if there exist $\mathcal{K}_\infty$ functions $\underline{\alpha}$, $\overline{\alpha}$ and $\kappa > 0$ that make the following hold for all $x, y \in \mathbb{R}^n$.

$$\underline{\alpha}(\|x - y\|) \leq V(x, y) \leq \overline{\alpha}(\|x - y\|) \tag{4}$$

$$\frac{\partial V}{\partial x}(x, y)f_p(x) + \frac{\partial V}{\partial y}(x, y)f_p(y) \leq -\kappa V(x, y) \quad \text{for all } p \in P \tag{5}$$

Theorem 4.6 ([12]). *Let* Σ *be a switched system. If there exists a common* δ-*GAS Lyapunov function* V *of* Σ, *then* Σ *is* δ-*GUAS.*   □

5 Constructing Approximate Bisimulation Between Delayed and Delay-Free Systems

In this section, we construct an approximate bisimulation relation between the transition systems $T(\Sigma_{\tau,\delta_0})$ and $T(\Sigma_\tau)$ that are constructed from the delayed system Σ_{τ,δ_0} and the delay-free model Σ_τ, respectively.

As preparation, we define the following function V' from δ-GAS Lyapunov function V.

Definition 5.1 (the function V'). Let $\Sigma = (\mathbb{R}^n, P, \mathbf{P}, F)$ be a switched system, and let $V : \mathbb{R}^n \times \mathbb{R}^n \to \mathbb{R}^+$ be a common δ-GAS Lyapunov function for Σ.

We define a function $V' : (\mathbb{R}^n \times \mathbb{R}^+ \times P) \times (\mathbb{R}^n \times \mathbb{R}^+ \times P) \to \mathbb{R}^+$ in the following manner:

$$V'\big((x,t,p),(x',t',p')\big) :=$$
$$\begin{cases} V(x,x') & \text{if } p = p' \text{ and } t \in [t', t' + \delta_0] \\ \infty & \text{otherwise.} \end{cases}$$

Our results rely on the following assumption.

Assumption 5.2 (bounded partial derivative). Let $\Sigma = (\mathbb{R}^n, P, \mathbf{P}, F)$ be a switched system, with $P = \{1, 2, \ldots, m\}$ and $F = \{f_1, f_2, \ldots, f_m\}$ being the set of vector fields associated with each mode. We say a function $V : \mathbb{R}^n \times \mathbb{R}^n \to \mathbb{R}^+$ has *bounded partial derivatives* if there exists a real number $\nu \geq 0$ such that, for any $p \in P$, the inequality

$$\left| \frac{\partial V}{\partial x}(x, y) f_p(x) \right| \leq \nu$$

holds for each $x, y \in \mathbb{R}^n$.

Remark 5.3. Assumption 5.2 is not assumed in the previous works on approximate bisimulation for switched systems, such as [12]. The objective of [12] is to discretize the state space and their framework is designed so that it can accommodate the error caused by the discretization (using [12, Equation 9]). Their framework does not consider time-delays and they rely on the fact that the switchings of the two systems occur at the same time instants. Therefore if one just fixes the dwell time $\tau - \delta_0$ in the results described in [12], it does not take into account the error caused while the two systems are operated in different modes.

In our results, to deal with this kind of error in an appropriate manner, we make the switchings occur at the same time instants by using retimings and use Assumption 5.2 to bound the effect of retimings. (Note that in our previous work [14], we used [14, Assumption 5.1] to bound the error caused while the two systems are operated in different modes.)

Imposing the assumption on δ-GAS Lyapunov functions, however, is not a severe restriction. In [12], they assume that there exists $\gamma \in \mathbb{R}^+$ such that, for all $x, y, z \in \mathbb{R}^n$,

$$|V(x,y) - V(x,z)| \leq \gamma(\|y - z\|) \tag{6}$$

(we do not need this assumption in the current work). It is claimed in [12] that (6) is readily guaranteed if the dynamics of the switched system is confined to a compact set $C \subseteq \mathbb{R}^n$, and if V is class $\mathcal{C}^1$ in the domain C. We can use the same compactness argument to ensure Assumption 5.2.

Our main technical lemma is as follows.

Lemma 5.4. *Let $\Sigma_\tau = (\mathbb{R}^n, P, \mathbf{P}_\tau, F)$ be a τ-periodic switched system, and $\Sigma_{\tau,\delta_0} = (\mathbb{R}^n, P, \mathbf{P}_{\tau,\delta_0}, F)$ be a τ-periodic switched system with delays within δ_0. Assume that there exists a common δ-GAS Lyapunov function V for Σ_τ, and that V satisfies the additional assumption in Assumption 5.2.*

We consider a relation $R_\varepsilon \subseteq (\mathbb{R}^n \times \mathbb{R}^+ \times P) \times (\mathbb{R}^n \times \mathbb{R}^+ \times P)$ defined by

$$(q, q') \in R_\varepsilon \overset{\text{def.}}{\Longleftrightarrow} V'(q, q') \leq \underline{\alpha}(\varepsilon) . \tag{7}$$

Here V' is from Definition 5.1. If we fix $\varepsilon = \underline{\alpha}^{-1}\left(\frac{\nu\delta_0}{1 - e^{-\kappa\tau}}\right)$ where ν is from Assumption 5.2, then, the relation R_ε is an approximate bisimulation between the transition systems $T(\Sigma_{\tau,\delta_0})$ and $T(\Sigma_\tau)$. Moreover, $T(\Sigma_{\tau,\delta_0}) \sim_\varepsilon T(\Sigma_\tau)$. $\square$

Proof. To prove that R_ε is an approximate bisimulation relation, we need to prove the conditions in Definition 3.5.

For $q_{\tau,\delta_0} = (x_{\tau,\delta_0}, t_{\tau,\delta_0}, p_{\tau,\delta_0})$ and $q_\tau = (x_\tau, t_\tau, p_\tau)$, we assume that $(q_{\tau,\delta_0}, q_\tau) \in R_\varepsilon$ holds. From the construction of the transition system $T(\Sigma_\tau)$, we have

$$t_\tau = k\tau \text{ for some } k \in \mathbb{N}. \tag{8}$$

By the definition (7) of the relation R_ε and Definition 5.1, we have

$$p_{\tau,\delta_0} = p_\tau, \tag{9}$$
$$t_{\tau,\delta_0} \in [t_\tau, t_\tau + \delta_0], \text{ and} \tag{10}$$
$$V(x_{\tau,\delta_0}, x_\tau) \leq \underline{\alpha}(\varepsilon). \tag{11}$$

By (4), we have

$$\underline{\alpha}(\|x_{\tau,\delta_0} - x_\tau\|) \leq V(x_{\tau,\delta_0}, x_\tau). \tag{12}$$

Then, by (11) and (12), we can say that $\underline{\alpha}(\|x_{\tau,\delta_0} - x_\tau\|) \leq \underline{\alpha}(\varepsilon)$. Thus, using the monotonicity of $\underline{\alpha}$, we have $\|x_{\tau,\delta_0} - x_\tau\| \leq \varepsilon$. By this equation with side conditions (8)–(10), we have $d(q_{\tau,\delta_0}, q_\tau) \leq \varepsilon$. This proves Condition 1.

Then, we will prove Condition 2. For q_{τ,δ_0} and q_τ, we additionally assume that $q_{\tau,\delta_0} \xrightarrow[\tau,\delta_0]{p_\tau} q'_{\tau,\delta_0} = (\mathbf{x}(t'_{\tau,\delta_0} - t_{\tau,\delta_0}, x_{\tau,\delta_0}, p_\tau), t'_{\tau,\delta_0}, p'_{\tau,\delta_0})$. Then, we define q'_τ by $q'_\tau = (\mathbf{x}(\tau, x_\tau, p_\tau), t'_\tau, p'_\tau)$ where

$$t'_\tau = (k+1)\tau, \text{ and}$$
$$p'_\tau = p'_{\tau,\delta_0}.$$

This definition of q'_τ guarantees $q_\tau \xrightarrow[\tau]{p_\tau} q'_\tau$. Now we show $(q'_{\tau,\delta_0}, q'_\tau) \in R_{g(\varepsilon)}$ for this q'_τ in the following manner.

$$
\begin{aligned}
&V'(q'_{\tau,\delta_0}, q'_\tau) \\
&= V(\mathbf{x}(t'_{\tau,\delta_0} - t_{\tau,\delta_0}, x_{\tau,\delta_0}, p_\tau), \mathbf{x}(\tau, x_\tau, p_\tau)) \\
&\le e^{-\kappa\tau} V(x_{\tau,\delta_0}, x_\tau) + \nu|t'_{\tau,\delta_0} - t_{\tau,\delta_0} - \tau| \\
&\le e^{-\kappa\tau} V(x_{\tau,\delta_0}, x_\tau) + \nu\delta_0 \\
&\le e^{-\kappa\tau} \underline{\alpha}(\varepsilon) + \nu\delta_0 \\
&= \underline{\alpha}(g(\varepsilon)).
\end{aligned}
$$

Thus we have $(q'_{\tau,\delta_0}, q'_\tau) \in R_{g(\varepsilon)}$ and this proves Condition 2.

Condition 3 can be proved in a similar way. It is easy to check that $T(\Sigma_{\tau,\delta_0}) \sim_\varepsilon T(\Sigma_\tau)$. □

6   Upper Bound of Skorokhod Metric

In Lemma 5.4, we constructed an approximate bisimulation that bound the cost d between the states by ε. Note that there is timing discrepancy between states we compare, and therefore this bound ε does not bound the pointwise error (the error in the continuous state space at the same time instant). Instead, what we obtain is actually an upper bound of the Skorokhod metric. The following definitions are taken from [7] and adapted to our setting.

First we define retiming functions.

Definition 6.1 (retiming). A function $\mathsf{r} : \mathbb{R}^+ \to \mathbb{R}^+$ is a *retiming* if it is order-preserving, bijective and continuous. The set of all retiming functions is denoted by Ret. The identity retiming is denoted by $\mathcal{I} \in$ Ret.

Then, we define the Skorokhod metric using the sup norm $\|\_\|_\infty$ on the set of retimings Ret.

Definition 6.2 (Skorokhod metric). Let r be a retiming, and $\pi, \pi' : \mathbb{R}^+ \to \mathbb{R}^n$ be two trajectories. Note that $\|\mathsf{r} - \mathcal{I}\|_\infty = \sup_{t\in\mathbb{R}^+} |\mathsf{r}(t) - t|$, and that $\|\pi \circ \mathsf{r} - \pi'\|_\infty = \sup_{t\in\mathbb{R}^+} \|\pi(\mathsf{r}(t)) - \pi'(t)\|$. Here, $\|\_\|$ on $\mathbb{R}^n$ is the usual Euclidean norm. The *Skorokhod distance* between the trajectories π and π' is defined by

$$
\mathcal{D}_\mathcal{S}(\pi, \pi') = \inf_{\mathsf{r}\in\mathsf{Ret}} \max\left(\|\mathsf{r} - \mathcal{I}\|_\infty, \|\pi \circ \mathsf{r} - \pi'\|_\infty\right).
$$

The transference of temporal specifications enables one of the most important applications of the Skorokhod metric—the application to conformance testing. In this paper, we do not refer the full transference theorem for temporal specifications in [7], since we only use the Skorokhod metric for reachability analysis, not complicated temporal properties. For reachability, the following obvious proposition is enough.

Proposition 6.3. *Let Σ and Σ' be switched systems. Assume that for every trajectory π of Σ, there exists a trajectory π' of Σ' such that $\mathcal{D}_S(\pi, \pi') \le \varepsilon$. Then, the reachable set of Σ is included in the ε-expansion $E_\varepsilon(S)$ of the reachable set S of Σ', where the ε-expansion $E_\varepsilon(S)$ is $\{x \in \mathbb{R}^n \mid \text{there exists } y \in S \text{ such that } \|x - y\| \le \varepsilon\}$.* $\qquad\square$

The following is our main theorem. It ensures that we can compute an over-approximation of the Skorokhod distance using the approximate bisimulation relation given in Lemma 5.4.

Theorem 6.4. *Assume the same assumptions as in Lemma 5.4. Let $\mathbf{p}_\tau$ be a τ-periodic switching signal, and $\mathbf{p}_{\tau, \delta_0}$ be the same signal but with delays within δ_0. That is, for each $s \in \mathbb{R}^+$,*

$$\mathbf{p}_{\tau, \delta_0}(s) = \begin{cases} \mathbf{p}_\tau(s) \text{ or } \mathbf{p}_\tau(s - \delta_0) & \text{if } s \in \bigcup_{k \in \mathbb{N}, k \ge 1}[k\tau, k\tau + \delta_0) \\ \mathbf{p}_\tau(s) & \text{otherwise.} \end{cases}$$

Given a state $x_0 \in \mathbb{R}^n$, we define two trajectories $\pi_{\tau, \delta_0, x_0}, \pi_{\tau, x_0} : \mathbb{R}^+ \to \mathbb{R}^n$ by

$$\pi_{\tau, \delta_0, x_0}(t) = \mathbf{x}(t, x_0, \mathbf{p}_{\tau, \delta_0}), \text{ and}$$
$$\pi_{\tau, x_0}(t) = \mathbf{x}(t, x_0, \mathbf{p}_\tau).$$

Then, we obtain an upper bound of the Skorokhod distance $\mathcal{D}_S(\pi_{\tau, \delta_0, x_0}, \pi_{\tau, x_0})$ by, for any $t \in \mathbb{R}^+$,

$$\mathcal{D}_S(\pi_{\tau, \delta_0, x_0}, \pi_{\tau, x_0}) \le \max\left(\delta_0, \underline{\alpha}^{-1}\left(\frac{\nu\delta_0}{\kappa\tau}\right), \underline{\alpha}^{-1}\left(\frac{\nu\delta_0}{1 - e^{-\kappa\tau}}\right)\right).$$

Proof. Note that $\mathbf{p}_\tau$ is a τ-periodic switching signal, and $\mathbf{p}_{\tau, \delta_0}$ is the same signal but with delays within δ_0. For $k \in \mathbb{N}$, the k-th switching of $\mathbf{p}_\tau$ occurs at $t = k\tau$. The k-th switching time of $\mathbf{p}_{\tau, \delta_0}$ is denoted by $\mathbf{st}_{\mathbf{p}_{\tau, \delta_0}}(k)$. We define a retiming r as follows: for every $k \in \mathbb{N}$ and $t \in [0, \tau)$,

$$\mathsf{r}(k\tau + t) = \frac{(\tau - t)\mathbf{st}_{\mathbf{p}_{\tau, \delta_0}}(k) + t\,\mathbf{st}_{\mathbf{p}_{\tau, \delta_0}}(k + 1)}{\tau}. \tag{13}$$

Intuitively, this retiming r adjust each switching time of the periodic signal to that with delays, and the interval between switchings are rescaled uniformly. It is easy to check that this r is order-preserving, bijective and continuous.

For this r, we have

$$\|\mathsf{r} - \mathcal{I}\|_\infty \le \delta_0. \tag{14}$$

Then, our next goal is to show that

$$\sup_{t \in \mathbb{R}^+} \|\pi_{\tau, \delta_0, x_0}(\mathsf{r}(t)) - \pi_{\tau, x_0}(t)\|$$

$$\le \max\left(\underline{\alpha}^{-1}\left(\frac{\nu\delta_0}{\kappa\tau}\right), \underline{\alpha}^{-1}\left(\frac{\nu\delta_0}{1 - e^{-\kappa\tau}}\right)\right). \tag{15}$$

Using the result of Lemma 5.4, we have, for all $k \in \mathbb{N}$,

$$\|\pi_{\tau,\delta_0,x_0}(\mathsf{r}(k\tau)) - \pi_{\tau,x_0}(k\tau)\| \leq \underline{\alpha}^{-1}\left(\frac{\nu\delta_0}{1 - e^{-\kappa\tau}}\right). \tag{16}$$

Note that $\mathsf{r}(k\tau) = \mathsf{st}_{\mathbf{p}_{\tau,\delta_0}}(k)$.

We can see from (13) that in $t \in [k\tau, (k+1)\tau]$, the application of r quickens or slows down time progress uniformly by multiplying $\frac{\mathsf{st}_{\mathbf{p}_{\tau,\delta_0}}(k+1) - \mathsf{st}_{\mathbf{p}_{\tau,\delta_0}}(k)}{\tau}$. In other words, in $t \in [k\tau, (k+1)\tau]$, $\frac{dr(t)}{dt} = \frac{\mathsf{st}_{\mathbf{p}_{\tau,\delta_0}}(k+1) - \mathsf{st}_{\mathbf{p}_{\tau,\delta_0}}(k)}{\tau}$.

This means that after the application of r, the trajectory $x = \pi_{\tau,\delta_0,x_0} \circ \mathsf{r}$ is according to

$$\dot{x} = (\pi_{\tau,\delta_0,x_0} \circ \mathsf{r})\dot{} = \frac{d\pi_{\tau,\delta_0,x_0}(\mathsf{r}(t))}{dr(t)}\frac{dr(t)}{dt}$$

$$= \frac{\mathsf{st}_{\mathbf{p}_{\tau,\delta_0}}(k+1) - \mathsf{st}_{\mathbf{p}_{\tau,\delta_0}}(k)}{\tau}f_p(x), \tag{17}$$

where p is the mode after k-th switching. By (5) and (17), we have

$$\frac{\partial V}{\partial x}(x,y)(\pi_{\tau,\delta_0,x_0} \circ \mathsf{r})\dot{} + \frac{\partial V}{\partial y}(x,y)f_p(y)$$

$$\leq -\kappa V(x,y) + \frac{\mathsf{st}_{\mathbf{p}_{\tau,\delta_0}}(k+1) - \mathsf{st}_{\mathbf{p}_{\tau,\delta_0}}(k) - \tau}{\tau}\frac{\partial V}{\partial x}(x,y)f_p(x).$$

Using $\mathsf{st}_{\mathbf{p}_{\tau,\delta_0}}(k) \in [k\tau, k\tau + \delta_0]$ and $\mathsf{st}_{\mathbf{p}_{\tau,\delta_0}}(k+1) \in [(k+1)\tau, (k+1)\tau + \delta_0]$, we have

$$\frac{\partial V}{\partial x}(x,y)(\pi_{\tau,\delta_0,x_0} \circ \mathsf{r})\dot{} + \frac{\partial V}{\partial y}(x,y)f_p(y)$$

$$\leq -\kappa V(x,y) + \frac{\delta_0}{\tau}\left|\frac{\partial V}{\partial x}(x,y)f_p(x)\right|.$$

Using Assumption 5.2, we can say that

$$\frac{\partial V}{\partial x}(x,y)(\pi_{\tau,\delta_0,x_0} \circ \mathsf{r})\dot{} + \frac{\partial V}{\partial y}(x,y)f_p(y) \leq -\kappa V(x,y) + \frac{\delta_0}{\tau}\nu.$$

We can see that the right hand side of this inequality is negative when $V(x,y) \geq \frac{\nu\delta_0}{\kappa\tau}$.

By combining this result with (16), we obtain (15) as desired. $\square$

7   Example

We demonstrate our framework using the example of the boost DC-DC converter from [4]. It is a common example of switched systems. For this example we have a common δ-GAS Lyapunov function V.

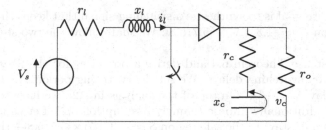

Fig. 4. The boost DC-DC converter circuit.

System Description. The system we consider is the boost DC-DC converter in Fig. 4, taken from [4]. Here we extend the analysis in [12]. The circuit includes a capacitor with capacitance x_c and an inductor with inductance x_l. The capacitor has the equivalent series resistance r_c, and the inductor has the internal resistance r_l. The input voltage is v_s, and the resistance r_o is the output load resistance. The state $x(t) = \begin{bmatrix} i_l(t) \\ v_c(t) \end{bmatrix}$ of this system consists of the inductor current i_l and the capacitor voltage v_c.

The dynamics of this system has two modes $\{ON, OFF\}^2$, depending on whether the switch in the circuit is on or off. By elementary circuit theory, the dynamics in each mode is modeled by

$$\dot{x}(t) = A_p x(t) + b \quad \text{for } p \in \{ON, OFF\} \ , \text{ where}$$

$$A_{ON} = \begin{bmatrix} -\frac{r_l}{x_l} & 0 \\ 0 & -\frac{1}{x_c(r_o+r_c)} \end{bmatrix}, \quad b = \begin{bmatrix} \frac{v_s}{x_l} \\ 0 \end{bmatrix} \text{ and}$$

$$A_{OFF} = \begin{bmatrix} -\frac{r_l r_o + r_l r_c + r_o r_c}{x_l(r_o+r_c)} & -\frac{r_l r_o + r_l r_c + r_o r_c}{x_l(r_o+r_c)} \\ \frac{r_o}{x_c(r_o+r_c)} & -\frac{1}{x_c(r_o+r_c)} \end{bmatrix} .$$

We use the parameter values from [4], that is, $x_c = 70$ p.u., $x_l = 3$ p.u., $r_c = 0.005$ p.u., $r_l = 0.05$ p.u., $r_o = 1$ p.u. and $v_s = 1$ p.u.

Analysis. Following [12], we rescale the second variable of the system and redefine the state $x(t) = \begin{bmatrix} i_l(t) \\ 5v_c(t) \end{bmatrix}$ for better numerical conditioning. The ODEs are updated accordingly.

[12] shows that the dynamics in each mode is δ-GAS, finding by SDP optimization a common δ-GAS Lyapunov function $V(x,y) = \sqrt{(x-y)^T M (x-y)}$ with $M = \begin{bmatrix} 1.0224 & 0.0084 \\ 0.0084 & 1.0031 \end{bmatrix}$, such that $\underline{\alpha}(s) = s, \overline{\alpha}(s) = 1.0127s$ and $\kappa = 0.014$. We use the same function V as an ingredient for our approximate bisimulation.

---

2 In the formalization of Sect. 2, the set P of modes is declared as $\{1, \cdots, m\}$. Here we instead use $P = \{ON, OFF\}$ for readability.

Our ultimate goal is to synthesize a switching signal that keeps the dynamics in a safe region $\mathcal{S} := [1.3, 1.7] \times [5.7, 5.8]$. We shall follow the two-step workflow in Fig. 1.

Let us first use Theorem 6.4 and derive a bound ε_1 for the Skorokhod distance caused by switching delays. We set the switching period $\tau = 0.5$ and the maximum delay $\delta_0 = \frac{\tau}{1000}$. On top of the analysis in [12], we have to verify the condition we additionally impose (namely Assumption 5.2). Let us now assume that the dynamics stays in the safe region $\mathcal{S} = [1.3, 1.7] \times [5.7, 5.8]$—this assumption will be eventually discharged when we synthesize a safety controller. Then it is not hard to see that $\nu = 0.33$ satisfies Assumption 5.2. By Theorem 6.4, we obtain that the Skorokhod distance between Σ_{τ,δ_0} (the boost DC-DC converter with delays) and Σ_τ (the one without delays) is bounded by $\varepsilon = 0.023655$, which is smaller than the pointwise error bound $\varepsilon = 0.0294176$ found in [14]. As suggested in Proposition 6.3, this bound can be used to reduce the reachability of the delayed system to that of its delay-free model.

We sketch how we can combine the above analysis with the controller synthesis in [9], in the way prescribed in Fig. 1. Our goal is to synthesize a safety controller for the system Σ_{τ,δ_0} with delays, for the safe set $[1.3, 1.7] \times [5.7, 5.8]$.

In [12] they use the same Lyapunov function as above to derive a discrete symbolic model T_τ^{symb} and establish an approximate bisimulation between $T(\Sigma_\tau)$ and the symbolic model. Their symbolic model T_τ^{symb} can be constructed so that any desired error bound ε_2 is guaranteed (a smaller ε_2 calls for a finer grid for discretization and hence a bigger symbolic model).

Now following the workflow in [9], we consider a shrunk safe region $[1.3 + (\varepsilon_1 + \varepsilon_2), 1.7 - (\varepsilon_1 + \varepsilon_2)] \times [5.7 + (\varepsilon_1 + \varepsilon_2), 5.8 - (\varepsilon_1 + \varepsilon_2)]$ for the symbolic model T_τ^{symb}. Then, we can employ an algorithm from supervisory control [20] and synthesize a set of safe switching signals that confine the dynamics of T_τ^{symb} to the shrunk safe region. This is the horizontal arrow at the bottom of Fig. 1. From the resulting controller, using [9, Theorem 1], we can construct a safety controller for the original system with delays, for the safe set $[1.3, 1.7] \times [5.7, 5.8]$. For a more detailed description of the resulting controllers, see [12, Figure 3].

8   Conclusion and Future Work

We have introduced an approximate bisimulation-based framework to analyze the effect of the time delays. Our framework constructs an approximate bisimulation relation between a delayed system and its delay-free model, which results in an upper bound of the Skorokhod distance. The construction of the approximate bisimulation relation uses Lyapunov functions for δ-GUAS. An example of a boost DC-DC converter has been analyzed successfully.

A possible direction of future work is to use the upper bound of the Skorokhod metric found by this framework to verification or controller synthesis for temporal logic specifications.

References

1. Abbas, H., Fainekos, G.E.: Towards composition of conformant systems. CoRR abs/1511.05273 (2015)
2. Abbas, H., Mittelmann, H.D., Fainekos, G.E.: Formal property verification in a conformance testing framework. In: Twelfth ACM/IEEE International Conference on Formal Methods and Models for Codesign, MEMOCODE 2014, Lausanne, Switzerland, 19–21 October 2014, pp. 155–164 (2014)
3. Angeli, D.: A Lyapunov approach to incremental stability properties. IEEE Trans. Autom. Control **47**(3), 410–421 (2002)
4. Beccuti, A.G., Papafotiou, G., Morari, M.: Optimal control of the boost dc-dc converter. In: Proceedings of the 44th IEEE Conference on Decision and Control, pp. 4457–4462, December 2005
5. Borri, A., Pola, G., Di Benedetto, M.D.: A symbolic approach to the design of nonlinear networked control systems. In: Proceedings of the 15th ACM International Conference on Hybrid Systems: Computation and Control, HSCC 2012, pp. 255–264. ACM, New York (2012)
6. Davoren, J.M.: Epsilon-tubes and generalized Skorokhod metrics for hybrid paths spaces. In: Majumdar, R., Tabuada, P. (eds.) HSCC 2009. LNCS, vol. 5469, pp. 135–149. Springer, Heidelberg (2009). https://doi.org/10.1007/978-3-642-00602-9_10
7. Deshmukh, J.V., Majumdar, R., Prabhu, V.S.: Quantifying conformance using the Skorokhod metric. In: Kroening, D., Păsăreanu, C.S. (eds.) CAV 2015. LNCS, vol. 9207, pp. 234–250. Springer, Cham (2015). https://doi.org/10.1007/978-3-319-21668-3_14
8. Frehse, G., et al.: SpaceEx: scalable verification of hybrid systems. In: Gopalakrishnan, G., Qadeer, S. (eds.) CAV 2011. LNCS, vol. 6806, pp. 379–395. Springer, Heidelberg (2011). https://doi.org/10.1007/978-3-642-22110-1_30
9. Girard, A.: Controller synthesis for safety and reachability via approximate bisimulation. Automatica **48**(5), 947–953 (2012)
10. Girard, A., Pappas, G.J.: Approximation metrics for discrete and continuous systems. IEEE Trans. Autom. Control **52**(5), 782–798 (2007)
11. Girard, A., Pappas, G.J.: Approximate bisimulation: a bridge between computer science and control theory. Eur. J. Control **17**(5–6), 568–578 (2011)
12. Girard, A., Pola, G., Tabuada, P.: Approximately bisimilar symbolic models for incrementally stable switched systems. IEEE Trans. Autom. Control **55**(1), 116–126 (2010)
13. Khatib, M.A., Girard, A., Dang, T.: Verification and synthesis of timing contracts for embedded controllers. In: Proceedings of the 19th International Conference on Hybrid Systems: Computation and Control, HSCC 2016, Vienna, Austria, 12–14 April 2016, pp. 115–124 (2016)
14. Kido, K., Sedwards, S., Hasuo, I.: Bounding Errors Due to Switching Delays in Incrementally Stable Switched Systems (Extended Version). ArXiv e-prints, December 2017
15. Kido, K.: Reachability analysis of hybrid systems via predicate and relational abstraction. Ph.D. thesis, The University of Tokyo (2018)
16. Majumdar, R., Prabhu, V.S.: Computing the Skorokhod distance between polygonal traces. In: Proceedings of the 18th International Conference on Hybrid Systems: Computation and Control, HSCC 2015, pp. 199–208. ACM, New York (2015)

17. Majumdar, R., Prabhu, V.S.: Computing distances between reach flowpipes. In: Proceedings of the 19th International Conference on Hybrid Systems: Computation and Control, HSCC 2016, pp. 267–276. ACM, New York (2016)
18. Pola, G., Girard, A., Tabuada, P.: Approximately bisimilar symbolic models for nonlinear control systems. Automatica **44**(10), 2508–2516 (2008)
19. Pola, G., Pepe, P., Benedetto, M.D.D.: Alternating approximately bisimilar symbolic models for nonlinear control systems with unknown time-varying delays. In: Proceedings of the 49th IEEE Conference on Decision and Control, CDC 2010, Atlanta, Georgia, USA, 15–17 December 2010, pp. 7649–7654 (2010)
20. Ramadge, P.J., Wonham, W.M.: Supervisory control of a class of discrete event processes. SIAM J. Control Optim. **25**(1), 206–230 (1987)
21. Zamani, M., Mazo Jr., M., Khaled, M., Abate, A.: Symbolic abstractions of networked control systems. IEEE Trans. Control Netw. Syst. **PP**(99), 1 (2017)

Formal Analysis of Robotic Cell Injection Systems Using Theorem Proving

Adnan Rashid[✉] and Osman Hasan

School of Electrical Engineering and Computer Science (SEECS),
National University of Sciences and Technology (NUST), Islamabad, Pakistan
{adnan.rashid,osman.hasan}@seecs.nust.edu.pk

Abstract. Cell injection is an approach used for the delivery of small sample substances into a biological cell and is widely used in drug development, gene injection, intracytoplasmic sperm injection (ICSI) and in-virto fertilization (IVF). Robotic cell injection systems provide the automation of the process as opposed to the manual and semi-automated cell injection systems, which require expert operators and involve time consuming processes and also have lower success rates. The automation of the cell injection process is achieved by controlling the injection force and planning the motion of the injection pipette. Traditionally, these systems are analyzed using paper-and-pencil proof and computer simulation methods. However, the former is human-error prone and the later is based on the numerical algorithms, where the approximation of the mathematical expressions introduces inaccuracies in the analysis. Formal methods can overcome these limitations and thus provide an accurate analysis of the cell injection systems. Model checking, i.e., a state-based formal method, has been recently proposed for the analysis of these systems. However, it involves the discretization of the differential equations that are used for modeling the dynamics of the system and thus compromises on the completeness of the analysis of these safety-critical systems. In this paper, we propose to use higher-order-logic theorem proving, a deductive-reasoning based formal method, for the modeling and analysis of the dynamical behaviour of the robotic cell injection systems. The proposed analysis, based on the HOL Light theorem prover, enabled us to identify some discrepancies in the simulation and model checking based analysis of the same robotic cell injection system.

Keywords: Robotic cell injection system · Higher-order logic · Theorem proving

1 Introduction

Biological cell injection is a method used for the insertion of small amount of substances, i.e., bio-molecules, sperms, genes and proteins, into the suspended or adherent cells. It is widely used in gene injection [19], drug development [21], intracytoplasmic sperm injection (ISCI) [27] and in-vitro fertilization (IVF) [26].

© Springer Nature Switzerland AG 2019
R. Chamberlain et al. (Eds.): CyPhy 2017, LNCS 11267, pp. 127–141, 2019.
https://doi.org/10.1007/978-3-030-17910-6_10

For example, in IVF, the sperm is injected into matured eggs for the treatment of infertility. Similarly, drug development involves the injection of drugs into a cell and the observation of its implication at the cellular level.

Robotic cell injection systems can automatically perform the task of cell injection as opposed to the traditionally adopted manual and semi-automated injection procedures, which require trained operators and time-consuming processes and also have lower success rates. The most important factor in a robotic cell injection system is the injection force [18] as a slight excessive force may damage the membrane of the cell [17] or an insufficient force may not be able to pierce the cell [10]. Moreover, these robotic systems consist of an injection manipulator, digital cameras, sensors and microscope optics [18] and thus the accuracy of the orientation and movement of these fundamental components is vital for the reliability of the overall system. Thus, the robotic cell injection system designs need to be analyzed and verified quite carefully to ensure that these requirements are exhibited by the final systems.

The first step in the analysis of a robotic cell injection system is to model the coordinate frames corresponding to the orientations of its various components, i.e, the injection manipulator, cameras and images. This model allows us to capture the movement and thus the positions of these components during the process of cell injection. Moreover, the relationship between these coordinates provides the relative positions of these components, which is quite vital for a successful cell injection procedure. Next, in order to perform the process of injection, the motion planning of the injection pipette is modeled using some force control algorithms, such as the contact-space-impedance force control [18,25] and the image-based torque controller [17]. These controllers capture the overall dynamics of the system and are mainly responsible for the smooth functionality of the system during the process of cell injection.

Traditionally, the robotic cell injection systems have been analyzed using paper-and-pencil techniques. However, these manual analysis methods are prone to human error and also are not scalable for analyzing complex models like the robotic cell injection systems. Moreover, in some cases, all the required assumptions are not documented in the mathematical analysis, which may lead to erroneous design and analysis. Similarly, the computer simulations and the numerical methods have been used for the analysis of these systems. However, due to the continuous nature of the analysis and the limited amount of computer memory and the computational resources, the system is analyzed for a certain number of test cases only and thus the absolute accuracy cannot be achieved. Computer algebra systems, such as Mathematica [20], have also been used for analyzing these systems [22]. However, the symbolic algorithms residing in the core of these systems are unverified [9], which puts a question mark on the accuracy of these analyses. Due to the safety-critical nature of robotic cell injection systems, the above-mentioned traditional techniques cannot be relied upon as they are either error prone or incomplete, which may lead to an undetected error in the analysis that may in turn lead to disastrous consequences.

Formal methods [16] are computer-based mathematical analysis techniques that can overcome the above-mentioned inaccuracies. Primarily, these techniques involve the development of a mathematical model of a system and verification of its properties using computer-based mathematical reasoning. Sardar et al. [24] recently used probabilistic modeling checking [7], i.e., a state-based formal method, to formally analyze the robotic cell injection systems. However, their methodology involves the discretization of the differential equations that model the dynamics of these systems, which compromises the accuracy of the corresponding analysis. Moreover, the analysis also suffers from the inherent state-space explosion problem [8]. Higher-order-logic theorem proving [13] is an interactive verification technique that can overcome these limitations. It primarily involves the mathematical modeling of the system based on higher-order logic and verification of its properties based on deductive reasoning. Given the high expressiveness of higher-order logic, it can truly capture the behavior of the differential equations, which is not possible in model checking based analysis.

In this paper, we propose to use the higher-order-logic theorem proving to formally analyze the robotic cell injection systems [17] using the HOL Light theorem prover [12]. The main motivation for the selection of HOL Light is the availability of reasoning support for real calculus [5], multivariate calculus [3], vectors [6] and matrices [6], which are some of the foremost requirements for formally analyzing robotic cell injection systems. The major contributions of the paper are:

- *Formalization of the cell injection system*, which includes the formal modeling of camera, stage and image coordinates and formal verification of their interrelationships in higher-order logic. It also includes the formal modeling of their dynamical behaviour (dynamics of two degrees of freedom (DOF) motion stage) using a system of differential equations and the formal verification of their solutions.
- *Formalization of the motion planning of the injection pipette*, which includes the formal modeling of the contact-space-impedance force control and the image-based torque controller and formal verification of their interrelationship.
- *Identification of the discrepancies in the simulation and model checking based analysis of these systems*, i.e., the mathematical expression representing the image-based torque controller used in both simulation and model checking based analysis of the same system was found to be wrong based on the reported formalization in this paper.

The rest of the paper is organized as follows: Sect. 2 provides an introduction about the HOL Light theorem prover, multivariate calculus theories of HOL Light and the robotic cell injection system. Section 3 presents the formalization of robotic cell injection system. We present the formalization of motion planning of the injection pipette in Sect. 4. This also includes the identification of the discrepancies in the simulation and model checking based analysis of the same system. Finally, Sect. 5 concludes the paper.

2   Preliminaries

This section presents an introduction to the HOL Light theorem prover, multivariate calculus theories of HOL Light and the robotic cell injection system.

2.1   HOL Light Theorem Prover

HOL Light [12] is a theorem proving environment that belongs to the family of HOL theorem provers. It is implemented in the meta language (ML) [23], which is a functional programming language and is widely used for the construction of the mathematical proofs in the form of theories. A theory in HOL Light consists of types, constants, definitions, axioms and theorems. The HOL Light theories are ordered in a hierarchical fashion and the child theories can inherit the types, definitions and theorems of the parent theories. Every new theorem has to be verified based on the primitive inference rules and basic axioms or already verified theorems present in HOL Light, which ensures the soundness of this technique. HOL Light provides an extensive support for the analysis based on Boolean algebra [2], real arithmetics [4], multivariable calculus [14] and vectors [6]. There are many automatic proof procedures [15], available in HOL Light, which are very useful in verifying the mathematical results automatically.

2.2   Multivariable Calculus Theories in HOL Light

A $\mathbb{N}$-dimensional vector is represented as a $\mathbb{R}^{\mathbb{N}}$ column matrix with each of its element as a real number in HOL Light [14]. All of the vector operations are thus performed using matrix manipulations. Similarly, all of the multivariable calculus theorems are verified in HOL Light for functions with an arbitrary data-type $\mathbb{R}^{\mathbb{N}} \to \mathbb{R}^{\mathbb{M}}$.

Some of the frequently used HOL Light functions in the reported formalization are explained below:

Definition 1. Vector
⊢ ∀ l. vector l = (lambda i. EL (i - 1) l)

The function `vector` accepts a list `l : α list` and returns a vector having each component of data-type α. It utilizes the function `EL m L`, which returns the mth element of a list L. Here, the `lambda` operator in HOL is used to construct a vector based on its components [14].

Definition 2. Real Cosine and Real Sine Functions
⊢ ∀ x. cos x = Re (ccos (Cx x))
⊢ ∀ x. sin x = Re (csin (Cx x))

The real cosine and real sine are represented as $\cos : \mathbb{R} \to \mathbb{R}$ and $\sin : \mathbb{R} \to \mathbb{R}$ in HOL Light [11], respectively. These functions are formally defined using the complex cosine $ccos: \mathbb{R}^2 \to \mathbb{R}^2$ and complex sine $csin: \mathbb{R}^2 \to \mathbb{R}^2$ functions, respectively.

> **Definition 3.** Real Derivative
> ⊢ ∀ f x. real_derivative f x =
>   (@f'. (f has_real_derivative f') (atreal x))

The function `real_derivative` accepts a function f : ℝ → ℝ and a real number x, which is the point at which f has to be differentiated, and returns a variable of data-type ℝ, which represents the differential of f at x. The function `has_real_derivative` defines the same relationship in the relational form.

We build upon the above-mentioned fundamental functions of multivariable calculus to formally analyze the robotic cell injection system in Sects. 3 and 4 of the paper.

2.3   Robotic Cell Injection Systems

A robotic cell injection system mainly comprises of three modules, namely executive, sensory and control modules as depicted in Fig. 1. The executive module consists of positioning table, working plate and the injection manipulator. The cells that need to be injected are placed on a working plate, which is mounted on a positioning table ($XY\theta$-axis) and the injection manipulator is mounted on Z-axis as shown in Fig. 1.

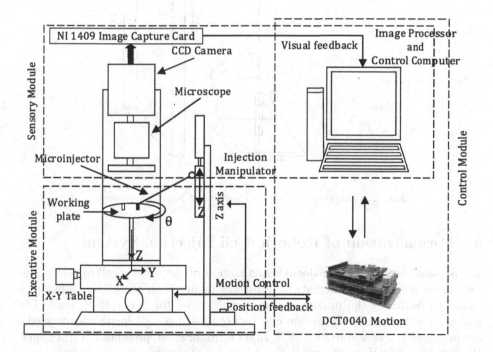

Fig. 1. Robotic cell injection systems

The sensory module comprises of a vision system that has four parts, namely optical microscope, charged coupled device (CCD) camera, peripheral component interconnect (PCI) image capture and a processing card. The CCD camera is used to capture the cell injection process using a PCI image capture. The control module contains a host computer and a DCT0040 motion control system. Figure 2 depicts the configuration of a robotic cell injection system. The axis $o - xyz$ represents the stage (table and working plate) coordinate frame, where o is the origin of these coordinates representing the center of the working plate and z is along the optical axis of the microscope. Similarly, $o_c - x_c y_c z_c$ is the camera coordinate frame with o_c representing the center of the microscope. The coordinate frame in image plane is represented as $o_i - uv$, where o_i is the origin and the axis uv is perpendicular to the optical axis.

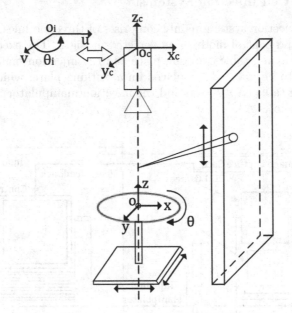

Fig. 2. Configuration of the robotic cell injection systems

3   Formalization of Robotic Cell Injection System

We present the higher-order-logic formalization of the robotic cell injection system using standard mathematical notations rather than the HOL Light notations, to facilitate the understanding of the paper for a non-HOL user. The source code for our formalization can be obtained from [1] for the readers who are interested to view the exact HOL Light formalization, presented in this paper. We consider 2-DOF to represent the dynamics of the robotic cell injection system. The camera, stage and image coordinates are two-dimensional coordinates, which are modeled as follows in HOL Light:

Definition 4. Two-dimensional Coordinates

$$\vdash \forall\ \texttt{x}\ \texttt{y}\ \texttt{t.}\ \texttt{twod\_coord}\ \texttt{x}\ \texttt{y}\ \texttt{t} = \begin{bmatrix} \texttt{x(t)} \\ \texttt{y(t)} \end{bmatrix}$$

---

where x and y with data-type $\mathbb{R} \to \mathbb{R}$ representing the respective axes and t is a variable representing the time.

Next, we model the rotation matrix from the stage coordinate frame ($o - xyz$) to the camera coordinate frame ($o_c - x_c y_c z_c$), and the two-dimensional displacement vector between the origins of both these frames:

Definition 5. Rotation Matrix and Displacement Vector

$$\vdash \forall\ \texttt{alpha.}\ \texttt{rot\_mat}\ \texttt{alpha} = \begin{bmatrix} \texttt{cos (alpha)} & \texttt{sin (alpha)} \\ \texttt{-sin (alpha)} & \texttt{cos (alpha)} \end{bmatrix}$$

$$\vdash \forall\ \texttt{dx}\ \texttt{dy.}\ \texttt{disp\_vec}\ \texttt{dx}\ \texttt{dy} = \begin{bmatrix} \texttt{dx} \\ \texttt{dy} \end{bmatrix}$$

The verification of the relationship between stage, camera and image coordinates provides key information for the reliable operation of the cell injection system by ensuring the accuracy of the orientation and movement of its various components, i.e., stage frame, microscope, camera and injection manipulator. Firstly, we verify the relationship between camera and stage coordinates as:

Theorem 1. Relationship Between Camera and Stage Coordinates

$\vdash \forall\ \texttt{xc}\ \texttt{yc}\ \texttt{x}\ \texttt{y}\ \texttt{alpha}\ \texttt{dx}\ \texttt{dy}\ \texttt{t.}$
    [A1]: $0 < \texttt{dx}\ \wedge$
    [A2]: $0 < \texttt{dy}$

$$\Rightarrow \Big(\texttt{rel\_cam\_sta\_coord}\ \texttt{xc}\ \texttt{yc}\ \texttt{x}\ \texttt{y}\ \texttt{alpha}\ \texttt{dx}\ \texttt{dy}\ \texttt{t} \Leftrightarrow$$

$$\begin{bmatrix} \texttt{xc(t)} \\ \texttt{yc(t)} \end{bmatrix} = \begin{bmatrix} \texttt{x(t) * cos (alpha) + y(t) * sin (alpha) + dx} \\ \texttt{- x(t) * sin (alpha) + y(t) * cos (alpha) + dy} \end{bmatrix} \Big)$$

---

where the HOL Light function `rel_cam_sta_coord` models the relationship between camera and stage coordinates. The two assumptions of the above theorem provide the design constraints for the relationship. The above theorem is verified using the properties of vectors and matrices alongside some real arithmetic reasoning. Next, to verify the relationship between image and camera coordinates, we first model the display resolution matrix as the following HOL Light function:

Definition 6. Display Resolution Matrix

$$\vdash \forall\ \texttt{fx}\ \texttt{fy.}\ \texttt{disp\_res\_mat}\ \texttt{fx}\ \texttt{fy} = \begin{bmatrix} \texttt{fx} & \texttt{0} \\ \texttt{0} & \texttt{fy} \end{bmatrix}$$

Now the image-camera coordinate frame interrelationship is verified as:

Theorem 2. Relationship Between Image and Camera Coordinates
⊢ ∀ xc yc u v t fx fy.
   [A1]: 0 < fx ∧
   [A2]: 0 < fy

$$\Rightarrow \left(\texttt{rel\_ima\_cam\_coord xc yc u v t fx fy} \Leftrightarrow \right.$$

$$\left. \begin{bmatrix} \texttt{u(t)} \\ \texttt{v(t)} \end{bmatrix} = \begin{bmatrix} \texttt{fx * xc(t)} \\ \texttt{fy * yc(t)} \end{bmatrix} \right)$$

---

where the HOL Light function `rel_ima_cam_coord` models the relationship between the image and the camera coordinates. The two assumptions of Theorem 2 provide the design constraints for the relationship. Next, we model the transformation matrix between image and stage coordinate frames, which is used in the verification of their interrelationship and is given as follows:

Definition 7. Transformation Matrix
⊢ ∀ fx fy alpha. transf_mat fx fy alpha =

$$\begin{bmatrix} \texttt{fx * cos (alpha)} & \texttt{fx * sin (alpha)} \\ \texttt{-fy * sin (alpha)} & \texttt{fy * cos (alpha)} \end{bmatrix}$$

Now, we verify an important relationship between the image and stage coordinates as the following HOL Light theorem:

Theorem 3. Relationship Between Image and Stage Coordinates
⊢ ∀ x y u v t fx fy dx dy alpha xc yc.
   [A1]: 0 < dx ∧
   [A2]: 0 < dy ∧
   [A3]: 0 < fx ∧
   [A4]: 0 < fy ∧
   [A5]: twod_coord u v t = disp_res_mat fx fy **
                           twod_coord xc yc t ∧
   [A6]: twod_coord xc yc t = rot_mat alpha **
                twod_coord x y t + disp_vec dx dy
  ⇒ twod_coord u v t = transf_mat fx fy alpha **

$$\texttt{twod\_coord x y t} + \begin{bmatrix} \texttt{fx * dx} \\ \texttt{fy * dy} \end{bmatrix}$$

---

where ** represents the matrix-vector multiplication. The first four assumptions (A1–A4) model the design constraints for the relationship between image and stage coordinates. The next assumption (A5) presents the relationship between image and camera coordinates. The last assumption (A6) presents the relationship between camera and stage coordinates. The verification of Theorem 3 is mainly based on Theorems 1 and 2, and some classical properties of the vectors and matrices. The verification of these relationships raise our confidence about the orientation of the vital components of a cell injection system, i.e., injection manipulator, working plate, camera and microscope.

Next, we model and verify the dynamics of the cell injection system. The dynamics of the 2-DOF motion stage, based on Lagrange's equation, is mathematically expressed as:

$$
\begin{bmatrix} m_x + m_y + m_p & 0 \\ 0 & m_y + m_p \end{bmatrix} \begin{bmatrix} \dfrac{d^2x}{dt} \\ \dfrac{d^2y}{dt} \end{bmatrix} + \begin{bmatrix} 1 & 0 \\ 0 & 1 \end{bmatrix} \begin{bmatrix} \dfrac{dx}{dt} \\ \dfrac{dy}{dt} \end{bmatrix} = \begin{bmatrix} \tau_x \\ \tau_y \end{bmatrix} - \begin{bmatrix} fex^d \\ fey^d \end{bmatrix} \tag{1}
$$

where m_x, m_y and m_p are the masses of the xy positioning tables and working plate, respectively. Similarly, τ_x and τ_y represent the components of the input torque to the driving motor. Similarly, fex^d and fey^d represent the components of the desired force applied to the actuators during the process of the cell injection. We formalize Eq. (1) as the following HOL Light function:

Definition 8. Dynamics of the 2-DOF Motion Stage

⊢ ∀ mx my mp x y t taux tauy fexd feyd.
    dyn_2_dof_mot_sta mx my mp x y t taux tauy fexd feyd ⇔
    mass_mat mx my mp ** sec_ord_der_sta_coord x y t +
        pos_tab_mat ** fir_ord_der_sta_coord x y t =
            tor_vec taux tauy - des_force_vec fexd feyd

---

where mass_mat is the matrix containing the respective masses and pos_tab_mat is the diagonal matrix. Similarly, tor_vec and des_force_vec are the vectors with their elements representing the components of the applied torque and desired force. The HOL Light functions fir_ord_der_sta_coord and sec_ord_der_sta_coord model the vectors having first-order and second-order derivatives of the stage coordinates:

Definition 9. First and Second-order Derivative Vectors

⊢ ∀ x y t. fir_ord_der_sta_coord x y t = deriv_vec_fir [x; y] t
⊢ ∀ x y t. sec_ord_der_sta_coord x y t = deriv_vec_sec [x; y] t

---

where deriv_vec_fir and deriv_vec_sec accept a list containing the functions of data-type $\mathbb{R} \to \mathbb{R}$ and return the corresponding first and second-order derivative vectors [1].

If the applied torque and force vectors are zero, then the injection pipette does not touch the cells. Thus, Eq. (1) can be transformed for this particular scenario as follows:

$$
\begin{bmatrix} m_x + m_y + m_p & 0 \\ 0 & m_y + m_p \end{bmatrix} \begin{bmatrix} \dfrac{d^2x}{dt} \\ \dfrac{d^2y}{dt} \end{bmatrix} + \begin{bmatrix} 1 & 0 \\ 0 & 1 \end{bmatrix} \begin{bmatrix} \dfrac{dx}{dt} \\ \dfrac{dy}{dt} \end{bmatrix} = \begin{bmatrix} 0 \\ 0 \end{bmatrix} \tag{2}
$$

We verify the solution of the above equation as the following HOL Light theorem:

Theorem 4. Verification of Solution of Dynamical Behaviour of Motion Stage

⊢ ∀ x y mx my mp taux tauy fexd feyd alpha x0 y0 xd0 yd0.

[A1]: 0 < mx ∧ [A2]: 0 < my ∧ [A3]: 0 < mp ∧

[A4]: x(0) = x0 ∧ [A5]: y(0) = y0 ∧

[A6]: $\dfrac{dx}{dt}$(0)= xd0 ∧ [A7]: $\dfrac{dy}{dt}$(0)= yd0 ∧

[A8]: $\begin{bmatrix} \text{taux} \\ \text{tauy} \end{bmatrix} = \begin{bmatrix} 0 \\ 0 \end{bmatrix}$ ∧

[A9]: $\begin{bmatrix} \text{fexd} \\ \text{feyd} \end{bmatrix} = \begin{bmatrix} 0 \\ 0 \end{bmatrix}$ ∧

[A10]: (∀ t. x(t) = (x0 + xd0 * (mx + my + mp))

$$- \text{xd0} * (\text{mx} + \text{my} + \text{mp}) * e^{\frac{-1}{\text{mx+my+mp}}t} \wedge$$

[A11]: (∀ t. y(t) = (y0 + yd0 * (my + mp))

$$- \text{yd0} * (\text{my} + \text{mp}) * e^{\frac{-1}{\text{my+mp}}t}$$

⇒ dyn_2_dof_mot_sta mx my mp x y t taux tauy fexd feyd

The first three assumptions (A1–A3) model the condition that all the masses, i.e., mx, my and mp are positive. The next four assumptions (A4–A7) present the values of coordinates x and y and their first-order derivatives $\frac{dx}{dt}$ and $\frac{dy}{dt}$ at $t = 0$. The next two assumptions (A8–A9) model the condition that the torque and force vectors are zero. The next two assumptions (A10–A11) provide the values of xy coordinates at any time t. Finally, the conclusion presents the dynamics of the 2-DOF motion stage. The proof-process of Theorem 4 involves the properties of real derivatives, transcendental functions, matrices and vectors alongwith some real arithmetic reasoning. Next, we verify an alternate form of the relationship between the image and stage coordinates, which depends on the dynamics of the motion stage (Definition 8) and is a vital property for the analysis of cell injection systems. For this purpose, we first model the positioning table matrix and inertia matrix:

Definition 10. Positioning Table and Inertia Matrices

⊢ ∀ fx fy alpha.

    pos_tab_mat_fin fx fy alpha =

        pos_tab_mat ** matrix_inv (transf_mat fx fy alpha)

⊢ ∀ mx my mp fx fy alpha.

    iner_mat mx my mp fx fy alpha =

     mass_mat mx my mp ** matrix_inv (transf_mat fx fy alpha)

---

where the HOL Light function `matrix_inv` accepts a matrix $A : \mathbb{R}^{MN}$ and returns its inverse. Now, the alternate representation of the image-stage coordinate frame interrelationship is verified as the following HOL Light theorem:

Theorem 5. Alternate Form of Relationship Between Image and Stage Coordinates

⊢ ∀ xc yc u v x y fx fy dx dy mx my mp taux tauy fexd feyd alpha.
    [A1]: 0 < dx ∧ [A2]: 0 < dy ∧
    [A3]: 0 < fx ∧ [A4]: 0 < fy ∧
    [A5]: invertible (transf_mat fx fy alpha) ∧
    [A6]: (∀ t. u real_differentiable atreal t) ∧
    [A7]: (∀ t. v real_differentiable atreal t) ∧
    [A8]: (∀ t. $\frac{du}{dt}$ real_differentiable atreal t) ∧
    [A9]: (∀ t. $\frac{dv}{dt}$ real_differentiable atreal t) ∧
    [A10]: (∀ t. rel_ima_cam_coord xc yc u v t fx fy) ∧
    [A11]: (∀ t. rel_cam_sta_coord xc yc x y alpha dx dy t) ∧
    [A12]: dyn_2_dof_mot_sta mx my mp x y t taux tauy fexd feyd
      ⇒ iner_mat mx my mp fx fy alpha **
                sec_ord_der_ima_coord u v t +
      pos_tab_mat_fin fx fy alpha **
                fir_ord_der_ima_coord u v t =
           tor_vec taux tauy - des_force_vec fexd feyd

The first four assumptions (A1–A4) describe the design constraints for the image-stage interrelationship. The next assumption (A5) ensures that the transformation matrix (`transf_mat`, Definition 7) is invertible, i.e., its inverse exists. The next four assumptions (A6–A9) model the differentiability condition for the image coordinates and their first-order derivatives. The next two assumptions (A10–A11) provide the image-camera and camera-stage coordinate frames interrelationships. The last assumption (A12) represents the dynamics of the 2-DOF motion stage. Finally, the conclusion of Theorem 5 is the alternate representation of the image-stage coordinate frame interrelationship. The verification of Theorem 5 is based on the properties of the real derivative, matrices and vectors alongwith some real arithmetic reasoning.

4 Formalization of the Motion Planning of the Injection Pipette

The injection motion controller is another vital part of the cell injection systems and its verification is necessary for a reliable system. It mainly includes the control of the applied injection force and the torque applied to the deriving motor. So, we formalize the force and torque controls and formally verify the implication relationship between both of these controllers. The impendence force control for a cell injection system is represented as follows:

$$m\ddot{e} + b\dot{e} + ke = f_e \tag{3}$$

where m, b and k represent the desired impendence parameters. Similarly, f_e is the two-dimensional vector having f_{ex} and f_{ey} as its elements, which represent the x and y components of the applied force. Moreover, e, $\dot{e}$ and $\ddot{e}$ are the vectors representing the position errors of the xy stage coordinates, their first-order and second-order derivatives, respectively, and are mathematically expressed as:

$$e = \begin{bmatrix} x_d \\ y_d \end{bmatrix} - \begin{bmatrix} x \\ y \end{bmatrix}, \ \dot{e} = \begin{bmatrix} \dfrac{dx_d}{dt} \\ \dfrac{dy_d}{dt} \end{bmatrix} - \begin{bmatrix} \dfrac{dx}{dt} \\ \dfrac{dy}{dt} \end{bmatrix}, \ \ddot{e} = \begin{bmatrix} \dfrac{d^2 x_d}{dt} \\ \dfrac{d^2 y_d}{dt} \end{bmatrix} - \begin{bmatrix} \dfrac{d^2 x}{dt} \\ \dfrac{d^2 y}{dt} \end{bmatrix} \tag{4}$$

where x and y are the actual axes and x_d and y_d are the desired axes of the stage coordinate frame. Now, the image-based torque controller for the xy stage coordinates is mathematically expressed as:

$$\begin{bmatrix} \tau_x \\ \tau_y \end{bmatrix} = \begin{bmatrix} m_x + m_y + m_p & 0 \\ 0 & m_y + m_p \end{bmatrix} \begin{bmatrix} f_x \cos\alpha & f_x \sin\alpha \\ -f_y \sin\alpha & f_y \cos\alpha \end{bmatrix} \begin{bmatrix} \dfrac{d^2 x_d}{dt} \\ \dfrac{d^2 y_d}{dt} \end{bmatrix} +$$

$$\begin{bmatrix} m_x + m_y + m_p & 0 \\ 0 & m_y + m_p \end{bmatrix} \begin{bmatrix} f_x \cos\alpha & f_x \sin\alpha \\ -f_y \sin\alpha & f_y \cos\alpha \end{bmatrix}$$

$$m^{-1}(b\dot{e} + ke - f_e) + \left(\begin{bmatrix} 1 & 0 \\ 0 & 1 \end{bmatrix} \begin{bmatrix} f_x \cos\alpha & f_x \sin\alpha \\ -f_y \sin\alpha & f_y \cos\alpha \end{bmatrix}^{-1} \right) \tag{5}$$

$$\begin{bmatrix} f_x \cos\alpha & f_x \sin\alpha \\ -f_y \sin\alpha & f_y \cos\alpha \end{bmatrix} \begin{bmatrix} \dfrac{dx}{dt} \\ \dfrac{dy}{dt} \end{bmatrix} + \begin{bmatrix} fex^d \\ fey^d \end{bmatrix}$$

Equation (5) can be alternatively written as:

$$\vec{\tau} = MT \begin{bmatrix} \dfrac{d^2 x_d}{dt} \\ \dfrac{d^2 y_d}{dt} \end{bmatrix} + MTm^{-1}(b\dot{e} + ke - f_e) + NT \begin{bmatrix} \dfrac{dx}{dt} \\ \dfrac{dy}{dt} \end{bmatrix} + \vec{f_{ed}} \tag{6}$$

where M, N and T in the above equation denote the inertia, positioning table and transformation matrices. The above equation was wrongly presented in simulations [17] and model checking [24] based analysis as follows:

$$\vec{\tau} = M \begin{bmatrix} \dfrac{d^2x_d}{dt} \\ \dfrac{d^2y_d}{dt} \end{bmatrix} + Mm^{-1}(b\dot{e} + ke - f_e) + N \begin{bmatrix} \dfrac{dx}{dt} \\ \dfrac{dy}{dt} \end{bmatrix} + \overrightarrow{f_{ed}} \qquad (7)$$

$$\vec{\tau} = MT \begin{bmatrix} \dfrac{d^2x_d}{dt} \\ \dfrac{d^2y_d}{dt} \end{bmatrix} + MTm^{-1}(b\dot{e} + ke - f_e) + NT \begin{bmatrix} \dfrac{dx}{dt} \\ \dfrac{dy}{dt} \end{bmatrix} + \overrightarrow{f_e} \qquad (8)$$

In Eq. (7) (used in the simulations based analysis [17]), the transformation matrix (T) is missing, which includes the amount of applied force and the angles at which the injection pipette is pierced into the cell and its absence can lead to disastrous consequences, i.e., excess substance injection, damaging cell tissues etc. Similarly, in Eq. (8) (used in the model checking based analysis [24]), f_{ed} is wrongly interpreted as f_e, i.e., the desired force, is taken equal to the applied force, which can never happen in a real-world system. We caught these wrong interpretations of Eq. (6) in the simulations and model checking based analyses during the verification of the implication relationship between force control and torque controller. We first started the verification of this relationship using Eq. (7) and ended up with the identification of this issue. Next, we took Eq. (8) and again, during its verification, identified its wrong interpretation, which enabled us to obtain its right interpretation as given in Eq. (6). We verified the image-based torque controller (Eq. (6)) as the following HOL Light theorem:

Theorem 6. Verification of the Implication Relationship Between Force Control and Torque Controller
⊢ ∀ xd yd x y t mx my mp fx fy
           alpha taux tauy fex fey fexd feyd m b k.
  [A1]: 0 < m ∧
  [A2]: 0 < k ∧
  [A3]: 0 < b ∧
  [A4]: invertible (transf_mat fx fy alpha) ∧
  [A5]: force_cont xd yd x y t m b k fex fey ∧
  [A6]: dyn_2_dof_mot_sta mx my mp x y t taux tauy fexd feyd
    ⇒ torque_cont xd yd x y t mx my mp fx fy
           alpha taux tauy fex fey fexd feyd m b k

The first three assumptions (A1–A3) ensure that the desired impendence parameters are positive. The next assumption (A4) provides the condition that the transformation matrix (**transf_mat**) is invertible. The next assumption (A5) models the impendence force control (Eq. (3)). The last assumption (A6) presents the dynamics of the 2-DOF motion stage. Finally, the conclusion represents the image-based torque controller (Eq. (5)). The verification of Theorem 6 is mainly based on the properties of real derivative, vector and matrices.

Due to the undecidable nature of the higher-order logic, the verification results presented in Sects. 3 and 4, involved manual interventions and human guidance. However, we developed some tactics to automate the verification process. For example, we developed a tactic VEC_MAT_SIMP_TAC, which simplifies the matrix and vector arithmetics involved in the formal analysis of the robotic cell injection system. Thus, the proof effort involved only 745 lines-of-code and 17 man-hours. The details about these tactics and rest of the formalization can be found in our proof script [1]. The distinguishing feature of our formal analysis is that all the verified theorems are universally quantified and can thus be specialized to the required values based on the requirement of the analysis of the cell injection systems. Moreover, our approach allows us to model the dynamics of the cell injection systems involving differential and derivative (Eqs. (1), (3), (5)) in their true form, whereas, in their model checking based analysis [24], they are discretized and modeled using a state-transition system, which may compromise the accuracy and completeness of the corresponding analysis.

5   Conclusion

In this paper, we presented a formal analysis of robotic cell injection systems. We first formalize the stage, camera and image coordinate frames, which are the main components of a robotic cell injection system, and formally verified their interrelationship using the HOL Light theorem prover. We also formalized the dynamics of the 2-DOF motion stage based on differential equations and verified their solutions in HOL Light. Finally, we formalized the impedance force control and image-based torque controller and verified their implication relationship. Our formalization helped us to identify some key discrepancies in the simulation-based and model checking based analysis of these systems, which shows the usefulness of using higher-order-logic theorem proving in the formal analysis of critical systems.

References

1. Formal Analysis of Robotic Cell Injection Systems using Theorem Proving (2018). http://save.seecs.nust.edu.pk/projects/farcistp/
2. HOL Light Boolean Algebra (2018). https://github.com/jrh13/hol-light/blob/master/bool.ml
3. HOL Light Multivariate Calculus (2018). https://github.com/jrh13/hol-light/blob/master/Multivariate
4. HOL Light Real Arithmetic (2018). https://github.com/jrh13/hol-light/blob/master/real.ml
5. HOL Light Real Calculus (2018). https://github.com/jrh13/hol-light/blob/master/Multivariate/realanalysis.ml
6. HOL Light Vectors and Matrices (2018). https://github.com/jrh13/hol-light/blob/master/Multivariate/vectors.ml

7. Clarke, E.M., Grumberg, O., Peled, D.: Model Checking. MIT Press, Cambridge (1999)
8. Clarke, E.M., Klieber, W., Nováček, M., Zuliani, P.: Model checking and the state explosion problem. In: Meyer, B., Nordio, M. (eds.) LASER 2011. LNCS, vol. 7682, pp. 1–30. Springer, Heidelberg (2012). https://doi.org/10.1007/978-3-642-35746-6_1
9. Durán, A.J., Pérez, M., Varona, J.L.: The Misfortunes of a Mathematicians' Trio using Computer Algebra Systems: Can We Trust? CoRR abs/1312.3270 (2013)
10. Faroque, M., Nizam, S.: Virtual Reality Training for Micro-robotic Cell Injection. Deakin University, Australia, Technical report (2016)
11. Harisson, J.: HOL Light Transcendental Theory (2018). https://github.com/jrh13/hol-light/blob/master/Multivariate/transcendentals.ml
12. Harrison, J.: HOL light: a tutorial introduction. In: Srivas, M., Camilleri, A. (eds.) FMCAD 1996. LNCS, vol. 1166, pp. 265–269. Springer, Heidelberg (1996). https://doi.org/10.1007/BFb0031814
13. Harrison, J.: Handbook of Practical Logic and Automated Reasoning. Cambridge University Press, New York (2009)
14. Harrison, J.: The HOL light theory of euclidean space. J. Autom. Reasoning 50(2), 173–190 (2013)
15. Harrison, J., et al.: Formalized Mathematics. Turku Centre for Computer Science, Turku (1996)
16. Hasan, O., Tahar, S.: Formal Verification Methods. Encyclopedia of Information Science and Technology, pp. 7162–7170. IGI Global Pub. (2015)
17. Huang, H., Sun, D., Mills, J.K., Li, W.J.: A visual impedance force control of a robotic cell injection system. In: Robotics and Biomimetics, pp. 233–238. IEEE (2006)
18. Huang, H., Sun, D., Mills, J.K., Li, W.J., Cheng, S.H.: Visual-based impedance control of out-of-plane cell injection systems. Trans. Autom. Sci. Eng. 6(3), 565–571 (2009)
19. Kuncova, J., Kallio, P.: Challenges in capillary pressure microinjection. In: Engineering in Medicine and Biology Society, vol. 2, pp. 4998–5001. IEEE (2004)
20. Mathematica (2017). https://www.wolfram.com/mathematica/
21. Nakayama, T., Fujiwara, H., Tastumi, K., Fujita, K., Higuchi, T., Mori, T.: A new assisted hatching technique using a piezo-micromanipulator. Fertil. Steril. 69(4), 784–788 (1998)
22. Nethery, J.F., Spong, M.W.: Robotica: a mathematica package for robot analysis. IEEE Robot. Autom. Mag. 1(1), 13–20 (1994)
23. Paulson, L.C.: ML for the Working Programmer. Cambridge University Press, Cambridge (1996)
24. Sardar, M.U., Hasan, O.: Towards probabilistic formal modeling of robotic cell injection systems. In: Models for Formal Analysis of Real Systems, pp. 271–282 (2017)
25. Sun, D., Liu, Y.: Modeling and impedance control of a two-manipulator system handling a flexible beam. In: Proceedings of the 1997 IEEE International Conference on Robotics and Automation, vol. 2, pp. 1787–1792. IEEE (1997)
26. Sun, Y., Nelson, B.J.: Biological cell injection using an autonomous microrobotic system. Robot. Res. 21(10–11), 861–868 (2002)
27. Yanagida, K., Katayose, H., Yazawa, H., Kimura, Y., Konnai, K., Sato, A.: The usefulness of a piezo-micromanipulator in intracytoplasmic sperm injection in humans. Hum. Reprod. 14(2), 448–453 (1999)

Workshop on Embedded and Cyber-Physical Systems Education

FPGA Based Big Data Accelerator Design in Teaching Computer Architecture and Organization

Chao Wang(✉), Yuming Cheng, Lei Gong, Bo Wan, Aili Wang, Xi Li,
and Xuehai Zhou

School of Computer Science, University of Science and Technology of China,
Suzhou, China
{cswang,wangal,llxx,xhzhou}@ustc.edu.cn,
{yumingc,leigong0203,wanborj}@mail.ustc.edu.cn

Abstract. In the past few years big data applications are becoming diverse and ubiquitous. There is a renewed interest in teaching senior level students to be professional in accelerator based computer architecture design and engineering. However, it poses a significant challenge to tutor the students with sufficient knowledge and practical skills in this area. In this paper, we propose a big data accelerator design project implemented on field-programmable gate array (FPGA) in teaching a computer architecture and organization course. The experimental system is carried out on a heterogeneous architecture using Xilinx Virtex 5 development boards. To achieve a modular accelerator implementation, several milestones are set to facilitate the on-time complete of the project. With the assistance of the FPGA-based experiment, most students have obtained a much more comprehensive understanding of the processor architecture and the accelerator design paradigm. Student feedback and survey illustrates the effectiveness and popularity of the FPGA-based project with milestones over simulation based experiments.

Keywords: Applications in subject areas · Simulations · FPGA

1 Introduction

Big data is common sense. To tackle the challenge of the data-intensive applications, modern computer architectures are becoming more heterogeneous, diverse, ubiquitous and complex, especially in the big data computing fields. To build fast prototyping computer architecture, Field-programmable gate array (FPGA) different multicore platforms which contain both processors, and reconfigurable logic resources are suitable for rapid prototyping of computer architecture projects in the embedded computing domain. Using FPGAs to teaching computer architecture and embedded systems is a challenging task since it involves diverse knowledge and skills, ranging from processor architecture, platform based hardware/software co-design, and reconfigurable computing technologies [1].

© Springer Nature Switzerland AG 2019
R. Chamberlain et al. (Eds.): CyPhy 2017, LNCS 11267, pp. 145–158, 2019.
https://doi.org/10.1007/978-3-030-17910-6_11

Often, computer architecture courses are carried out without any practical experiments or using only simulation-based projects. [2] presents an FPGA-based platform for processor design, which provides an excellent opportunity for senior grade students to put hands on a real hardware system. To provide more practical knowledge in both big data applications and computer architecture, it is desirable to integrate a custom accelerator design on FPGA.

Meanwhile, the design complexity of the big data accelerator increases the use of register transfer level (RTL) design methodologies. Hardware description language (HDL) like Verilog HDL and VHDL is now standard routine in electronic design automation (EDA). Furthermore, to facilitate component reuse, the intellectual property (IP) and platform-based design paradigm is used to reduce the design time and the time-to-market (TTM). Once the RTL based hardware accelerators are packaged into IP core, they could be shifted and reused directly to multiple different projects.

As a consequence, the merge of FPGA hardware and HDL language provides an optimal design paradigm for students to experience a particular customized dual processor in computer architecture classes. With the help of computer-aided design (CAD) tools and educational boards from FPGA vendors, students are capable of developing their custom processor from the very beginning. The students are only responsible for implementing the RTL code of the custom processor under specifications, verifying the correctness of the hardware module, and integrating it into the FPGA development board. Toolchains and software environment are no longer an issue for students so that the entire project could be finished in two or three months.

This paper proposes an accelerator design project based on FPGA Xilinx Virtex 5 development board in teaching computer architecture and organization course. The dual processor system is composed of a customized accelerator for big data, attached to a local Microblaze (MB) processor on FPGA. The MB processor is integrated to provide straightforward application interfaces to students, while the accelerator is deployed for customized functionality implementation, including neural networks, machine learning, data mining, and genome sequencing. Taking the student's background into account, the primary target of this experiment is not to implement a processor with all the functions fully implemented, but let them grasp the basic engineering skills for processor design and system integration, based on the utilization of FPGA boards and CAD tools. To facilitate the arrangement of the projects by the teacher and ensure the completion of the projects on time by the students, totally six milestones were arranged every one or two weeks.

We have been teaching the Computer Architecture and Organization course (No. G430113460) since 2009 fall semesters, at School of Software Engineering, University of Science and Technology of China, Suzhou, China. The technical detail of this course is to educate the students with the basic knowledge and principles of designing a Microprocessor. In the earlier two years, no such project was assigned, and a project was assigned from 2011 to 2015. In each year a course survey was taken, and statistics indicate the effectiveness and success of the dual processor system design experiment based on FPGA educational boards.

The organization of this paper is as below. Section 2 outlines the related studies and points the highlight of this work. In Sect. 3 we present the experiment details including the FPGA-based framework, the software toolchain, and the design flow. After that, a customized accelerator design with the milestones is illustrated in Sect. 4. After that Section, Sect. 5 reports the course statistics, student survey, and feedback. Section 6 explains the cost and teaching effort in the project. Finally, Sect. 7 is the conclusion.

2 Related Studies and Motivation

As FPGA is becoming more powerful, in the past decade there is a renewed interest using FPGA as an experimental platform in computer architecture and embedded systems courses. For example, ESE [3] introduces a FPGA-based accelerator for sparse LSTM efficient speech recognition engine, not only makeing the algorithm smaller, but also supporting compressed deep learning algorithm. [2] proposes a generic FPGA-based design with multiple embedded processors and predefined peripherals to explore both the hardware and software issues with embedded computer designs. [4] presents an experiment platform for embedded software programmers with a DCT co-processor for JPEG application on an Altera Nios II development kit. DLAU [5] is a scalable deep learning accelerator Unit on FPGA, which utilizes tile techniques to explore locality and employs three pipelined processing units to improve the throughput. [6] introduces an FPGA-based system based on a five-stage pipelined processor. Students can observe pipelined registers by tracing and debugging the pipelined processor registers.

On the hardware logic resources on an FPGA, a study [7] depicts that the hardware logic on Virtex-4 is sufficient to accompany the Pentium processor. [8] evaluate and survey the simulation based approaches appropriate for lecturing computer organization and architecture courses. [9] integrates a computer architecture course with software and hardware codesign. Moreover, [10] present an experimental simulation literature for project-based multicore education in computer architecture and organization courses.

Similarly, Teaching and Design Workbench framework [11] reports a general infrastructure for teaching embedded systems and computer architecture. A new architectural feature for embedded processors using a research simulator is introduced. [12] presents a digital electronics course, in which the authors integrate programmable logic into a development board. [13] shows an FPGA-based pipelined CPU design project into a computer architecture course. The project is constructed on the Altera DE2 board and involves a 32-bit accelerator design with five pipelined stages. [14] proposes an FPGA-based framework with multiprocessors and network-on-chip platform. The projects stimulate more industry applications with the real-time requirement. [15] utilizes FPGA hardware platform on teaching embedded systems. The course includes several projects to allow students to define their project on the FPGA-based hardware. [16] describes integrated system composed of microcontrollers and peripherals. Likewise, [17] presents an embedded system coursework including components such as integrated control, system-on-chip, networking, computer peripherals. [18] illustrates a design project using a soft processor and custom hardware logic on a programmable system-on-chip. A similar system-on-chip project is described in [19], where a servo controller for a robotic arm is implemented on an Excalibur chip with an embedded ARM processor and programmable logic. Hansson et al. [20] propose a design project where students partition and map JPEG decoder onto a multiprocessor platform running on an FPGA.

Unlike the above projects, this paper provides unique highlights from previous work in following two aspects:

(1) First, the implemented accelerator in this project can improve the performance of the novel big data applications significantly. The students could design and implement their accelerators on Xilinx FPGA board, such as machine learning and neural networks.
(2) Second, the accelerator is attached as a co-processor to the local Microblaze on FPGA board; therefore the students work on a heterogeneous system. The system level design could facilitate them gaining a "big picture" and hands-on experiences of the computer systems rather than processor architecture.

Based on the above contributions, students can implement the essential functionality of the big data accelerator to solve the real problems. With the hands-on learning approach, students are capable of getting familiar with their practical knowledge in new big data domain and skills learned from the computer architecture lecture.

3   Generic Hardware and Software Environment

With the increasing resources of the FPGA chip, it is now acceptable to bring more than one CPU processor into a single chip. Therefore in this project, the custom accelerator is implemented as an attached coprocessor of the central processor (For Xilinx V5 board is Microblaze processor). Another reason to build a dual core system is to alleviate the burden of writing running application codes with cross-compilers. In this Section, we present the FPGA-based framework along with both hardware configuration and software environment.

3.1   Hardware Configuration

The custom processor project is carried out on a Xilinx Virtex V5LX110T FPGA board from Xilinx University Program. The V5LX110T board offers some input/output peripherals and other modules, including serial terminal controllers, timer, and Ethernet module. Other than the Microblaze processor, following IP cores are also integrated into the system:

(1) The custom accelerator processor: The use of custom processor demonstrates the application-specific design and implementation of the big data oriented accelerator, with significant knowledge in the application domain required.

(2) Fast Simplex Link (FSL): FSL provides a straightforward data path from the register files in Xilinx Microblaze to the custom accelerator. The write and read transactions of the FSL could be directly invoked through unique PUT (including put, cput, nput and ncput) and GET (get, cget, nget and ncget) instructions.

(3) Processor Local Bus (PLB): This bus allows various peripherals to be instantiated and connected as slave modules. The Microblaze processor can communicate with these peripherals arbitrated by PLB.

(4) DDR SDRAM controller: The DDR memory is used for storing the program code for the Microblaze processors and also serves as data memory.

(5) UART and Timer controller: The serial ports are useful for PC-FPGA communication. Thus the debugging messages could be displayed on the screen through serial ports. The timer controller modules allow Microblaze to keep track of the execution on the accelerator and ensure the real-time behavior by interrupts.

Figure 1 illustrates the block diagram of the dual processor system. The architecture constructed in this project is generic that it can support a variety of other similar projects. The custom accelerator can incorporate with specific hardware modules, such as neural networks and genome sequencing.

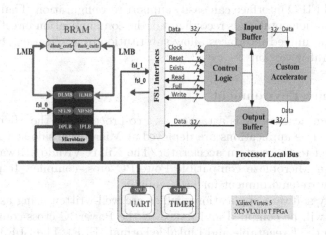

Fig. 1. Architecture of the FPGA chip, the communication interfaces between MB processor and accelerator is based on FIFO interface

3.2 FPGA Based Heterogeneous Framework

In the FPGA chip, the custom accelerator is attached to a local Microblaze processor via FSL channels. The FSL based communication interfaces are illustrated in the right part of Fig. 1. Using Microblaze processor allows the applications to be defined using C language, which is part of the application since the custom accelerator is hard to be programmed and compiled into the binary executable files. Furthermore, different customized modules to the processor architecture can be added or reconfigured through the Xilinx Vivado tool suite [21,22].

To support a fast data transfer of on-chip data communication, the Microblaze processor, and the accelerator are connected via a pair of FIFO based Xilinx FSL channels. The MB-to-Accelerator interface offloads the execution to the accelerator via FSL bus channels, and the accelerator can run each forwarded instruction and return the results to the MB. The message transferred by FSL contains following signals: Data, Clock, Reset, Exists, Read, Full, and Write signals. The FIFO packet also includes the input buffer, output buffer, and control logic. The input buffer receives the offload functions and stores them temporarily, while the output buffer stores the execution results. The control logic is responsible for manipulating the process of the custom big data services.

The custom accelerator can raise interrupt signals and communicate with the MB through specific, explicit instructions. These instructions can access read/write MB configuration registers and execute custom operations on the accelerator side. Communication between MB and the accelerator is utilized in a master-slave manner. For the particular task distribution stage, Microblaze acts as a master which sends an explicit instruction to drive the FIFO based interconnection. The custom accelerator serves as masters when a back FIFO sends a return value to MB processor. As the accelerator could be customized, the proposed FIFO interface can easily support reconfiguration. That is after the accelerator implementation is reconfigured, the communication interfaces remain the same. The unified interfaces allow substitution of applications between different accelerator versions.

3.3   Software Environment

As the custom accelerator is attached as a co-processor to the Microblaze processor, the source applications are deployed at Microblaze side at the start and then offloaded to the custom accelerator. The Xilinx Vivado software tool suit is based on a Microblaze compatible PowerPC cross-compiler. It provides an efficient software environment for programming.

The ready software applications, which are well-written using assembly and C-language, will be compiled and linked by the PowerPC cross-compiler into a binary file in the Executable and Linkable Format (ELF). The ELF file could be offloaded on the SD card on the FPGA chip or downloaded by the cable from the PC end.

3.4   Processing Flow

As the Microblaze is a PowerPC compatible instruction set processor, therefore all the applications running on Microblaze is first processed to the ELF file, by the cross compiler from Xilinx Vivado tool suite. This section illustrates the detailed hardware/software co-processing flow using FPGA and Vivado toolset. The entire flow mainly consists of five stages, which are marked with the related labels in Fig. 2:

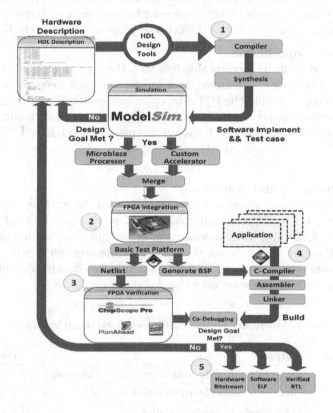

Fig. 2. Project design flow using Xilinx FPGA and tools

(1) Custom Accelerator Hardware Design
Hardware description and design is the first phase in which HDL sources are implemented into the custom accelerator. The register-transfer-level (RTL) description code will undergo a procedure including both compilation and synthesis steps. Sample applications are designed to verify the behavior and timing correctness of the custom accelerator. Taking Xilinx tools as a demonstration, both front and back end simulations are operated within Xilinx ISim or Model-Sim simulation environment.

(2) Heterogeneous System Integration
After the hardware implementations are verified, the primary design goal for the accelerator has been met. Then we can integrate MB and the accelerator into the heterogeneous system. In this project, students carry the module integration with Xilinx Platform Studio (XPS) and IMPACT tools.

(3) BSP and Netlists Generation
Now hardware platform design files are generated for verification and debugging, including both netlists and board support packages (BSP). The netlists are used for hardware bitstream generation, while the BSP files provide original hardware description running essential environments for diverse applications. Therefore the BSP files are also regarded as the necessary input factors as the C Compilers.

(4) Software Compilation
Applications are built into executable files with the cross-compilation toolchains, including a C-compiler, assembler, and linker. Students need to configure the cross toolchains, including the BSP file, optimization levels and running modes, which in the case could have a potential effect on the performances. Besides, hardware bitstreams in stage 3 should be programmed into FPGA chip at first, and then executable elf files can be downloaded for hardware/software co-debugging.

(5) Co-debugging and Analysis
The co-debugging operations are constructed with Xilinx ChipScope, PlanA-head, and ISE tools. If the design goal is met, we can get the final design files including platform hardware specification bitstreams, executable elf files, and verified RTL implementations for the custom accelerator. Otherwise, the performance optimization and tuning operations should be considered, which leads to the hardware redesign to start over the design flow.

Table 1. Milestones for the custom accelerator implementation

Milestones	Purpose	Duration
1	Gaining familiarity with experimental environment	1 week
2	Simulation and algorithm analysis	2 weeks
3	RTL design of the accelerator	2 weeks
4	Pipelined implementation	1 week
5	System integration	1 week
6	Trade-offs analysis	2 weeks

Each week has 6 h.

4   Project Setup snd Milestones

This accelerator is a pipelined design with selected kernel instructions and custom functionalities. To educate the students in two months, Table 1 lists the six milestones to help students with scheduling project by the end of the class.

First, Milestone 1 familiarizes students with the execution flow of the accelerator and experimental environment. This stage includes a prototype on FPGA, which is composed of a Microblaze processor, a custom accelerator, a memory block, and a UART controller. The initial accelerator, which has only one add instruction implemented, was given to the students. In this milestone, each student is required to display the results of a simple add instruction at the PC end through the UART controller. Students must program the demonstrative hardware module on the FPGA, understand communication scheme through the PC and the FPGA board, and return the results through the serial ports.

In Milestone 2 students could get a simulation with the selected big data application. The first step is to use Matlab to implementation the big data functions. Students should choose the particular algorithm, and profile the application to locate the hot spots for following algorithms:

(1) Convolutional Neural Networks
(2) Deep Neural Networks
(3) User-based Collaborative Filtering
(4) K-means clustering
(5) Genome Sequencing.

Milestone 3 is the RTL implementation of the accelerator. Based on the profiled hot spots, students should implement the particular hardware functions of the accelerator. Besides, the functions are also packaged in this milestone.

In Milestone 4 the accelerator is implemented in a pipelined manner. The pipeline includes five stages: Instruction Fetch, Instruction Decode, Execution, Memory Access and Write Back.

Milestones 5 and 6 are the two daunting tasks based on the pipelined accelerator. Both milestones pose challenges to the students, so the students will be divided into groups to finish those two milestones. Each group has 2 or 3 members, and we totally have about 35 groups. In milestone five the accelerator is integrated to the FPGA based system. This facilitates the students to obtain a better understanding of the platform-based design. In milestone 6, the students analyze the trade-offs among the speedup, power, and hardware cost. Both milestones take two weeks.

5   Project Evaluation

The computer architecture course was given in Fall semesters from 2009 to 2015. In the first two years 2009 and 2010, no project was assigned. Students only ran some simulation experiments using WinDLX, DLXView, and Simplescalar tools. Then in 2011–2015 a project was assigned. From 2012 to 2015 the FPGA board and milestones are adopted in the project, while in 2011 the project is based on the ModelSim simulation and no milestones are arranged in the project. Table 2 illustrates the primary survey results of the feedback from 2009 to 2015.

Table 2 shows that the overall numerical score of 2009 and 2010 is 4.33 and 4.51, both are without the project. Meanwhile, the evaluation score gets between 4.96 and 4.93 when the experiment is carried out and optimized on FPGA from 2012 and 2015. As in 2011, there is only ModelSim simulation on the processor, and no milestones are set. Therefore the overall numerical score of 2011 is relatively low at 4.62. Table 3 shows the project statistics from 2011 to 2015, with the custom accelerator experiment. The dramatic difference between 2011 and

Table 2. Course survey and basic feedback results

Module	2009	2010	2011	2012	2013	2014	2015
Number of students	80	39	79	78	87	100	100
Number of respondents	22	3	77	75	85	95	97
Percentage of respondents	28%	87%	98%	96%	98%	95%	97%
Overall score	4.33[a]	4.51[a]	4.62[a]	4.96[a]	4.93[a]	4.94[a]	4.93[a]

[a]The maximum score is 5.

Table 3. Project statistics

Year	2011	2012	2013	2014	2015
Project goal	**Custom accelerator design**				
Class size	79	78	87	100	100
Milestones	No	Yes	Yes	Yes	Yes
ModelSim	Used	Used	Used	Used	Used
Xilinx FPGA	Not	Used	Used	Used	Used
Student finished 4	30	75	81	90	89
Student finished 5	12	40	42	65	73
Student finished 6	3	20	27	53	68

2012–2015 comes from two reasons: First, the milestone management facilitates the students to divide the final target into achievable steps. Second, the enforcement of the FPGA development board also contributed to the success from 2012 to 2015. Instead of just using simulators like ModelSim for the processor design specification and validation, the hands-on experiments using real FPGA boards provide students a practical experience to accomplish the processor design Furthermore, by integrating both an MB processor and an accelerator into one system, student could accomplish a dual processor system rather than one raw CPU processor, which could raise the motivation of finishing the project.

Table 4 shows the survey results taken from 2009 to 2015. For each item in this inquiry, students should choose one from the total five options: Strong Disagree (1.00), Weak Disagree (2.00), Borderline (3.00), Weak Agree (4.00), and Strong Agree (5.00). The maximum score is 5.00. Most students report that the workload of the experiment is adequate (rating 4.93/4.89 from 2012 to 2015). Moreover, students indicate it is useful to design a real processor in the computer architecture and organization course (score 4.99/4.91 from 2012 to 2015), even it occupies much more attention and engineering effort during the class. Table 4 also reports that the experiment on the FPGA board is far more helpful than simulators in studying architecture (from 4.32 to 4.99/4.96). After taking the course in 2012 and 2013, most students indicate the appropriate technical depth of the project (4.92/4.97), and a good number of students believe that they have gained and acquired enough knowledge and skills in designing a processor (4.95/4.87), and therefore the project is popular with students (4.97/4.88).

Table 4. Scoresheet of Feedbacks from the Students

ID	Module	2009	2010	2011	2012	2013	2014	2015
1	Is the Workload of the experiment adequate?	3.23	3.38	3.13	4.93	4.89	4.95	4.90
2	Is it necessary to involve the CPU design project?	—	—	3.14	4.99	4.91	4.97	4.93
3	Teacher's attitude	4.45	4.47	4.6	4.95	4.91	4.92	4.89
4	Is the project well organized?	4.45	4.53	4.65	4.93	4.96	4.97	4.92
5	The technical depth of the lecture and the project?	4.55	4.5	4.7	4.95	4.94	4.92	4.98
6	The technical width of the lecture and the project?	4.23	4.44	4.64	4.97	4.92	4.89	4.96
7	Is the experiment helping me sort the clues?	4.32	4.53	4.65	4.99	4.96	4.90	4.90
8	Popularity	4.18	4.29	4.53	4.97	4.88	4.92	4.95
9	Gain and acquisition	4.27	4.47	4.57	4.95	4.87	4.93	4.92
10	Is the milestone management helpful?	—	—	—	4.97	4.95	4.96	4.98
11	Are the milestones fair and adequate?	—	—	—	4.97	4.87	4.97	4.96
12	Is the teaching assistant helpful in the project?	4.05	4.41	4.47	4.96	4.89	4.91	4.89
13	Total evaluation	4.33	4.51	4.62	4.96	4.93	4.94	4.93

Regarding the milestone management, a majority of students believe that the milestone management is quite helpful (4.97/4.95), and the division of six milestones is adequate (4.97/4.87). The feedback indicates that this project with FPGA and the scheduled milestones has a significant positive influence on the comprehensive understanding of computer architecture. The utilization of the FPGA is not only bringing extensive skills of computer architecture knowledge to students but also raising their motivation designing their custom processors.

6   Discussion of the Costs and Efforts

For other institutions which would like to introduce such projects into the course, it will be useful to depict more details about the cost and budget when establishing the project. To our best knowledge, the cost and teaching effort include following aspects:

6.1   Hardware and Software Cost

As the experiments are deployed at the real FPGA development board, the total cost includes the purchase of the FPGA board and the use of the software. We totally have 40 Zynq boards and 20 Virtex five boards, all from Digilent China. We highly recommend Zynq boards as it has following two benefits:

(1) To control the cost. Each Zynq only costs approximately $500, while is much cheaper than Virtex 5 ($1650), while the hardware resources on Zynq is sufficient to build the target dual processor system.
(2) Although the design flow for Virtex 5 and Zynq FPGA boards are quite similar, the ARM-based Zynq board has a wider scope of readers and audiences than using Microblaze based Virtex 5 board.

6.2   Efforts in Organizing the Experiments

In order to help the students to get the basic knowledge and the "big picture" in designing a dual processor system, we provide a framework using VHDL with only one single instruction implemented. The three teaching assistants take about 8 hours to implement, simulate and verify the structure on the Virtex 5/Zynq board. To make sure that all the on-site questions and problems from students are quickly answered and solved, three teaching assistants are employed for this course. As there are totally 80 90 students enrolled in this course, we divided them into two classes during the project, ensuring each student has his/her board in the experiment. Finally, please note the budget may be slightly different in the various countries/regions, in particular for the FPGA development boards. Anyway, we sincerely hope this information could be potentially useful to other institutions.

7   Conclusion

Teaching computer architecture can be quite challenging since it involves different aspects such as processor architecture, system-on-chip, and reconfigurable computing technologies. In this paper, we have presented an FPGA-based accelerator for big data applications in teaching computer architecture and organization class. The students obtain hands-on experiences of designing a custom accelerator with the help of FPGA educational boards and software tools. The accelerator is attached to a Microblaze processor on the Xilinx Virtex 5 educational boards. A course survey is distributed after class and the feedback from the students reveal that a majority of students have gained more practical understanding and skills than simulators. The real FPGA board is bringing much more attention and benefits, while it needs more effort and involvement. Most students report high ratings for the milestone management during the project setup, which helps them to achieve the target project step by step.

Finally, we can conclude that this project can be useful by other universities those have relevant courses such as computer architecture, computer organization, and embedded systems. Since the experiences on this project could educate students with more practical engineering skills, therefore it could help them pursue a career in hardware design and computer architect more quickly.

Acknowledgements. This work is partially supported by the National Key Research and Development Program of China (under Grant 2017YFA0700900), Anhui Provincial Natural Science Foundation (No. 1608085QF12), Jiangsu Provincial Natural Science Foundation (No. BK20181193), Youth Innovation Promotion Association CAS (No. 2017497), and Fundamental Research Funds for the Central Universities (WK2150110003).

References

1. Jackson, D.J., Caspi, P.: Embedded systems education: future directions, initiatives, and cooperation. ACM SIGBED Rev. **2**(4), 1–4 (2005)
2. Kumar, A., Fernando, S., Panicker, R.C.: Project-based learning in embedded systems education using an FPGA platform. IEEE Trans. Educ. **56**(4), 407–415 (2013)
3. Han, S., et al.: ESE: efficient speech recognition engine with sparse LSTM on FPGA. In: FPGA, pp. 75–84 (2017)
4. Mitsui, H., Kambe, H., Koizumi, H.: Use of student experiments for teaching embedded software development including HW/SW co-design. IEEE Trans. Educ. **52**(3), 436–443 (2009)
5. Wang, C., Gong, L., Yu, Q., Li, X., Xie, Y., Zhou, X.: DLAU: a scalable deep learning accelerator unit on FPGA. IEEE Trans. Comput. Aided Des. Integr. Circuits Syst. **36**(3), 513–517 (2017)
6. Bulić, P., Guštin, V., Šonc, D., Štrancar, A.: An FPGA-based integrated environment for computer architecture. Comput. Appl. Eng. Educ. **21**(1), 26–35 (2013)
7. Lu, S.L.L., Yiannacouras, P., Suh, T., Kassa, R., Konow, M.: A desktop computer with a reconfigurable pentium®. ACM Trans. Reconfigurable Technol. Syst. (TRETS) **1**(1), 5 (2008)
8. Nikolic, B., Radivojevic, Z., Djordjevic, J., Milutinovic, V.: A survey and evaluation of simulators suitable for teaching courses in computer architecture and organization. IEEE Trans. Educ. **52**(4), 449–458 (2009)
9. Schaumont, P.: A senior-level course in hardware–software codesign. IEEE Trans. Educ. **51**(3), 306–311 (2008)
10. Ozturk, O.: Multicore education through simulation. IEEE Trans. Educ. **54**(2), 203–209 (2011)
11. Soares, S.N., Wagner, F.R.: T&D-bench—innovative combined support for education and research in computer architecture and embedded systems. IEEE Trans. Educ. **54**(4), 675–682 (2011)
12. Todorovich, E., Marone, J.A., Vazquez, M.: Introducing programmable logic to undergraduate engineering students in a digital electronics course. IEEE Trans. Educ. **55**(2), 255–262 (2012)
13. Lee, J.H., Lee, S.E., Yu, H.C., Suh, T.: Pipelined CPU design with FPGA in teaching computer architecture. IEEE Trans. Educ. **55**(3), 341–348 (2012)
14. Ttofis, C., Theocharides, T., Michael, M.K.: FPGA-based laboratory assignments for NoC-based manycore systems. IEEE Trans. Educ. **55**(2), 180–189 (2012)
15. Edwards, S.A.: Experiences teaching an FPGA-based embedded systems class. ACM SIGBED Rev. **2**(4), 56–62 (2005)
16. Bruce, J.W., Harden, J.C., Reese, R.B.: Cooperative and progressive design experience for embedded systems. IEEE Trans. Educ. **47**(1), 83–92 (2004)
17. Koopman, P., et al.: Undergraduate embedded system education at carnegie mellon. ACM Trans. Embed. Comput. Syst. (TECS) **4**(3), 500–528 (2005)
18. Hall, T.S., Hamblen, J.O.: System-on-a-programmable-chip development platforms in the classroom. IEEE Trans. Educ. **47**(4), 502–507 (2004)
19. Bindal, A., Mann, S., Ahmed, B.N., Raimundo, L.A.: An undergraduate system-on-chip (SoC) course for computer engineering students. IEEE Trans. Educ. **48**(2), 279–289 (2005)

20. Hansson, A., Akesson, B., Van Meerbergen, J.: Multi-processor programming in the embedded system curriculum. ACM SIGBED Rev. 6(1), 9 (2009)
21. Feist, T.: Vivado design suite. White Paper 5 (2012)
22. O'Loughlin, D., Coffey, A., Callaly, F., Lyons, D., Morgan, F.: Xilinx Vivado high level synthesis: case studies (2014)

Author Index

Abbas, Houssam   94
Aoki, Toshiaki   63

Cheng, Yuming   145

Eo, Jeongyoon   27

Fainekos, Georgios   11

Goldsztejn, Alexandre   79
Gong, Lei   145

Hasan, Osman   127
Hasuo, Ichiro   3, 109

Ingibergsson, Johann Thor Mogensen   43
Ishii, Daisuke   63, 79

Kido, Kengo   109
Kim, Hokeun   83
Kim, Kang-Wook   27
Kraft, Dirk   43

Lee, Chang-Gun   27
Lee, Edward A.   83
Li, Xi   145

Mangharam, Rahul   94
Murakami, Toru   63

O'Kelly, Matthew   94

Rashid, Adnan   127
Rodionova, Alena   94

Schultz, Ulrik Pagh   43
Sedwards, Sean   109

Takeuchi, Shigeki   63
Tomita, Takashi   63

Wan, Bo   145
Wang, Aili   145
Wang, Chao   145
Wasicek, Armin   83

Yaghoubi, Shakiba   11
Yonezaki, Naoki   79

Zhou, Xuehai   145

Printed in the United States
By Bookmasters